The

ART
SPANDER
Collection

ALSO BY ART SPANDER
Golf: The Passion & the Challenge

Series Editor, Carlton Stowers

The
ART
SPANDER
Collection

Introduction by
AL MICHAELS

TAYLOR PUBLISHING COMPANY
Dallas, Texas

To my parents, who never understood
why I didn't become a lawyer, and my wife,
Liz, who doesn't understand why anyone
would become a journalist.

Published by Taylor Publishing Company
1550 West Mockingbird Lane
Dallas, Texas 75235

The columns included in this collection
originally appeared in *The San Francisco Examiner*.
Reprinted by permission. All rights reserved.

Library of Congress Cataloging-in-Publication Data

Spander, Art.
    The Art Spander collection / introduction by Al Michaels.
        p. cm. — (The Sportswriter's eye)
    "The columns included in this collection originally appeared in
the San Francisco examiner"—T.p. verso.
        Includes index.
        ISBN 0-87833-649-4 : $14.95
        1. Sports—United States.   2. Sports.   3. Newspapers—Sections,
    columns, etc.—Sports.   I. Title.   II. Series.
    GV583.S64 1989   88-28633
    070.4'49796'0973—dc19   CIP

Printed in the United States of America
0 9 8 7 6 5 4 3 2 1

Introduction

When questioned by those who've never met him to describe Art Spander, I feel like a chemist asked to explain a test tube with five dozen components. At a time when attention spans seem shorter and microwaved answers are accepted without much contemplation, I'd prefer giving no description rather than relate just one or two little morsels that tend to conjure up a caricature. Because to describe Art in rapid order is similar to explaining away China as "big."

Even these few hundred words can barely make a nick, but maybe a story or two in this preamble and the compilation of columns that follow will allow a glimpse into the head of a man whose brain, if attached to an RPM gauge, would rival the reading on a car taking the checkered flag at Indianapolis. And that's when he's sleeping.

Let's go back to March of 1985. I'd traveled to Paris to cover a welterweight fight between Milton McCrory and Pedro Vilella for ABC's "Wide World of Sports," the type of matchup that's become a staple for the three major networks' anthology series. That is to say . . . hopefully interesting, generally not compelling, pretty routine. Four thousand or so Frenchmen were expected to show up at the Palais Omnisports de Bercy for this Saturday-night bout. The start of the match had been geared for the American television audience and thus, to coincide with "Wide World's" 4:30 Eastern Time start, the first round was scheduled shortly after 10:30 P.M., Paris time.

By coincidence, Art and Liz Spander had been traveling through Europe for several days and, in a trip planned months in advance, had elected to make Paris the last stop on their vacation before heading home. I know exactly what Liz had in mind. The perfect ending to this late-winter odyssey was going to be a Saturday-night dinner at an eatery with an appropriate number of stars in the *Michelin Guide*. There'd be candlelight and coquilles St. Jacques, champagne and chardonnay, foie gras and fresh flowers. Hey, Monday meant getting the kids off to school, repairing the dishwasher, business as usual at the office, soup on the stove.

The Spanders love life as much as any couple, and I'm certain Art was relishing to the same extent the thought of such a conclusion to a perfect trip. But hold it! Wait a second. There was a column to be written for Monday. Oh, sure. Art had written a few thousand columns through the years. No big deal. Think of a subject, peck away at the keyboard. Still can't get into it? No problem. Rewrite an old column with a couple of updated twists. You're entitled. You've earned that right. You said what, Art? You can't do that. You want to go to the fight? To the Milton McCrory–Pedro Vilella fight? For Monday's column? What about Liz? What about dinner? You want to know if Domino's delivers to the Place de la Concorde? Help!

So what is it with Art Spander? Is it dedication, obsession, compulsion, loyalty, drive, single-mindedness, craziness, madness, just what? After fifteen years of friendship, I think I've got it. It's curiosity. It's not only being interested in everything (EVERYTHING!!) but being fascinated all day, every day, by why birds chirp, what weight and what grade oil a turbine engine needs, how a cornfield gets replanted after a drought, how many quail in a covey, who's the head of state in New Zealand, who's the governor of North Dakota, and does he have any relatives in Fargo? This, of course, is in addition to knowing who finished fourth in the National League in 1934, who kicked field goals for the Lions in 1957, and the string tension of Ron Laver's racket the first time he won a major.

The fact of the matter that Saturday night in Paris was this— Art had digested a lot of great meals in his lifetime but he'd never been to a boxing match in France. And that made him curious. He'd learn something he didn't know. He'd observe something he hadn't seen. And he'd be fascinated by it. He could have a snack after midnight, anyway. Hello, Milton McCrory. Au revoir, Maxim's.

I'd made that trip to Paris with Alex Wallau, then a member of our production team and now the superb boxing analyst for ABC. I'd introduced Alex to Art at the fight and knew they'd be on the same flight back to the United States the next day. Alex would be home in New York for a few days before heading for a fight at Harrah's Hotel in Stateline, Nevada, on the south shore of Lake Tahoe. As he left our hotel that Sunday morning,

Alex asked me how long it would take to drive from the airport in Reno to Harrah's. I told him Art would be on his flight and he could ask him for directions. I was to remain in Paris for a few days, and late that evening my phone rang. It was Alex Wallau calling from New York.

Alex: Al, how long will it take me to drive from Reno to Harrah's?

Me: I told you to ask Spander.

Alex: I did.

Me: What'd he tell you?

Alex: Well, he told me there were three possible routes depending on the weather and contingent upon the completion of a particular road-construction project. He said the state transportation department had hoped to be finished by now but work had been held up by the unexpected discovery of an ancient Indian burial ground. He said if I followed the first route I'd see twenty-six different species of flora and then he named them all and said that seven might not be in full bloom yet because of a late-winter cold snap. He said to look for a particular spot on the second route where some old prospectors' skeletons were found three months ago and he then proceeded to quote the price of gold each year from 1849 to the present. He said the third route might be best because I'd be able to stop at a roadside stand that had the best caramel custard he'd tasted outside of a sampling from a roadside pushcart in Düsseldorf in 1978. In addition, there was a gas station along the way that featured 94-octane unleaded, a brief glimpse at the summit of a mountain that had been scaled only by an extinct breed of bighorn sheep, and that from 4 to 7:45 P.M. the entrance to Harrah's parking lot would be more easily accessible from this direction.

Me: Anything else?

Alex: Yeah, he said to try to get a guy named Mario to park my car because he'd put it in a spot convenient to a quick retrieval and when I got inside I could kill some time at the crap table. He then gave me the complete rundown on the mathematical probabilities of making six consecutive passes and told me the four easiest ways a novice could spot loaded dice. He then began to expound on the evolution of baccarat and the emergency flood-control procedures currently in effect at the hotel, but by that time we were at baggage claim and he had to run to pick up the latest copies of *Scientific American, Chocolatier,* and *The Sporting News* before he caught his connecting flight.

Me: So what do you need to know?
Alex: How long does it take to drive from Reno to Harrah's?
Me: About an hour.

And so it is with Art Spander's columns. They're like a grand tour. Or a ride you've never been on before. Or a panoramic view from an observation tower. Sit back and enjoy the scenery. And welcome to Art Spander's world. The whole wide world.

—Al Michaels

Contents

Trips, the Site Fantastic / 59

Getting Back to Basics / 77

Nothing Exceeds Like Success / 109

You Can't Choose Them All / 173

CONTENTS

Preface

Ernest Hemingway contended that there are two types of writers, those who have something to say and those who have to say something. After twenty-eight years in journalism, I'm still not certain where I fit. Or whether I fit.

"And what did you say you do for a living?" someone invariably asks at a party. You mumble something about the newspaper business, hoping he'll believe you have a delivery route.

"Oh, I read the *Examiner* (or *Daily Blat,* whichever seems more appropriate). Do you have a byline?" he asks.

"Uhm," you stammer, "I write a sports column." That response is followed immediately by, "Oh, I never read the sports pages." Or, "God, I wanted to be a sportswriter. You get paid to go to games? What's Joe Montana really like?"

What sportswriting is really like is a business of ambivalence, of great friendships with other writers and great frustration with your own prose, of deadlines that can't be missed and events that should be missed.

"This is a game for madmen," the late Vince Lombardi said of his job as a coach. "In football, we're all mad."

In sportswriting, maybe only 65 percent of us are mad. The other 35 percent are merely strange.

Normal people may start out in journalism but they quickly disassociate themselves from the business. What remains are individuals caught between the great American novel and some twenty-year-old center fielder who can't conjugate the verb "to be."

We spend half our time listening to college students asking how to get in and the other half wishing we could get out— although we're just fooling ourselves. Given the opportunity to change professions, few sportswriters do. Like the guy who cleans up after the elephants in the circus, we don't want to leave show business.

Really, I was going to go to law school when I graduated from UCLA in 1960. But somebody said I could earn $50 a week working for UPI as a chauffeur during the Democratic Convention. And that led to a job on the night desk. Which led to the *Santa Monica Evening Outlook*. Which led in 1965 to the *San Francisco Chronicle*. Which led to the job as sports columnist on the *San Francisco Examiner* in 1979.

Since then I've spent hours reading guys such as Jim Murray, Ed Pope, and Dave Kindred and wishing I could write like them.

The best description of a sports columnist may have been provided almost accidentally years ago by the *London Times's* Bernard Darwin, in discussing a fellow worker.

"For Neville Cardus," said Darwin, "cricket is his daily bread, but he spreads it with all manner of the most delicious jam."

The idea is to give a subject a flavor that's unique and, you hope, digestible. Yet one man's jam may be another man's pepper.

There are no set rules for writing a column, with this exception: Never take yourself seriously. Misplaced judgment or misplaced modifiers can be tolerated, immodesty cannot.

As the late Red Smith reminded, after publication the page may be serving as a shroud for haddock. Still, it ain't easy.

"Each time I sit behind a typewriter," said Smith, "I merely open a vein and let the blood trickle out."

These days we use computers—word processors—instead of typewriters, but a transfusion still proves necessary.

Writing a sports column is like riding a tiger. Once seated, it's impossible to get off. You become a columnist, not a person. There's always the worry about what you'll write the next day. And the day after that.

"Sports," said the author Roger Kahn, "tells anyone who watches intelligently about the times in which we live. About managed news and corporate politics; about race and terror. And about what the process of aging does to strong men. There is courage and high humor too."

A sports columnist's task is to embellish the courage and humor, to comprehend what is significant and what is not, to be wise and witty on demand.

"I complain a lot about writing sports," Red Smith said once, "but you don't have to lift anything."

Except, with luck, the reader's spirits.

Nothing Like
a Name

TWILIGHT OF A BASEBALL GOD

JULY 11, 1987

It is July for Mr. October. Soon the days grow short for Reggie Jackson, who already finds his career reaching autumn, despite the contradiction of the calendar.

Reggie remains a man of melodrama and real drama, at once engaging and arrogant, full of impetuosity, incandescence, and himself.

Through the season Reggie has done what is arbitrary and what is necessary, creating chaos and championships and a very big wake on an ocean of tranquility.

His life has been a remarkable blend of integrity, insecurity, instability, inspiration, and intimidation. He can stare down a journalist or knock down a teammate, his moods wavering like the confidence of some pitcher who had to face Jackson with the bases loaded.

He has transcended sport to become not merely a hero but a celebrity, who like Arnie or Zsa Zsa can be easily identified by his first name alone. Say "Reggie," and nobody wonders which Reggie you mean.

At age forty-one, the skills have eroded and the personality has mellowed. No longer is Jackson strictly power at the plate and bombast in the clubhouse, although he still can drive the ball out of the park and other players to distraction.

"I always wanted to be the bull in the ring," Jackson wrote in his autobiography.

Call the picadors and order the band to play a pasodoble. Reginald Martinez Jackson of the Oakland A's is about to come strutting into the arena, looking for action and attention—and invariably getting both.

So many things have been said about Reggie, many of them by himself. "He'll be talking twenty years after he's laid in the grave," someone joked before an A's game the other afternoon. Was that a remark of justification or of jealousy?

How do you describe Reggie Jackson, who has hit more home runs than every man who's played major-league baseball except five?

Who in his nineteen previous seasons has been in six World Series and eleven league championship series?

Who has been a fixture in the All-Star Game, having been selected fourteen times?

Who overcame a childhood of near-poverty to construct a lifestyle of sheer luxury?

The quintessential remark either was or wasn't made by Jackson himself, but whether the words are verbatim or paraphrased, they are accurate: "I'm the straw that stirs the drink." The comment appeared during his first spring training with the Yankees, 1977.

"I held up a glass and compared the Yankees to one of those complicated drinks a bartender can mix," said Jackson in his book.

"I talked about Munson and Rivers and Catfish and Nettles and Chambliss. And I said, 'Maybe I've got the kind of personality that can jump into a drink like that and stir things up and get it all going.' At least that's the way I remember it."

What we'll remember about Jackson are 550-plus home runs; strikeouts as turbulent as his personality; an incredible sense of timing; continual contributions to victory.

Bill Russell, the basketball player, once told Joe Morgan after he was traded, "It's funny how those winning teams keep following you around." So too did they keep following Reggie.

When he was with the A's, Oakland won five division and three world championships. When he was with the Yankees, New York won four division and two world championships. When he was with the Angels, California won two division championships.

Winning teams keep following him around, and so does controversy.

Whether he was wrestling with Billy North in the A's clubhouse or screaming at Billy Martin in the Yankees' dugout, Reggie seemed to be in the middle of a dispute when he wasn't in the middle of a rally.

Observations. Pitcher Catfish Hunter: "Reggie would give you the shirt off his back, but he would call a press conference to announce it."

Pitcher Darold Knowles: "There isn't enough mustard in the whole world to cover that hot dog."

Former manager George Bamberger: "From the seventh inning on, Reggie Jackson is the greatest player I've ever seen."

Current Tigers manager Sparky Anderson: "In all honesty, Reggie Jackson never changed from the time he started. I don't think there's a guy who played under more pressure than Reggie and accomplished more."

An assurance of fame is not a pressing problem with Jackson, but the compliments bring approval. The man has been splendid. And he enjoys hearing about it.

"I appreciate what Sparky said," Reggie averred. "He's a guy who's been around baseball for forty years, managed for around twenty. That kind of comment means that all the hard work has paid off."

Reggie is a driven man, and a driving man. He has more than eighty cars, numerous investments, and two auto-repair shops.

He owns a home in Oakland, another in Monterey, which is being remodeled, a condominium in Newport Beach. Wretched excess? Not to someone who remembers a boyhood when there was never enough to eat or to wear.

"I didn't taste steak until I was in high school," recalls Jackson of his days in the suburbs of Philadelphia. "Some nights my room was so cold I had to lay on top of the covers to get my bed warm enough to crawl in."

Reggie escaped—through talent, desire, and, as must be the case in all stories of success, good fortune.

He got a football scholarship to Arizona State, became a baseball star, and was drafted by the Kansas City A's—after he was bypassed by the New York Mets.

And, as Sinatra sings, through the good and lean years and all the in-between years, Reggie, *el toro,* kept charging every red cape. Charles Finley, George Steinbrenner, and others might taunt him, but nobody would faze him.

This is to be his final season, and so he returns to the team with which he started and the city where he lives, the A's and Oakland.

You can go home again, But you can't be young again.

Six weeks ago, Jackson was swinging so poorly there were hints he would retire at the All-Star break.

"Hey, I was hitting .180. I was taking up a roster spot. How in the hell could I not think of retiring? I'm a baseball player. And I'm Reggie Jackson. And I've got 500 home runs. But I'm human, and I'm thinking what you're thinking. You've got to be a realist."

Sometimes it is better to be a dreamer.

"If I could, I'd like to be thirty again. Why thirty? Because I knew enough about the game and there was nothing I couldn't do physically. Wouldn't it be great to be thirty all your life but keep growing mentally and have the knowledge of a guy seventy-five?"

Wouldn't it now? But life permits no such luxury.

Time is the opponent nobody can beat. For Mr. October, winter's call can be heard, even in July.

JACK CLARK'S YEAR OF FULFILLMENT

JULY 14, 1987

Jack Clark stood there, buttressed not only by the frame of a clubhouse dressing cubicle but the knowledge of potential realized.

How confident he seemed Monday deep within the walls of the Oakland Coliseum on the eve of his fourth All-Star Game. How patient. How deserving.

A journey from expectation to success was over. It was a trip many thought could never be made. Jack Clark proved them wrong. What fools these mortals be.

An argument is hereby presented: Despite Eric Davis, despite Don Mattingly, despite Wade Boggs, superior players all, Jack Clark of the St. Louis Cardinals is at this moment the most productive athlete in the major leagues.

He has driven in eighty-six runs. He has hit twenty-six homers. He is batting .311. And July still has days to go. More significantly, Clark's team has the best record in baseball. Jack the Ripper. Jack the Nimble. Jack the Repentant.

For eight seasons Clark labored across the Bay at Candlestick Park, a member of the San Francisco Giants, chilled by the repressive wind, frozen by the continuing boos. Discredited. Disenchanted.

He was only a kid, barely out of high school, not to mention the minor leagues, fighting his own disappointment and the Giants' inadequacies, lashing out at pitches in the dirt or demons in the brain.

He carried the baggage of anticipation, a load that figuratively brought him to his knees and brought Giants fans to a boil.

6

With every move he'd make, with every step he'd take, they'd be booing him to a fare-thee-well.

His strikeouts mounted, his disillusionment grew. The Giants sank. There were good times but all too few.

"I wasn't enjoying the game," Clark recalled. "I had made it to the big leagues, but I wasn't having any fun, wasn't enjoying baseball the way I had in the minors. I was making more money and wasn't enjoying it. The big leagues wasn't like it was supposed to be."

Neither was Jack Clark, who was supposed to be a savior, yes, another Willie Mays.

In Clark's second season with San Francisco, 1978, Jack caught a great many pitches on the fat of the bat, and, it now turns out, too many compliments.

That year, twenty-year-old Jack Clark hit .306 and twenty-five home runs. And the Giants, for one of the infrequent occasions during the decade, were in the pennant race. Oh, the accolades. Oh, the pressure.

"I can't remember a player being so good, so young," said Joe Altobelli, Clark's manager at the time. "You have to go back when Mickey Mantle broke in."

Said teammate Jim Barr: "He's like Mays in that every time he comes up, he seems to make things happen."

Said Chuck Tanner, then managing the Pirates: "Jack immediately reminded me of DiMaggio at the plate. The swing isn't quite as smooth, but there's a physical resemblance."

There: Mantle, Mays, DiMaggio. There were no comparisons with Babe Ruth or Babe Zaharias but the next year, when he slumped, they compared him to Baby Jane.

The spectators jeered. Jack whined, management scoffed. It was a case of inexperience embellished with insensitivity. Jack kept begging to be traded. Management kept begging to be criticized.

"If I could go back, I would change things," thirty-one-year-old Jack Clark concedes midway through his eleventh complete season in the majors.

"I said a lot of things that were uncalled for, but there was a lot of frustration. It was not until other people came into the picture, Joe Morgan and Darrell Evans with the Giants, that I found out about the game.

"They expect when you get to the big leagues you should know

7

it all, produce right away. If you don't, they talk about it, put pressure on you. It took me time to find out, to play the game-within-the-game that it takes to win.

"I didn't have anybody really teach me the ropes for a while, so it took me longer.

"And I wasn't very good at handling the press. I'd get myself in trouble. They don't teach you that stuff in classes in school. I was a quiet, shy person, and all of a sudden you're in front of people in the stands or reporters asking questions."

The question asked primarily was this: Will Jack Clark ever be consistently good? The answer has been given in the two-and-a-half seasons since Clark was traded to the Cardinals.

Jack needed teammates with talent and a positive attitude. Jack needed warm weather. Jack needed direction from his manager. In St. Louis he has all three—and eighty-six runs batted in at the All-Star break.

"It's a combination of everything," said Clark. "I'm a better player and a person than I was seven or eight years ago. I could help any team now—the Cardinals, the Giants.

"I can hit. I can do something to a baseball somebody else can't. As a matter of fact, Joe Morgan called me the other day and said, 'Stop telling people you're not hitting the ball good.' I agreed. He's right.

"I'm not Mickey Mantle or Frank Robinson, but I can hit."

He can hit. Last week he powered a ball into the upper deck at Busch Stadium and then, like Reggie Jackson, stood transfixed at home plate, seemingly awed by his own handiwork.

"I wasn't trying to show up anybody," Clark insisted. "I wasn't calling attention to myself. I just thought the ball was going foul, so I was leaning over trying to make it be fair."

Have we been fair to Jack Clark? Does society demand too much from its possible heroes? Would they be better off left to grow and improve without our scrutiny?

"It took me a long time to get where I am. There was a lot of learning. I wish I could have done it different. But now I'm more polished, more patient. And I'm reaping the benefits."

If only the San Francisco Giants could make the same statement.

DALY CITY'S
"SPORTS BUMS"

OCTOBER 23, 1983

ANAHEIM—Nearly forty years ago they roamed the streets of Daly City, two kids with dreams and dirty tennis shoes.

"We were sports degenerates," John Robinson recalled. "In summers, we'd get up in the morning, and all day long we'd play game after game. You look back, it was sort of crazy."

You imagine a father complaining. Why didn't they make something of themselves, get a job? Why waste time on the sandlots? Who did they think they were? Joe DiMaggio? Sammy Baugh?

"Actually, thinking back," remembered Robinson, "we were pretty bad athletes."

Perhaps, but the two boyhood pals, Robinson and John Madden, became damned fine coaches. More important, they developed into men with an appreciation for life.

Having led the Raiders, then of Oakland, to a Super Bowl victory, Madden took leave from the profession to become, arguably, the best and certainly the most amusing television color announcer extant.

Having led USC to a national championship and several bowl victories, Robinson moved to the pros to become coach of, arguably, the best and certainly the most surprising football team in its division, the Los Angeles Rams.

This weekend the Rams, for the second time during the season, play the 49ers, whom both Robinson and Madden rooted for as kids. This weekend Madden is on assignment in New York broadcasting the game between the Falcons and the Jets. "I got the real titanic," Madden said, sarcastically.

Madden never has draped the truth with diplomacy. Honesty is a trademark. Ask him a question and you receive an unadulterated answer, even about his best friend, John Robinson.

Over these four decades, you wonder, what memory does Madden treasure most about Robinson? His awards as a prep football player at Serra High? His work as an assistant coach to Madden on the Raiders? His quick resurrection of a Rams franchise thought to be moribund?

"No," said Madden. "I'll tell you what I think of when I think of John Robinson.

"When we were kids, we never had any money. So if one of us had a nickel, usually me, and you bought an ice cream cone, the other guy would say, 'Bites,' and then he could take a bite. And hell, he'd eat half your cone.

"You had to say, 'No bites' before he said, 'Bites.' But usually you didn't. So to keep the other guy from getting your ice cream, the trick was to spit on it. Well, John was the only guy who would still eat your ice cream cone."

Madden, forty-seven, and Robinson, forty-eight, met at Our Lady of Perpetual Help Grammar School. From there Madden went to local Jefferson High, while Robinson crossed the hills to San Mateo and Serra. "But as soon as school was over, John would be back in Daly City with me," said Madden.

Has success changed John Robinson? Not at all. Neither has it made much of a dent in Madden, now surely one of the nation's more recognizable celebrities.

"Both of us are about the same," insisted Madden. "We don't hang out in Marchbank Park or the pool hall any longer, but we enjoy people and we still love sports.

"We went to baseball games at Seals Stadium, 49ers games at Kezar. We never had a cent. We sneaked in. Never paid anywhere. We couldn't. Never had any money. His dad didn't do a heck of a lot. My dad was a mechanic. I guess our families had some money, but we never saw any."

What the two friends did see, even then, was a future in athletics.

"We thought we were really students of the game," Madden said.

"In those days, everybody's favorite 49er players were Joe Perry and Hugh McElhenny. John liked Billy Wilson, because he was an end and John was an end. But both of us liked Bob Toneff, #74, a defensive lineman. We'd watch the line play, the pass rushes and talk about it."

Robinson went to the University of Oregon. Madden enrolled at College of San Mateo, then transferred to Oregon. "I didn't adjust," said Madden. He graduated from Cal Poly of San Luis Obispo.

"We used to tell each other the first guy who got a head coaching job would hire the other," mused Madden. "It took me three times to get Robinson to work for me on the Raiders. Then he only stayed one year because he got the head job at USC.

"John cares about people, not business. Some people still have the first dollar they earned. John doesn't know where his last dollar is."

As long as John Madden buys the ice cream, John Robinson will never have to worry.

DEATH SO SOON

JANUARY 7, 1988

The news arrived, like that of so many other tragedies, on the car radio. Pete Maravich was dead, said a disembodied voice.

I remembered the November morning another voice on another car radio told me John F. Kennedy had been shot. Now as then came a crushing feeling of disbelief.

Pete Maravich dead. And the Warriors would play the San Antonio Spurs. And the 49ers were preparing for Minnesota. And so we beat on, boats against the current . . . .

Each person begins and ends the same. But what happens between birth and death, what we make of our lives, differentiates one from another.

For a few years that in retrospect now seem only a few moments, Maravich, "Pistol Pete" as he was invariably known, separated himself from almost everybody. He was the most exciting basketball player in the land.

Obituaries are meant to be written by young people about old. But the plot does not always follow the script.

The dry disbelief in the words of Kareem Abdul-Jabbar echoed our own thoughts. "He was younger than I am," Kareem said barely above a whisper when asked to recall Maravich and his deeds.

Athletes are not supposed to age. Or weaken. Or perish. In the mind's eye we see them on the fields and courts of friendly strife diving for loose balls or leaping into the end zone, going on and on.

Don Sutton, age forty-two, signs a contract to pitch with the Los Angeles Dodgers. And the same day, Pete Maravich, age forty, collapses and dies. Logic fails us.

This month's issue of *Hoop*, the National Basketball Association program, has a long feature on "The Early Showmen: Cousy, Monroe, Maravich." Do not tell me the timing is coincidental. I will believe otherwise. There is an eeriness about the scenario.

The NBA of the 1980s is a league of flash and fame, where,

12

paying obeisance to the television camera, the seminal play is the dunk or stuff shot.

Maravich's skill was in getting the ball to the basket, not putting it through, although he was almost unequaled at making points.

He dribbled through his legs, he passed behind his back, and then he'd throw up a jumper.

"I always felt Pete was one of the most unique players to come into the league," Jerry West, another unique player, told *Hoop*. "But he carried this stigma of being a hot dog. I think he never really got with the right team or the right coach in his pro career."

You see, we were naive. We still believed the essence of basketball was to hit the open man—which Maravich damned well did—not to provide a lot of "oohs" and "aahs." Pete was in the avant-garde. He understood sport was entertainment as well as competition.

Now everyone's a hot dog. Or a Polish sausage. We get 360-degree spins, over-the-back dunks, and enough slapping of palms to create a percussion section for a marching band.

An athlete, it has been written, floats above the complex and disagreeable, which become for him the unreal. His private world is the real world.

Yet often it is a world he cannot fathom.

Pete kept dribbling and shooting. And kept being criticized. He sought answers. He found them in diet, becoming a vegetarian, and in religion.

The pattern is familiar. The rest of us claw and scrape under the misconception that a mountain must be scaled, and we spend much of our lives trying, if failing. Athletes reach the top almost immediately. And then what?

"A shame you did it all at twenty-six," sings the man in *Evita*. "There are no mysteries now. Nothing can thrill you, no one fulfill you."

Maravich's fulfillment came from the church. Nobody boos in a sanctuary.

"The most important thing to me," Maravich said not long ago, "was people saying, 'We've never seen a basketball game before, and we'll never miss another one.' I'd rather be remembered for those happy faces than anything else."

Pete gave us a lot of smiles and so much more. He was too young to die. We all are.

TWO-UP ON THE GAME OF LIFE

AUGUST 14, 1987

RANCHO MURIETA—So there he stood, with hat of straw and swing of legend, all wrinkles and wonder, a man for many seasons, a golfer for one reason, Samuel Jackson Snead.

He is greatness preserved, history personified, a link to simpler times—a myth who's part icon and part con man, a hero with twinkling eyes and larcenous thoughts.

He turned pro in 1935, when milk was eight cents a quart but nobody could spare a dime. And now, fifty-two years later, with too many contemporaries gone, Snead not only survives but persists, grousing about his putting yet conceding that he's two-up in the game of life.

Snead is seventy-five now, the same age as Ben Hogan and Byron Nelson, against whom he made birdies, headlines, and a reputation that will last as long as men and women battle fate and nature in that most frustrating of sports, golf.

Hogan is a near-recluse in Texas, refusing to submit his pride to the embarrassment of three-putt greens. Nelson plays only for enjoyment, a champion who retired much too young.

But Snead, cantankerous, agile, admirable, comes out of his haven in Virginia to add to the record and our memories. He recalls the way he was. We're grateful for the way he is.

Sam showed up in the Sierra foothills, at Rancho Murieta, southeast of Sacramento, for the Senior Gold Rush. It's only his second PGA Senior Tour event of a year that is now making the turn for home.

He rides a golf cart. He has trouble seeing, because of what he says is a wrinkled retina in his right eye. "People across the way look like they're about twelve feet tall, on stilts," said Snead.

14

He lurches a trifle in the completion of a swing that used to be as sweet as praline pie.

But he still makes birdies. The way he played the par-four seventeenth hole at Rancho Murieta on the opening day of the pro-am was wonderful. A great drive. An iron eight feet from the cup. A putt into the hole. Plop. Pleasure. Birdie.

The kids who populate the regular golf tour, bland, blond, think of the game as a business. They're so serious. And so silent. Faces in a crowd of faceless people. A lot of fine rounds. Very few ingratiating looks.

The old guys, the seniors, fifty and older, may be rich and famous but they can tell of days long gone, when the obstacles were large and the purses small and hardly anyone would offer a penny for your thoughts much less for use as a ball marker.

Snead's magical mystery tour through the oaks and expensive homes at Rancho Murieta was full of self-deprecation and keen observation. He laughed about the inability of his amateur partners and whined about the competency of his own game.

"What's that yardage?" Snead asked a caddie who carried a burden if not clubs, Sam's red-and-white Wilson bag being hauled on the back of his cart.

"I guess it's about 165," the young man responded.

"I don't like guessing," snapped Snead. "I want to know. And, what hole is this?"

A missed shot on the hole, the par-three sixteenth sent the ball into a bunker. Slammin' Sam? He slammed the club into the caddie's chest. "Here," he grunted. "Can't do much worse unless they blindfolded me."

We can't do much better, even watching a player past his prime. Hey, the guy was earning money when Babe Ruth was still active. He won the Oakland Open at Claremont Country Club fifty years ago, 1937—and still can tell you every detail of the final round.

That's when a photographer took his picture and sent it to the wires. The next day the photo ran in the New York papers and, we've been told, Snead, in his country naiveté, gasped, "How'd they get that picture? I was never in New York."

Snead claims he never made the remark. "Fred Corcoran invented it," laughed Sam about his late manager and PGA Tour director. "He told everyone I said it. A lot of things about me aren't true."

And a lot of them are. Snead has won eighty-four PGA tournaments officially. Other records indicate he's won more than 130. But he never won a U.S. Open. And he never plays for fun.

"I got to have something going, even now," said Snead. "For me to play with somebody, unless it was a president or something, doesn't matter. And even with a president I might play halfway. I just can't get up.

"I remember I was playing with four guys down at Greenbrier," said Snead about the days when he was the pro at the West Virginia resort.

"I parred the first four holes, and one of them said, 'Hey, we want to see you shoot a good round.' I told him I couldn't knuckle down just playing around. He said, 'Oh, would you like to play us for $10 a hole?' I said, 'All of you, $10 apiece each hole?' He said fine. I had eight birdies from there in."

The only flaw in his career was a failure to win the U.S. Open. He had so many chances. And so many misses. In the late 1930s at Philadelphia, for example, he took an eight on the final hole when a bogey-six would have put him in a playoff.

"I'd be lying if I said I don't think about it," sighed Snead. "But it doesn't bother me. Sometimes I lost it by foolish things. Sometimes because I didn't know what score was already in. And sometimes because I got bad pairings."

An aberration? An indication? A sign that this golfer was still human after all?

"I've got no complaints. I owe everything I have to golf. I could stop playing today, I think, and be satisfied."

But he won't. He'll keep playing. Which keeps us satisfied. Keep going, Sam. We love every swing and every memory.

WILLIE
HAD DOUBTS

JANUARY 10, 1986

NEW YORK—He wore a three-piece suit, handling questions the way he once did fastballs, nostalgia flowing, sentiment oozing, honesty showing.

Willie Lee McCovey was always a difficult man to understand. For opposing pitchers. For the public. In a world that had become too public, he sought to retain his privacy.

Perhaps it was a defense mechanism, a method of keeping his fears and foibles far from the madding crowd. Perhaps it still is.

"If I hadn't been selected to the Hall of Fame," he said a few hours after he had been, "it would have bothered my friends a lot more than it would me.

"The last few weeks, people thought it was a foregone conclusion that I'd be chosen. I don't think a day passed in the Bay Area without one of the papers doing something. I think among all the people I knew, I was the one who had some doubt.

"It had reached a point where I would not have been so disappointed as downright embarrassed for my friends. I knew I could handle it, but my friends would have thought it was an injustice."

The scales balanced. Justice prevailed. Willie McCovey, twenty-two years a major leaguer, the greatest left-handed home-run hitter in National League history, for all intents then and now a San Francisco Giant, was chosen.

Excluding the five legends from the original year, 1936, a half-century past, Ruth, Cobb, Wagner, Mathewson, and Walter Johnson, only sixteen players have been elected their first year of eligibility. McCovey is one.

"It's a thrill," he conceded. "And now I don't have to go through the anticipation year after year."

"Stretch," they called him, and on a dais of a conference room at the Sheraton Centre Hotel, where a short while earlier he had offered a brief bit of oratory, Willie McCovey was stretched out in a chair.

His left hand was decorated by a ring bearing his uniform number, 44. The baby finger of his right hand was embellished by a ring with his initials, WM. His voice was untarnished by a sleepless night.

Willie Mac had been advised of his honor by phone Wednesday at 5:30 P.M. Pacific Standard Time.

Not long before, he had arrived home from an abbreviated round of golf at his club, Lake Merced in Daly City, where the bunkers and trees gave him fewer problems than the members, repetitively asking how he could so admirably control his emotions.

They should have known. Willie almost always controlled his emotions. As he would admit, "As a ballplayer, I kept a little mystery about myself."

A 10 P.M. flight from San Francisco International, the euphemistic "red-eye," brought him three time zones east.

"I didn't sleep," McCovey would concede. "Not because I was thinking about getting into the Hall of Fame. I've never been able to sleep on airplanes."

A secret disclosed, but it's too late for Don Drysdale and Bob Gibson. If only they had known, the time to face Willie was after an all-night, cross-country flight. Willie, yesterday morning, faced a spate of journalists from the Big Apple. There were no yawns, maybe because there was no recognition of reality. "What time is it?" he would ask later. "I'm still on California time."

His play, however, will remain timeless.

A plaque will be hung at Cooperstown in upstate New York, the community synonymous with baseball skill, and kids from generations unborn will know his name.

"What it's all about," the late Jimmy Cannon wrote once, "is a man being good at something." Cannon was alluding to Joe Namath. The thought holds for Willie McCovey. He was good at hitting a baseball. No. He was great at hitting a baseball.

Chub Feeney is now the National League president. In 1959, when McCovey arrived in San Francisco, Feeney was general manager of the Giants.

"I had seen him in Arizona that spring," Feeney said. "I knew what he could do. But we were rather surprised by that first game."

Who wasn't? A few hours out of the Pacific Coast League, chauffeured to Seals Stadium in the limo of team owner Horace Stoneham, McCovey began his major-league career with two triples and two singles off the Phillies' Robin Roberts.

"It could have been three triples," said Chub, "but one ball was hit so hard it bounced off the wall right to the fielder."

How do you define greatness? Through the endless statistics? Through the testimony of observers? Maybe best of all by memories.

The highlight of his career, said McCovey, impossibly trying to separate so many spectacular days, was the 1962 World Series—and please, no, don't refer once more to the final out, a McCovey liner at Bobby Richardson. "Somebody," sighed McCovey, "always has to ask about that."

McCovey recalls that 1962 World Series, the one and only for the Giants. He recalls an evening at Pittsburgh's Forbes Field when he drilled—no other word is so appropriate—a ball over the center-field fence.

"That place was so big," reminded McCovey, "they would put the batting cage in the center because they didn't think anyone could hit a ball that far."

Willie McCovey could.

"I also came in as a pinch-hitter one time and hit a grand-slam homer off Don Drysdale," said McCovey. "I remember that.

"I had been trying to get a raise. I went in to see Chub. He told me to call him 'Mr. Feeney.' In the clubhouse after the homer, I said, 'Mr. Feeney.' He said, 'Now you can call me Chub.' "

Others called Drysdale McCovey's cousin. Not McCovey. "My eyes didn't light up when I saw he was going to face us. I had to bear down. But I was able to hit him."

Did Drysdale, notorious for his intimidation, ever hit McCovey? "No, I never got thrown at by anybody. I never fraternized much. There was that mystery about me. People didn't know if I'd come after them. But Don threw at Willie Mays."

Memories. McCovey spoke of conversations with Ted Williams and Stan Musial about—what else?—hitting.

"One thing I noticed," said McCovey. "Most of the nicest big leaguers were baseball's biggest names. Players were great to me. After I got going in San Francisco, the fans were great to me.

"I feel my induction into the Hall of Fame next summer will be for the whole city of San Francisco, the whole Bay Area. I think it means more to them than it does to me."

And, though he may try to tell us differently, it means a great deal to Willie McCovey. That's no secret.

THE NFL'S MACHIAVELLI

JANUARY 15, 1984

The calculated gamble that passes for Al Davis's life often blurs the assets and erudition of a man as charming as he is reputed to be devious.

Behind the shiny-toothed leer and below the greased-down hair exists the last of America's rugged individualists, and possibly the most fascinating character we've ever met.

Or the most despised.

Name the people, inside sport or out, who in this land equal fifty-four-year-old Al Davis's reputation for a combination of success, secrecy, and sacrilege.

Who else can be so outrageous? So clever? So intense? So combative? So farsighted? Or, most of all, since victory remains his consuming wish, so triumphant?

"I only want to win," he sighs repetitively.

And win he does, vicariously through his football team, an alter ego called the Raiders, or directly in courtrooms or business deals.

Who stops Al Davis?

Not the system of jurisprudence. Despite rules to the contrary, Davis moved the Raiders from Oakland to Los Angeles. Not the other NFL teams. Despite forecasts to the contrary, the Raiders are in Super Bowl XVIII.

Who is this man who talks about the future and affects styles out of the past? Who talks in half-sentences? Who quotes Theodore Dreiser and Machiavelli? Who claims his idols are Rocky Marciano, George Blanda, Jackie Robinson, and Henry Kissinger? Who will tell you anything except a lie?

"I think Al Davis has the serial number of the unknown soldier."—Sam Rutigliano, head coach of the Cleveland Browns.

"If Al Davis had decided that he wanted to become president

21

of this country, he could have done it. He's that brilliant."— Edward Stancyzk, athletic director at Adelphi University, where Davis coached.

"Al Davis has spent most of his life looking for weaknesses in people because he believes that in life there are only winners and losers."—Ed Heafey, attorney for the Oakland Coliseum, who opposed Davis in the infamous antitrust trials.

"Al Davis has done more toward promoting Oakland as a big-league city than has been accomplished in the previous sixty years."—A spokesman in January 1964, when Davis was named "Outstanding Young Man of the Year" by the Oakland Junior Chamber of Commerce.

"I hired Al Davis as head coach in 1963 because everybody hated his guts. Al Davis wants to win, and he'll do anything to win, and after losing all those games I wanted to win any way I could."—Wayne Valley, the former Raiders owner.

Allow Al Davis a few choice words:

"I don't want to be the most respected man in football; I want to be the most feared.

"I don't treat people the way I would like to be treated. I treat them the way they want to be treated.

"Am I ruthless? I know this. When it gets down to the end, I hate to lose.

"I don't want to give the feeling I'm above and beyond, but I've always had the perception to understand the game. Do you follow me? As a kid, I was the organizer.

"I'm not for anarchy. Nobody loves football more than I do. But I'll be damned if I'm going to let the Oakland Coliseum hold me hostage. Where's the island that Napoleon was sent to—Elba? Maybe they'll put up a stadium there.

"What I do is dominate with philosophy."

Only two current NFL owners have been coaches, Davis and Paul Brown. Al perceives the big picture, not just a single image. He understands what makes teams winners—great players. He understands what keeps great players satisfied—big contracts.

As football's version of the Emma Lazarus poem on the base of the Statue of Liberty, Davis takes not so much the huddled masses yearning to be free as the mavericks and malcontents other teams can't handle.

"I'm a strong believer in environment," he says. "A change in environment means a lot." The idea came from reading

Dreiser's *Sister Carrie.* At Syracuse, the third college he attended as an undergraduate, Davis earned a degree in English.

Abrasive, manipulative, dictatorial, honest, Al Davis worked his way through the ranks until taking over the Raiders before the 1963 season.

Oakland was 1-13 in 1962. Oakland was 10-4 in 1963. As we are informed by the litany out of the Raiders' office, since Al arrived the team has the best record in pro football.

When the old American Football League decided to attack the NFL, Davis was elevated to commissioner. It was similar to Iran elevating the Ayatollah Khomeini.

The AFL tried to steal everything from the NFL that wasn't tied down. The white flag went up. A merger was negotiated. Pete Rozelle was the czar of football. Al Davis was back in Oakland, screaming about a sellout and holding a grudge against Rozelle that will never die.

Al opposed a common draft. A common draft was instituted. Al opposed a championship game between the two leagues. Ironically, his club repeatedly arrives in the Super Bowl.

"We had them," he wistfully recalled about the battle. "There was no alternative to peace. If you study foreign affairs, you'll find there's a rule that the guerrilla wins if he doesn't lose. If he exists he wins, and time is on his side because the patience of the establishment wears thin."

Two decades later, Al is a tenuous part of the establishment, the NFL. The United States Football League is the guerrilla. Did USFL executives heed Davis's advice?

Davis justified his move to Los Angeles on a need for money. "In the 1960s and 1970s, the great organizations were built through hard work and intelligence and great players. In the 1980s, it's not going to be that way. Economics is going to be the factor."

There were guffaws. But with the USFL spending millions for Herschel Walker and Mike Rozier, the laughs have stopped. Davis is right once more.

"Life is two things," Davis insisted once. "Challenge and creativeness. That's what America is."

Patriotism has been called the last refuge of a scoundrel. Don't mention that to Al. He can't stand being last in anything.

THE RARE BIRD

JUNE 9, 1986

BOSTON—They are taking him from the court, this gem of an athlete, taking him sweaty and triumphant from people who would smother him with hugs the way they're now battering him with cheers.

It is a matter of safety as well as recognition. The Hope Diamond is being put back in the vault. King Tut's mask is being returned to the museum. Larry Bird is being taken to the Boston Celtics' locker room.

Thirty-nine seconds are on the clock, but the game is over. It has been over seemingly from the moment it began. From the moment Larry Bird walked onto the floor.

"I maintain the championship was won," chortles Bird's teammate Bill Walton, "the day Larry Bird was born."

Precognition. An exhibition. Larry Bird has painted a glorious portrait. And the Houston Rockets into a corner. Boston has crushed the Rockets, 114-97. The NBA season is finished. The Celtics are champs for the sixteenth time.

Bird has kept a promise and enhanced a reputation. He has played a basketball game for the ages. He is weary beyond belief. "Not a breath left in his body," Walton would notice.

Perspiration has pasted Bird's hair against his scalp. But he is a winner. Again. And the most valuable player. Again.

This is an era of hyperbole. Actors who couldn't memorize Olivier's lines are called great. A year-old golf tournament is called a classic. But Larry Bird's skills cannot be exaggerated.

Oscar Robertson was special. So were Elgin Baylor and Jerry West and Rick Barry. But now there is Larry Bird. And all you can think of is the line Bobby Jones used in 1965 about Jack Nicklaus winning the Masters by a mile: "He plays a game with which I'm not familiar."

We arrive with pre-fixed ideas, doubters who saw a Cousy, a Russell, a Walt Frazier, skeptics properly suspicious of everything and everyone new. But then Bird turns a loose ball into an assist, a bad dribble into a basket. And we are won over, converts prepared to testify.

"He's the greatest player ever," said Milwaukee Bucks coach Don Nelson about Bird. And Nelson played with Russell and Havlicek.

"He's from another planet," sighed Celtics scout Ed Badger. "Whatever you think he can do, he does it better. I can't believe there's been another like him."

Reactions. Results. The ball is bouncing out of bounds. Bird dives, saves, fires to Kevin McHale. Dunk. The twenty-four-second clock is running down. Bird dribbles, spins, and connects from beyond the three-point circle.

Numbers: Another triple-double for Larry Bird: twenty-nine points, twelve assists, eleven rebounds. Numbers: Another home-court victory for the Celtics, forty-nine times out of fifty chances this season at home.

"The best basketball player I've ever seen," said Walton—called by some the best basketball player *they'd* ever seen.

How? Why? What enables six-foot-nine Larry Bird to take away rebounds from seven-footers Akeem Olajuwon and Ralph Sampson? What enables 220-pound Larry Bird to get down the court faster than men sleeker and supposedly swifter than he?

"You saw the game," said Walton. "Describe it."

How do you describe a moonbeam? Or the taste of cherries jubilee? How do you freeze in time the magic and the motion? How do you embody the intangible?

"What makes him different from everyone is his mind," said Walton. "He's the quickest player on the court even though he may be the slowest getting down the court."

He is tough, mentally, physically. "The ball will be in my hands," Bird had forecast twenty-four hours before the game, "and that's all I care about. I know when I'm going to play well, and when I'm that way we all usually play well."

"I worked myself up so high," said Bird, "I had to settle down some and let the game come to me. I was tired, but I was so pumped up I wasn't tired. It's surprising how some players rise to the occasion."

Larry Bird rose. It was his destiny. "I have to do it when I have the chance." He had the chance. The Celtics had the championship.

KAREEM THE MYSTERIOUS

NOVEMBER 30, 1983

OAKLAND—In the purple raiment of royalty, Kareem Abdul-Jabbar stands imperiously at one end of the basketball court, a man in control of himself and, at times, the game.

His is a quiet presence, a subdued domination.

Magic Johnson offers the Los Angeles Lakers exuberance. Michael Cooper provides flash. But Kareem remains a lonely sentinel, going about his task silently, elegantly, efficiently.

The box score does not always reflect his contribution. The standings inevitably do.

When the Lakers rallied to beat Golden State last night at Oakland Coliseum Arena, 111-105, Magic was making the passes and Mike McGee was making the baskets. Kareem was pleased. "What matters," he said, "is we won. That's what always matters."

Success clings to this big man. Championships lie in his wake. Three consecutive NCAA titles were taken by UCLA when he was there. Three times he has been on NBA champions. He is perhaps the greatest player in history. He is perhaps the most mysterious player in history.

Secretive, somber, afflicted by the ills of society, seven-foot-two Kareem Abdul-Jabbar was determined to be the country's tallest recluse. He fought a private war against the media and the milieu of American sport. Anger and disdain seemed his primary motivation.

But as his enemies grew older, so did Kareem. He was coaxed out of a shell into a world of laughter and love, where he could enjoy his accomplishments and mankind.

The metamorphosis, and other details of a life long hidden are described, with the help of writer Peter Knobler, in an autobiography titled, appropriately enough, *Giant Steps*.

Candor is Kareem's virtue. He cannot hide on the court. He decided not to hide anything in his story. It is an attempt to set the record straight. It is also a catharsis.

Journalists and athletes invariably have an adversary relationship. Usually, they coexist, one side pushing against the other and making little headway. Kareem never believed in tolerance.

Postgame remarks were growled, when they were given at all. Interviews became confrontations, with Abdul-Jabbar, who held the cards, always triumphant.

Twelve years ago, while he was a member of the Bucks, I approached Kareem in a mirrored dressing room at Milwaukee Arena on an off-day during the play-offs. We performed our figurative dance. I was hemming and hawing. He was tersely responding. When he stood up to depart, we were both visibly relieved.

How different it is now. Kareem is no longer bitter. The press is no longer caustic. To help promote his book, Abdul-Jabbar willingly sits for questions and questioners he once believed foolish.

"I made a lot of mistakes," Kareem conceded last night. He was sitting in the Lakers' locker room an hour and a half before tipoff. He was polite, considerate, expansive.

"I painted myself into a corner. The press didn't like me. I didn't like the press. We never got time to understand each other.

"That's one reason I like the book. I had thought about doing it for years. I wanted people to understand me, to know me."

Two of those people were his parents, Al and Cora Alcindor.

His conversion to the Muslim faith, his name change from Lewis Alcindor to Kareem Abdul-Jabbar, his reclusive life, drove a wedge between Kareem and his mother and father. But the reconciliation has taken place. Both sides are thankful.

Each of us is shaped by his or her environment. Lew Alcindor, growing up in New York an only child, was a happy kid. But as years passed, "I noticed I was darker and taller than everyone else." Soon the differences would gnaw at his self-esteem and his sense of justice.

His sensitivity was interpreted as moodiness. His intensity was looked upon as arrogance. His satisfaction was limited to the basketball court and, after he accepted Islam, studying the religion.

A while back, a columnist in Boston, George Kimball, referred to the fact Kareem had smiled.

"What had I turned into?" Abdul-Jabbar asks, in print. "I had always smiled as a kid. Somewhere all of that had been squashed."

Kareem's hatreds and fears had gained the best of him. Racism evokes no happiness. But the man obviously believes that where there is life, there is hope, and a reason to smile.

"I had forced that gregarious kid inside myself. But I found that people want to like you. It's better this way."

Who could disagree?

PRESSURE GETS TO McENROE

SEPTEMBER 18, 1984

These are the lyrics of Paul Simon: "A man hears what he wants to hear and disregards the rest . . . . " On this late afternoon in the Cow Palace, it is time to hear the words of the world's best tennis player.

John McEnroe sits behind the baseline gnawing on a fingernail and his image. A couple of chairs down is his doubles partner, Peter Fleming. Two's company. Autograph-seekers are a crowd.

On the court, McEnroe's younger brother, Patrick, is losing a first-round match in the Transamerica tournament to Tom Gullikson. John studies the situation with clinical detachment.

"This match should have been held in the evening," John McEnroe whispers to nobody in particular. He gazes at perhaps 200 spectators in an arena that will hold 15,000. "It's a shame more people couldn't see this match."

What John McEnroe sees in this match he doesn't like but does understand. "My brother's just starting at Stanford," reminds Mac. "This match means experience. It's not easy being my brother. He's heard about it 50,000 times. But you've got to take the pluses with the minuses."

Was that a desultory smile on McEnroe's face? Yes, he was fully conscious of the remark. The guy who berates linesmen was preaching the power of positive thinking—and grasping the irony.

"I look for the good," said McEnroe. "It might not always seem that way. But I realize I've been lucky. I've tried to make the best of things. I wish the media and the public would understand what it's like for me."

What do we know of John McEnroe, Jr.? That he has a big

serve and little patience? That he is talented and can be abrasive? That he's at war with the British press and at peace with himself? He never promised us a rose garden. But he did promise himself he would accept the challenge.

"I have pressure," said McEnroe. "Not like the pressure of a guy with a wife and two kids trying to put food on the table. I realize that. I know I've made a lot of money. But the people who criticize don't understand what it's like to be in my position."

And what is it like at age twenty-five to be king of the mountain, to possess the skills most of us would kill for?

"It's a little scary," said John McEnroe, "to think the only thing you can do is go down."

The experts contend it will be a while until McEnroe sinks. On the contrary, he seems to be improving each year, getting better, not worse. In 1984 he has won sixty-six of sixty-eight matches. That's not tennis, that's domination.

"Playing as close to your potential as possible," said McEnroe. "That's what it's all about." McEnroe leans forward. He is wearing a gray sweatshirt and blue warm-up pants. The white socks have his name woven down the side. Your own sweatsocks. What would F. Scott Fitzgerald have said about this side of paradise? McEnroe is interrupted frequently. People, kids, adults thrust programs or slips of paper at him. He begs off. "Later," he sighs. "Later." Celebrity is an uncomfortable role.

"It's funny how you change," volunteered McEnroe. "When I was sixteen or seventeen I used to carry four or five rackets hoping someone would notice me and think I was a real tennis person. Now I try to get away from it.

"There's not a question I haven't been asked. But people ask them like it's the first time I've heard them. A guy asked me to sign a doctor's prescription. Told me I'd probably never been asked to do that before. I had.

"People have no idea what it's like. But I can understand that. Before I got to where I am, I had no idea either."

It's what he puts on his competitors that has bothered the public. They had grown weary of tantrums and blue language. His slick strokes were lost in a barrage of petulance.

"I'm maturing," insisted McEnroe. "I've tried to avoid controversies, especially since the French."

Ah, the French Open. What did he say to that photographer? Was it *"Bonjour, mon ami"*?

"Sometimes I just don't know what makes me do things. I don't plan them. They are spur-of-the-moment. The only time in my life I did something deliberate was against this guy." McEnroe nodded toward Bill Scanlon, the despised one.

Everyone has enemies. McEnroe also has his idols. Rod Laver was one when John was a kid. Jimmy Connors is one now that John is a man.

"I love the way Connors gets pumped up," said McEnroe, who beat Jimmy both at Wimbledon and in the U.S. Open this year. "No one plays as hard as Connors. It's amazing. In all the matches I've played him, for maybe a game and a half one match, he didn't seem to be trying. It freaked me out."

The tougher the match the better McEnroe likes it and the less he acts up. Early in a tournament is when he is most likely to lose his cool, if not the match.

"I was a kid when I first started playing pro tennis. I hope I've improved. I want people to look at me and say, 'Hey, this guy can play tennis.' "

They've always said that. What else they say is up to John McEnroe.

THREE CHEERS FOR RED SMITH

MARCH 16, 1981

It may be a sign of the times that the most effective way for anyone—even a newspaperman—to become famous is to appear on national television. Thus, last night, in his seventy-fifth year, did Red Smith possibly gain the recognition to which he has so long been entitled.

Certainly, those who have studied the sports pages of America over the years will not be unfamiliar with Red Smith or his marvelously literate prose.

But so many of us no longer are concerned with the written word, only the TV image.

We are enthralled by the fuzzy picture on the screen rather than the permanent record of ink on paper. We would rather be told what is happening by some guy with a teardrop hairdo instead of spending a few moments to read it ourselves.

We make heroes out of people who sell soap or sell themselves, people who invade our living rooms and our senses. Seeing, we have been told, is believing. Unfortunately, very few of us had ever seen Walter Wellesley "Red" Smith.

That oversight was corrected last night. There was a segment about Red Smith on CBS-TV's "60 Minutes." The evening crew in the sports department of the *Examiner* stopped working briefly to watch. You presume it was that way on other papers. One of our own was being honored.

For more than half a century, seventy-five-year-old Red Smith has been a working newspaperman, battling, at times, deadlines and the power structure and the misuse of grammar. He proved that sportswriters could be literate and perceptive—and caring. Everyone, I suppose, has heroes. Yours may be Pete Rose or Muhammad Ali, or Ronald Reagan or Ralph Nader. One of mine is Red Smith. He gave my profession a great deal of class. He also gave the American public a great deal of information.

It is fashionable these days for some sportswriters to spend most of their time being critical, either of their subjects or of their job. They don't like the athletes or the owners—or the fans. They don't like writing about people who catch baseballs or drop them. They complain about being unfulfilled.

Life, however, is what you make of it. And Red Smith has made all he could of his. Complain? Gripe? Not Red Smith. As he told Morley Safer of CBS last night, he loves his work. So do we.

A decade ago, when the Giants traded Willie Mays to the Mets, Smith reminisced about 1951, when Willie was called up from the minors. The late Garry Schumacher was the public-relations man then for the Giants, the New York Giants, and he was inordinately enthusiastic about Mays.

" 'We got to take care of this kid,' said Garry Schumacher of the Giants," Smith wrote. " 'We got to make sure he gets in no trouble because this is the guy—well, I'm not saying he's going to win pennants by himself, but he's the guy who'll have us all eating strawberries in the wintertime.' "

Smith used that last remark as the title for one of his anthologies. Said Red, "It captures, I think, some of the flavor of the sportswriter's existence, which is what the late Bill Corum was talking about when he said, 'I don't want to be a millionaire, I just want to live like one.' "

The only way Red Smith would be a millionaire would be if his wealth were measured by the number of words he has written since joining the *Milwaukee Sentinel* in 1927 after graduation from Notre Dame. Not that you'll hear him complaining.

"I set out to make a living, not to make a contribution," he remarked last night. Definitely, he's accomplished both.

He has approached the world of sport with this sort of balance: suspicion without cynicism, admiration without rapture.

Maybe the best sports columnist-reporter in the history of American journalism, Smith believes he is supposed to *tell* the story not *be* the story. This philosophy, of course, makes him the antithesis of an individual to whom he referred, Howard Cosell.

"I'm not a psychologist," said Smith once, "but I do know, for example, that a fellow like Howard Cosell is the braggart he is because of a massive insecurity. He has to be told every couple of minutes how great he is, because he's so insecure.

"And if you don't tell him, he tells you. He can't help this."
Smith, to be sure, has his faults. They are much less wearing.
As do others of his generation, Red dislikes basketball: "It
only bores me," he told the national television audience.

He also is prone to use his columns in *The New York Times*
to extol the virtues of trout fishing or Thoroughbred racing,
neither of which has the general audience appeal of, say, a piece
on Reggie Jackson or Bill Veeck.

Yet, even if the subject matter is not always the most interesting,
the prose used to describe it invariably is.

Smith's sense of humor was obvious last night when he exposed
his love affair with the game of college football. "I was almost
willing to rewrite the rule book into English for free," he
explained.

He never did. He simply kept writing his columns several times
a week. Not unlike others, it is the part of the business he
appreciates least.

"I sit down at a typewriter, cut open a vein, and bleed," he
has said about the agony of producing copy.

That agony has brought us plenty of ecstacy. Here's to Red
Smith, TV star. It's about time.

HIS DAY
TO SHINE

AUGUST 1, 1984

LOS ANGELES—On the victory stand, with "The Star-Spangled Banner" providing the most exhilarating of background music, the young man nicknamed Rowdy tried to retain his composure. He was not nearly as successful as he was in retaining a lead a brief while before.

What was that comment Churchill made about Field Marshal Montgomery? In defeat unbeatable, in victory unbearable? America's chlorine corps has not had to worry about defeat. And the American public has been offered no problems with victory. Our kids know how to win, mentally as well as physically.

Whether Ambrose Gaines IV should be described as a kid at age twenty-five is open to debate. That Gaines, like so many of his countrymen from G. Washington to C. Yeager, has the right stuff is undeniable. A few tears and some lingering doubts only enhanced his triumph.

Seemingly all bulging pectorals and blond hair, Gaines yesterday powered his way to victory in the fastest swimming race of them all, the men's 100-meter freestyle.

The event takes less than a minute. Actually, less than fifty seconds. The world record, set by Gaines four years ago, is 0:49.36. One lap in one direction, one in the other, and the race is history. Then, they either hang gold around your neck or the millstone of disappointment.

"There isn't any time to think," Gaines said after the race. Not until you're receiving accolades or condolences. And then the brain flails away like a drowning man trying to stay afloat.

The national anthem had started. The Stars and Stripes was being hauled up the flagpole. Gaines's right hand was over his heart. His left grasped a bouquet of flowers. His mind tried to grasp the magic of the moment.

"My mom was on the right side of the stadium," Gaines would

recall, "and my dad was on the left. They were both crying. I told myself to keep cool. Don't choke. Millions of people are watching you. But it didn't work. I started crying myself. I couldn't even get out the words to 'The Star-Spangled Banner.' "

Gaines will be permitted this faux pas. When he had to be perfect, in the pool, he was. He got the lead quickly and held off second-place Mark Stockwell of Australia and third-place Per Johansson of Sweden, finishing in 49.80 seconds. The other American, Mike Heath, who had beaten Gaines in the Olympic trials, was literally left on the block.

For a long time now, Rowdy has dearly wanted an Olympic gold. He was a cinch to win it in 1980. But then, well, the tale of the boycott and subsequent American frustrations has been told repeatedly.

"In 1980, I was in my prime," a somewhat wistful Gaines recalled. "Everything came easy in 1980. But now it was tough. I had to fight for it. I almost gave up the chance a year ago, but I stayed in there. I've had a lot of low points along the way. I almost quit. I started getting beat a lot. But it was all worth it."

Gaines, despite his troubles, was favored although Stockwell had a faster time in a morning prelim. Expectations are not easy baggage to carry. "The danger," said Richard Quick, Gaines' longtime coach, "is trying not to lose instead of swimming to win."

The burden on our young athletes is large. The television and newspaper exposure creates pressure. The joy of competition is subjugated to the demand for victory. In the evening they lie in bed musing about the future. Will it bring a medal? Or eternal regret?

Rowdy Gaines, nicknamed for Rowdy Yates on the old "Rawhide" TV series, had steeled himself for defeat. "I had a speech ready if I finished second," he conceded. The words need never be said.

"On the starting block, my legs were like rubber I was so nervous," Gaines said. "A couple of hours before the race, I had a couple of cups of coffee. I never drink coffee. I was bouncing off the walls of my room. But Tracy Caulkins came over and talked and calmed me down."

Caulkins, of course, is the young woman who has set so many American swimming records, received the Sullivan Award as the nation's outstanding amateur athlete in 1978, and Monday won a gold herself in the 400-meter individual medley.

"I knew he had it in him," Caulkins said later, after a congratulatory hug. "I just had to get him to remain calm. Attitude is so important in this sport. You have to believe in yourself."

A year ago, Gaines didn't believe in anything except retirement. "There was a three-month period last summer when I wanted to give up," Gaines said. "I wasn't improving. I was scared to lose. I wasn't trying to win. It didn't seem worth it.

"Then I said, 'What the heck. I've only got one more year. I'll only be twenty-five, and I'll have fifty more years to live after that.' If I had quit, I think twenty years down the line I would have jumped out a twentieth-floor window.

"This was my last race. If I had lost, I would have been proud of my records and my career."

He won the race and lost his composure. He'll take the trade-off anytime.

A TRUE
LIVING
LEGEND

NOVEMBER 28, 1986

"Some day," wrote Red Smith for the final sentence of his final column, "there would be another DiMaggio."

His suggestion was more a remembrance of things past than a prediction of items future.

There will never be another DiMaggio. Red knew it. We all know it.

Legends do not flourish under the scrutiny of the television camera. The world now is too public, the players now too expressive.

Joe DiMaggio emerged from an era when humility was an athletic virtue. He transcended baseball and grew into a mythical figure in popular culture.

DiMaggio swapped mastery for mystery and secured a place as the last American hero.

Roger Kahn, the author, understood this all too well. He tried to plumb depths hidden for years, to exploit the popularity of DiMaggio and the woman he loved, Marilyn Monroe.

Scandal sells. Roger Kahn is a craftsman, best known for his narrative on the Brooklyn Dodgers, *The Boys of Summer.*

This book is *Joe and Marilyn.* It's subtitled *A Memory of Love.* You can call it *The Boy and Girl of Autumn.* The writing is smooth, the treatment harsh. Reverence is tarnished by prurience.

A confession will be made by a forty-eight-year-old sports columnist: Joe DiMaggio is a hero. I don't want to read about his human frailties, about what makes him like the rest of us. Tell me only about his superhuman qualities, about what made him different.

Joe DiMaggio came home to San Francisco the other day. It was a sad journey. They were burying one of his boyhood pals, Reno Barsocchini.

Joe and brother Dominic, another skilled if less glamorized ballplayer from the 1940s and early 1950s, were two of the pallbearers.

"As time goes," mused Joe an hour before the funeral, "my dear friends keep going too."

Joe DiMaggio is seventy-two. His birthday was Tuesday, a day after Reno Barsocchini died of cancer. Joe is gray and, although in good shape, no longer young.

In the mind's eye, however, Joe DiMaggio will always be in his early thirties, wearing the pinstripes of the New York Yankees, and loping gracefully under fly balls.

It is not easy to interrogate one's hero.

I remember a spring afternoon in 1951 when, after an exhibition game between the Yankees and the Hollywood Stars at Gilmore Field in Los Angeles, I chased Joe's taxi a block and a half for an autograph still kept.

I place myself in a category created by a Hofstra University professor who said the problem with most American males forty-five or older is they wanted to grow up to be Joe DiMaggio.

I thought of Paul Simon's lyrics asking, "Where have you gone, Joe DiMaggio? A nation turns its lonely eyes to you." Simon explained later he did not plan to use DiMaggio, but liked the meter and rhythm of the lines. "And I was seeking a hero with a certain mystique."

DiMaggio sat on a bench at the Halsted-N-Gray funeral home. He wore a gray sharkskin suit and a white boutonniere. He spoke of the half century he had known Barsocchini, who for years ran the DiMaggio restaurant before opening his own.

And then I asked about Roger Kahn's book.

"I haven't read it and I won't," DiMaggio responded. He was civil, but hesitant. "I don't even know the man who wrote it. I know about him, but I don't know him."

Does he know about the book? "Yes. Friends have told me. It's disturbing."

Joe DiMaggio does not like to be disturbed. He is a private person, once terribly shy. "Sensitive, yes, I suppose so," he told a sportswriter. "I never want to hurt anyone's feelings, and I don't want to be embarrassed."

Roger Kahn's book, in truth, is embarrassing. Joe DiMaggio belongs in the Hall of Fame. Not on the cover of the *National Enquirer.*

Could DiMaggio understand if the book had been printed at the apex of his stardom? "Yes," he mumbled, "but why now?"

Why now? Why him? Joe DiMaggio is and was a man of noble dignity, self-effacing, with ability proved over an amount of time.

The man hit in sixty-one straight games for the San Francisco Seals. The man hit in fifty-six straight games for the New York Yankees.

Another DiMaggio? Never. Let us admire the one we have.

49ers'
WALSH STILL AN ENIGMA

OCTOBER 2, 1983

The photograph shows everything and reveals nothing. There, at the moment of ultimate triumph, rides Bill Walsh, his face reflecting, well, that's the problem. Who can say exactly what emotion is carved into the furrowed visage?

This was immediately after the final gun of Super Bowl XVI, poignant seconds of the man's finest hour. Walsh had ascended the shoulders of his troops and metaphorically to the heights of professional football, carried along on a tide of adulation toward the locker room of the Pontiac Silverdome.

His arms are lifted. He is smiling. Or is he? So enigmatic is the expression it must have been painted by Leonardo da Vinci. Is Walsh euphoric? Smug? Relieved? As always when dealing with Bill Walsh, one can only guess.

This much may definitely be stated about Bill Walsh, fifth-year coach of the San Francisco 49ers: His hair is white; his mind is sharp. Otherwise, he seems an individual of complexity and contradictions, saying one thing, doing another, and generally keeping the rest of the world a trifle off balance.

"Bill Walsh," conceded 49er quarterback Joe Montana some time ago, "is not an easily described man."

Perhaps it is best that way. Society is too quick to assign niches. Al Davis is devious; Vince Lombardi was truculent; John Madden is emotional. And Bill Walsh? Bill Walsh is, perhaps, what we wish him to be.

Calculating? Certainly he provides that impression. Even his former offensive coach, Sam Wyche, called him calculating. And yet would a calculating person so impetuously announce his resignation as did Walsh at the end of last season?

A genius? Allusions have been made to such status, and when Walsh goes about the merry business of aligning X's and O's his brilliance is noticeable. But would a genius have selected James Owens in the draft ahead of William Andrews? Or create a game plan that couldn't overcome the mediocre Philadelphia Eagles?

Is Walsh deceptive? Somewhat. But the coach's art requires deception, a compromising of the Golden Rule. "We won't blitz Atlanta the way we did St. Louis," Walsh will propose before a gathering of journalists. Why, then, did the 49ers blitz Atlanta on almost every play? Basically, because Walsh wanted to win.

Skeptics among the wayward journalists assigned to 49ers coverage dwell on Walsh's frailties. They consider him too slick, overly coy, far different from the glowing biographical sketches in national publications. They snicker at his suggestions, wonder about his judgment.

This week Walsh told Paul Zimmerman of *Sports Illustrated* the 49ers are flawed and flawed teams do not win the Super Bowl. Walsh is asked about the remark. "I can't think of any flaws," he responds. The writers are mystified. And more skeptical than ever.

But football, we have been told, is a form of warfare. In battle the element of surprise is a key to victory. Keep everyone guessing, including the press. Give only your name, rank, serial number, and current statistics.

"To be finally successful," Walsh told a writer after the Super Bowl victory, "there has to be a little larceny in you. I don't plead innocence to everything. There is manipulation."

Yet Walsh is not venal. He questions his motives as much as others question them. He is not above second-guessing himself; he simply is suspicious of others asking the questions.

"I have not read a newspaper in a month, except for glancing at the top of an article, if we've won a game but not if we lost," Walsh insists. This from a man who apparently adores the limelight, who rarely refuses an interview. Why this attitude, this ostrichlike affectation?

"I don't want to be distracted. It is tough enough to go out and play games without worrying about criticism. It is another distraction."

The 49ers have played excellently after a season-opening loss to the Eagles, a loss that still vexes Walsh.

"I was too conservative in that game," he explains. "We were running the ball well, so I kept going with the run. We couldn't get the ball in the end zone. Now we're back to passing, going for the score. That's the way we play football best."

That's the way the 49ers got to the Super Bowl. That's the way they may get there again. Who is Bill Walsh? Most of all, a damned fine coach.

A HEART-GRABBING EXIT FOR THE JUICE

DECEMBER 10, 1979

Yes, there would be one ultimate appearance, one final opportunity, one more time that O.J. Simpson would pull on shoulder pads and a jersey and come out of a locker room as a member of an organized team.

That would be next weekend in Atlanta, where Sherman marched and Margaret Mitchell wrote and in a few days one of the great running backs in the history of football would terminate a career.

But this was home, the shore of San Francisco Bay. And yesterday, on a pleasant December afternoon, a triumphant December afternoon, Orenthal James Simpson was being given a hurrah that if it wasn't the last was certainly the most affectionate.

Seconds before, as the game wound down, as the second 49ers victory of the agonizing season became inevitable, O.J. Simpson took a pitchout and began to sweep left—and to run to daylight. The yardage mounted, the cheers swelled, the memory was made.

It was a seventeen-yard gain, the longest scrimmage run of the game. It was vintage O.J. Simpson. The years had been turned back and the crowd had been turned on. Now O.J. Simpson could jog from the ravaged turf of Candlestick Park a hero, a guy who had fulfilled if not his fantasies then at least the hopes of the majority of 44,506 fans.

Sure there was delight with the 23-7 lead against Tampa Bay that would soon become the final score. But now the focus of their attention was on the figure on the sideline, the guy wearing #32. "Joose, Joose," they hollered again and again. And the Juice, O.J. Simpson, waved and smiled like an embarrassed teenager.

The other day, in the opulent splendor that is the office of 49ers owner Eddie DeBartolo, Simpson talked about the way he would have preferred to end his eleven-year career in the NFL. It was the stuff of dreams, or of movies, the profession O.J. has chosen to replace athletics.

"I have no regrets," said thirty-two-year-old O.J. Simpson, "but ideally it would have been great to finish in the Super Bowl, score the winning touchdown with no time on the clock, and then keep running right into the tunnel as the crowd went crazy."

He couldn't do that. But at least, with a career nearly reaching termination, he didn't simply end it in anonymity, in embarrassment. No, O.J. was able to display those skills one more time. It couldn't have happened to a nicer guy.

"I was still able to run away from a defensive back," laughed Simpson. "That was surprising."

It was surprising to some that 49ers coach Bill Walsh didn't utilize Simpson more, even though throughout the season, Walsh had explained why the Juice was mainly a spectator instead of a contributor. After all, this was O.J.'s day. And there had been a special pregame ceremony. Why not keep him in the lineup for a while? Why not let him score the fourth-quarter touchdown from a yard out that would be scored by Lenvil Elliott?

"Because," insisted Bill Walsh, "that would have been a slap in the face for O.J. Simpson, an insult.

"More dramatic than a one-yard touchdown, which is tokenism, pure tokenism," said Walsh, "is the run he made at the end of the game. There was just a little flash of the old brilliance, and that's what I hoped he would reveal. It's like a storybook to me.

"For him to break back on the pursuit as he's done so many hundreds of times and to make a sizable gain, and then be taken out of the game with the crowd receiving him is the ideal conclusion of his career here. And I just feel super about that."

O.J. felt pretty good about it, too. And, according to his public statement, he found no fault in Walsh allowing him to carry only six times for a total of twenty-six yards in this, his final home game.

"I knew the game plan," said O.J. Simpson. "Knew we were

going to pass an awful lot. Knew under the circumstances I wouldn't get to play much. The idea was to win, and we won."

You can't say they won it for the Juice, but they did give O.J. the game ball. And in the locker room, several players, Mike Hogan and Bob Bruer included, asked a photographer to take a picture of them standing alongside O.J., much as a kid might ask.

A short time earlier, several of the 49ers players had carried from the field Walsh and, no, not Simpson, but defensive tackle Al Cowlings, since high school one of O.J.'s closest friends. "I have no idea why," laughed Cowlings. "Maybe they felt sorry for me."

While Walsh and Cowlings rode, Simpson walked. First across the middle of the field to exchange greetings with Tampa Bay running back Ricky Bell, who was to follow O.J. at USC. Then, surrounded by a sea of humans who wanted one last glimpse, one last touch, into the dugout and the locker room.

There the crush began anew, reporters and photographers and TV cameras crowding around the dressing cubicle Simpson would never use again, asking questions, making remarks.

"I appreciated the ceremony before the game," said Simpson. "It was nice and simple." But then, with a wink, he added, "I did want a Rolls-Royce."

You can't have everything. And O.J. Simpson did have all those great years with USC, and the Buffalo Bills, all those rushing records and recognition. He also had two years with his hometown team, the 49ers, something that had been his wish since he was a kid.

And then yesterday, on his final carry as a football player in San Francisco, he had a seventeen-yard gain that gave everyone a chance to remember O.J. Simpson the way he should be remembered.

Could you ask for anything more?

MONTANA'S TRAVAIL

DECEMBER 8, 1985

Quarterback is a position that drives some men to drink, some to religion. Name your poison. Or your prayers. You might find help in a bottle or a pulpit.

Booing fans, interceptions, squandered expectations. Bobby Layne, Sonny Jurgensen, Billy Kilmer could find support on many a brass rail. Jim Zorn and Steve Bartkowski, on the other hand, escaped in the bosom of the Lord.

At the moment, Joe Montana endorses neither method. Until this season there was no reason. He was an icon in the Bay Area, a region of iconoclasts, Super Bowls, passing records, MVP awards. The only criticism we ever heard about Joe Montana was his own.

Not anymore. We've flagellated Joe. All of us. We've found he is not perfect. That he can't walk from Oakland to San Francisco. Or settle the national debt. We're disillusioned. No Santa Claus. No faultless quarterback. Off with his head.

Billy Loes was one of baseball's true prophets, not to mention true eccentrics. He lost a ground ball in the sun, but he never lost perspective. "Don't win twenty games," Loes warned, "because they'll expect you to do it every time."

Montana made a mistake. Grounding the ball in the end zone last Sunday against the Redskins. Anyone is capable of that. Montana's error was in winning two Super Bowls in four years, in becoming the all-time, #1 quarterback in the NFL's rating system.

Joe Montana wrote *Gone With the Wind* for his first novel, built the Taj Mahal as his first project. Then what? Then came the inevitable question: "What do you do for an encore?" What Joe did was prove he had blemishes. How dare he?

The other day, Joe Montana, with those sparkling blue eyes and cleft jaw, sprawled in one of the school desks the 49ers use for meetings and tried to sort out what it's like to go from a hero to a bum before the 1985 season has gone from start to finish.

Understand this, Montana is not oblivious to the stings. An audience that once wanted to put him on a pedestal now wants to put him on a slow boat to China. The man is hurt.

"I talked to Ron Jaworski before the Eagles game," said Montana of the Philadelphia quarterback. "He asked me, 'How's it going?' I said, 'You've been around long enough to know how it's going.' And we both laughed."

Joe may have lost games, yet he's retained a sense of humor. The bad back, the injured shoulder, the drug rumors at times left him discouraged. But the famous smile that glistened from *Time* and *Newsweek* not all that long ago is still readily available.

"I think Y.A. Tittle explained it best," said Montana of the great quarterback who played for the 49ers and the New York Giants. "He told me last year to enjoy every moment. He said when you're a quarterback, they love you when you're young, hate you in the middle, and love you when you're old."

Montana is twenty-nine, seven years a pro. Is he young, old, or in the middle? He certainly isn't hated, although on occasion Joe may believe as much.

He wrote a critical letter to a critical fan. He's knocked the press for knocking him. He's taking things personally—which is what we all might do under the circumstances.

"I don't regret writing the letter," said Montana. "Sometimes people forget you're human and have feelings. The guy who wrote me had no idea of what it's like to be in competition."

A few weeks ago, Montana became a father for the first time. A baby daughter makes a man sensitive.

"A lot of things never started bothering me until I had a family. The things people say about me, the drug rumors, the critical remarks, affect my family.

"My daughter was sick and I was sick, and we were both going to the hospital. A woman bus driver stops the bus in front of my driveway—there's no bus stop there—and says something unpleasant."

Was it Harry S Truman who said, "If you can't stand the heat, stay out of the kitchen?" Athletes must accept adversity. But do they have to accept irrationality?

"I've had some bad games," conceded Montana. "It's been

a strange year. Frustrating. There were times I was thinking I can't afford to make another mistake."

Said former Rams quarterback Pat Haden, "Joe's been the darling with both Notre Dame and the 49ers. Nothing he has known prepared him for what has happened. The thing that will make or break him now is his mental toughness."

For quarterbacks, it has always been thus.

—————————

DO PEOPLE BELIEVE IN AL MICHAELS? YES!

FEBRUARY 3, 1984

SARAJEVO, Yugoslavia—Do you believe in miracles? On an historic, triumphant evening four years ago, many Americans did. A rare spark of nationalism ignited a fire of emotion, embers of which still glow.

Do you believe in miracles? The phrase, so poignant, so appropriate, will be etched into our psyches as well as our culture.

Don't give up the ship. Remember the Alamo. Do you believe in miracles?

Now, an ocean's distance from that small arena in upstate New York where the delirium exploded in all directions like ripples on a pond, the man who asked that memorable question is himself being quizzed.

A new band on the run forms the nucleus of the 1984 U.S. Olympic hockey team. But if the faces are different, the voice calling the shots will be the same. In a sense, Al Michaels is under greater pressure than the athletes.

After 1980, after the victory over the Soviet Union, after the pride and the pandemonium, we were left with only pictures in the mind's eye, and, interestingly enough, Al Michaels.

The slick announcer who resides in Menlo Park never made a goal or a poke check or even a skate mark on the ice.

But after the champions disbanded, after Mike Eruzione took his rasping voice into TV color, after Jim Craig and Ken Morrow and even the coach, Herb Brooks, moved on to the pros, who was left but Michaels? He's the reincarnation of the moment.

"People who wanted to stand up and cheer, who wanted to

say thanks, didn't know who to write," said Michaels. "The hockey team didn't exist any longer. So they wrote to me. It was a case of identification."

With the upset, the team ascended Olympian heights. With his descriptions, so did Michaels.

The announcing combination of Michaels and former NHL goalie Ken Dryden didn't slop the canvas with blotches of color. Instead, they embellished with careful strokes a picture that nearly painted itself.

Presented a marvelous opportunity, others might have spewed out a Vesuvius of hyperbole or perhaps been so overcome they could only mumble. But Al kept his cool and his perspective.

"I tried to remain very professional," said Michaels. "As a fan and an American, I wanted to get caught up in it, and I was, in my own way. But my life's work is broadcasting, and I've been trained to know I could not get carried away and yell and scream and become the ultimate jingoist."

While the action went on and the drama expanded, Michaels reminded himself: Remain in control. He did.

Seconds remained. He blurted out the first thing that entered his thoughts: "Do you believe in miracles?" As the clock showed zero and the celebration began, Al answered his own deft question. "Yes."

What he can't answer now is where this year's U.S. hockey team will finish.

"But," he will say after having watched the world's best amateur teams the last few months, "don't expect another miracle."

ABC-TV is. From Michaels. Recently selected as the National Sportscasters and Sportswriters' "Sportscaster of the Year" for a second time, Al has been given an added assignment at the 1984 Winter Olympics.

"Ice skating," he said sardonically.

What does the man who used to be the Giants announcer, who has called the World Series and college football games, know about ice skating? "A great deal more than I knew three weeks ago."

He also knows the cost of a tuxedo. For some reason, at boxing matches, the cruelest sport, and skating, the most graceful, the people behind the microphones go formal.

"Never owned a tux until last week," said Michaels. "They're more than $300."

Hockey and ice skating alternate in the stadiums. Michaels will be taking up permanent residency. But the man will not confuse a double axel with a slap shot.

"The U. S. hockey team is in the same draw as Canada, Czechoslovakia, and Finland. We'll probably lose to the Czechs. They're the second-best team in the world next to the Soviets.

"That means the first match, Tuesday, against Canada, even before the opening ceremonies, could be the key for the United States. If we lose to Canada, right off the bat we're done."

Win or lose, Sarajevo will never duplicate Lake Placid.

"Emotions were high because of Afghanistan and Iran. It was accomplished by a group of ebullient kids. They were a mirror image for a lot of people. Their excitement was natural, not contrived. They were so happy they didn't know what to do."

Al Michaels did.

ELWAY: PROMISE FULFILLED

JANUARY 12, 1987

CLEVELAND—And there in the mammoth old stadium, with the wind swirling, the crowd hooting, and defeat lurking in the darkness, John Elway fulfilled his great promise.

The boy became a man. The Denver Broncos Sunday became AFC champions. The city of Cleveland, alas, became a pumpkin once more.

The mark of a quarterback is not his passing percentage or the style of his delivery.

Pro football isn't constructed on beauty but toughness of willpower and intensity so strong that dreams become reality when they could as easily have become nightmares.

The mark of a quarterback is what he can do when the situation is hopeless and his hands are freezing and his uniform is soaked with mud and sweat.

The mark of a quarterback is to win. Now and forever, John Elway is a winner.

John Elway did, well, not the impossible, because were it impossible no one could have done it. Shall we say the improbable? Or the remarkable? Or, as Dan Reeves, his phlegmatic coach was to muse, "the unbelievable."

Elway drove the Denver Broncos on and on, nearly the entire length of a muddy, icy football field, ninety-eight yards in all, for a tying touchdown in the closing minute. And then the Broncos beat the Cleveland Browns, 23-20 in overtime, to advance to Super Bowl XXI.

So John Elway finally makes it to the Rose Bowl, where in a fortnight the NFL tournament final will be held, Broncos against the New York Giants.

53

At Stanford, each season would climax in frustration. In the pros, he has achieved a goal.

There was skepticism about John Elway from the very beginning. He was another of those California Golden Boys with flaxen hair and gleaming teeth who are anathema to the hulks from the Midwest.

He had gone not to Auburn or Michigan but to Stanford, where football is only a game not an obsession.

His skill was such that Elway had been the first man taken in the 1983 draft, but that was by the Colts, then in Baltimore and then coached by Frank Kush, a martinet. Elway refused to sign with the Colts. His image took a pounding, as his body would in games he started as a rookie after the Colts traded his rights to Denver.

Perhaps Elway was a fraud, the cynics suggested. Dan Marino could be admired. Bernie Kosar would be applauded. But what had John Elway done but throw interceptions, like the one against the Steelers in the play-offs two seasons past?

The question becomes academic. John Elway becomes a hero.

Ninety-eight yards in fifteen plays.

With the Cleveland crowd firing dog biscuits at him from the bleachers. With the Cleveland weather chilling his fingers but not his heart.

"The thing I thought about before the game," said Elway in a locker room piled high with dirty uniforms and elation, "was that great quarterbacks come through in tough situations. They make the big plays in big games."

Again and again in this one in legendary old Cleveland Stadium, where Groza kicked and Feller pitched, where football is played without any concessions to modern technology, twenty-six-year-old John Elway made the big plays.

With his celerity and his strength, he transformed potential losses into gains. He transformed the Broncos into champions.

"I want to thank this man," said Broncos linebacker Jim Ryan, wrapping an arm about Elway's broad shoulders. "He got us to the Super Bowl."

No less indebted was Denver safety Dennis Smith, whose coverage failure on a long pass had enabled Cleveland to score a touchdown and go in front, 20-13, with some six minutes remaining.

"I would have been the goat, except for John Elway," sighed Smith. "I've got to send him a thank-you note."

Elway will just send his regards to Broadway. And Pasadena. Third down and eighteen on that ninety-eight-yard drive—Elway to Mark Jackson for twenty yards.

"Yeah," said Elway, "it reminded me of that completion on fourth and seventeen against Cal."

That was in 1982, on another memorable drive, when Stanford kicked a field goal to go ahead—and then Cal won seconds later on the bizarre five-lateral kickoff return known as "The Play."

"The Play" stung Elway. Now "The Drive" glorifies him. A promise is fulfilled.

BLACK
MILESTONE

JANUARY 27, 1988

SAN DIEGO—Doug Williams sat in the middle of a dozen questions, and all you could think of, besides the absurdity of the scene, were the lines from that Bob Dylan song: "How many roads must a man walk down," the words asked plaintively, "until they call him a man? . . . "

When will we begin to call Doug Williams a man? And not a black man? When will we begin to acknowledge his contribution? And not his color? When will America put away its racial and ethnic baggage and begin to judge people on performance?

Sad, so sad. One week it's Jimmy the Greek spouting half-truths; the next it's the flower of sporting journalism wondering about breaking precedent. All because our priority system is a shambles.

Stevie Wonder and Paul McCartney lyricize about ebony and ivory, but in the real world, the world of suspicion and suspense, life is hardly a musical interlude.

And for Doug Williams of the Washington Redskins, the days leading to Super Bowl XXII are hardly satisfying.

Understand this: Doug Williams will start at quarterback Sunday against the Denver Broncos. Never before has a black man played quarterback in a Super Bowl. But instead of putting him on a pedestal, we're placing him in a sideshow. Send in the clowns.

"How does it feel to be black?" asked an unthinking sort. Williams slid forward a few inches on the bleacher seat in San Diego Stadium and reminded, "I've been black all my life."

Taking every wrong direction on our lonely way back home.

The other quarterback, the Denver quarterback, isn't compelled to deal with the trivial. Nobody asks John Elway how it feels to be white. Only whether he can move the ball against the Redskins.

John Elway is blond and went to Stanford, so naturally we describe him as the "All-American boy." Doug Williams isn't blond and went to Grambling and he's been described as a great many things. The "All-American boy?" Now that you've mentioned it, yes.

"Doug Williams is apple pie," advised his college coach, Eddie Robinson. "In Doug Williams you have the typical American boy. He goes to church, comes from a large family, has humility and is a leader."

No allusion to pigmentation, only to probity. No testimonial to the incidental, only to the significant.

"It's been blown out of proportion," said Williams about the black-white business.

"It just so happens that I'm playing for the Redskins in the Super Bowl, and I'm black. I know it's going to mean a lot to some people in America, but we all have to put it in perspective. I'm not here holding up my hand, waving, and saying 'I'm black, I'm a quarterback, yay, yay, yay.' "

Perspective: Doug Williams was a first-round draft choice in 1978. The previous season he threw forty-two touchdown passes and finished fourth in the Heisman Trophy balloting. The man could play football. Can play football.

Perspective: In April 1983, Williams' bride of eleven months, Janice, died of complications from a brain tumor, leaving him with an infant daughter and a deep emotional scar. "Why me?" asked Williams at that time. Since, he has remarried.

Williams went from the Tampa Bay Bucs to the USFL to unemployment. The Redskins signed him in 1986 as a backup. He threw one pass that season. It was incomplete. He was disillusioned.

"When I think of twenty-eight quarterbacks in the NFL," he contended, "I don't think there are ten better than me."

Washington coach Joe Gibbs, who moved Williams ahead of Jay Schroeder, obviously doesn't think there is one better on the Redskins.

"When I look at a man," John Elway responded to a question about Williams, "I don't look at his skin color, only what he does."

For Doug Williams, then, what should matter are his completions—not his complexion.

Trips,
the Site
Fantastic

A MONUMENT
AND A MEMORY

DECEMBER 8, 1982

HONOLULU—The orange glow of dawn poked through windows in dark clouds. A brisk wind swept from the west. A motor launch moved away from the dock and back into time.

Forty-one years had passed since a similar morning burst into flame, since a surprise raid precipitated the entrance of the United States into World War II.

December 7, 1941, President Franklin Delano Roosevelt would declare the following day, was a date "which will live in infamy." Now it persists in memory.

Who had heard of Pearl Harbor before that morning? Who has not heard of it now? Warplanes from Japan swept upon the American naval base in what Roosevelt called an "unprovoked and dastardly" attack. History would be altered.

For a few minutes, it was hell on earth. Bombs fell. Ships exploded. Buildings burned. Hundreds died.

The primary target was the tightly packed flotilla along the eastern edge of Ford Island, "Battleship Row." Specially designed torpedoes pounded the vessels.

One ship, the *Nevada,* managed to get under way. Five others did not. The *Maryland, California, Tennessee,* and *Oklahoma* were damaged. The U.S.S. *Arizona* was destroyed.

Half an hour after the first Japanese plane dove from a clear sky, the *Arizona* sank, entombing more than 1,100 crewmen. The other battleships would sail again. The *Arizona* would stay on the bottom, in thirty-eight feet of water, a grim reminder.

Eventually, a winglike structure would be constructed above, but not touching the ship's hull. The U.S.S. *Arizona Memorial,* dedicated in 1962, has become a major Hawaiian tourist attraction.

This year alone it has been visited by more than a million people. But the first tourist boat to the memorial was delayed yesterday. First the dead would be honored with words and flowers.

When the motor launch arrived at the memorial, it was just after 7 A.M. A Navy band softly played a Sousa march. Patriotic and military organizations carried wreaths. Soon it would be a time for speeches. Now it was a time for contemplation.

The outline of the U.S.S. *Arizona's* hull can be seen below the surface. A rusting gun turret protrudes above water level. Forty-one years later, diesel fuel still seeps from tanks filled only the day before the disaster, an eerie, glistening reminder.

The massive mooring quay where once the *Arizona* was tied remains a lonely sentinel. On this special morning a Marine honor guard, soon to fire a salute, and a bugler, who will play taps, stand upon the enormous block of cement.

The minutes move. It is 7:55 A.M., the moment when a squadron of Japanese Kate 12 torpedo planes swooped in from the east. A Navy chaplain requests silence. A shipyard whistle echoes his demand. Heads bow. Then the silence is shattered by the roar of three jets flying over in the "missing man" formation.

The commemorative address is a saber-rattling speech from Joseph K. Taussig, Jr., deputy assistant secretary of the Navy, who is a military man through and through.

A third-generation Annapolis graduate, Taussig was an ensign aboard the battleship *Nevada* in Pearl Harbor the day of the attack.

Hit by metal from the exploding superstructure of the *Arizona*, Ensign Taussig refused to desert his antiaircraft battery. For this conduct he was awarded the Navy Cross. In 1946, after months of hospitalization, he was to lose his left leg. He never lost his jingoistic approach.

"Only two years ago," argues Taussig, "it seemed that the lessons of Pearl Harbor had been forgotten. For nearly thirty years the numbers of our naval forces had been dwindling . . . and most of our ships were simply getting older and older."

He calls Jane Fonda and Joan Baez traitors, those who evaded the Vietnam War cowards. He praises his own generation who had "fought to ensure that our women were not raped, our homes not ravaged."

In the small audience some smile, some wince. The words drift off in the breeze. Taps resounds. It is 8:35 A.M., ironically the time the U.S.S. *Arizona* hit bottom. The ceremonies conclude.

In the gathering are three major-league baseball managers attending the annual meetings—Ralph Houk of the Boston Red

Sox, Russ Nixon of the Cincinnati Reds, Rene Lachemann of the Seattle Mariners.

"I was driving to Augusta, Georgia, from San Diego when I heard Pearl Harbor had been bombed, said Houk. I wondered where it was," Houk enlisted, rose from private to major, saw action in Germany, and won a Purple Heart.

Others were not as personally involved. Last week, a booster of the University of Nebraska, which played Hawaii in football, stood on the *Arizona* Memorial and listened to a solemn explanation of the attack on Pearl Harbor.

"Yeah," sneers the fan, "but tell me one thing. Who's going to win the game?"

It is rewarding to say nobody laughed.

SARAJEVO SO-SO, BUT SARAJEVOANS GREAT

FEBRUARY 5, 1984

SARAJEVO, Yugoslavia—Rain was falling on a town praying for snow. A hockey controversy swirled like the wind on Mount Bjelasnica. Police with machine guns seemed to be at every corner. Welcome to the world of international fun and games.

The XIV Winter Olympics are about to start, literally below a cloud. But the weather is usually gray and oppressive in the Balkan backwater called Sarajevo. Fortunately, the citizens prove a charming contrast.

True, Sarajevo has had periods of inhospitality. Archduke Ferdinand brought his act here in 1914, and the rest is history. He bombed. Or a conspirator tried to bomb him and missed. Another, however, shot him. The incident embarrassed municipal authorities. It also triggered World War I.

The assassin, Gavrilo Princip, has been immortalized. The spot near the Miljacka River where he fired the fatal bullet is commemorated by footprints set in cement, possibly the world's most inconspicuous monument.

Nasty weather again raised a question. Why did a sooty industrial town of 450,000 get a sporting event supposed to be as beautiful as it is competitive? What happened to Christmas-tree villages in the Alps? Or the pristine loveliness of Scandinavia? Why in 1978 did the International Olympic Committee select Sarajevo over Göteborg, Sweden, or Sapporo, Japan?

Perhaps the answer lies in the soul of those who inhabit Yugoslavia. They are hardy and resolute, overcoming the control of the Ottoman Empire and the yoke of the Hapsburgs. Now they had the opportunity to raise Sarajevo into the public

63

consciousness. They clutched it with ferocity.

No matter what happens the rest of the way. No matter if the Nordic races go through mud, no matter if the United States and Canadian hockey teams accuse each other of treachery instead of merely violations of the amateur code, Sarajevo's image will forever be embellished. No longer will the town remain only a tragic footnote to a great conflict.

Yugoslavia, or Land of the South Slavs, is often described as one country with two alphabets, three religions, four main languages, five principal nationalities, six republics, and seven nations on its borders. It is a cultural mélange, a mingling of East and West. Most of all, with a unique capitalistic theme of communism, Yugoslavia is a survivor.

The contrasts overwhelm. Gray-clad members of the Milicija, the security force, loom at every turn. Yet a citizen ran half a block through a storm to give an American journalist a small booklet dropped on a sidewalk.

Embarking on a Jugoslovenski Aerotransport flight from Frankfurt to Zagreb, the traveler first is bused to a place on the tarmac, far from the terminal, then under the baleful gaze of police told to identify his luggage before it will be placed aboard.

The DC-9 contains graffiti on seat backs and two grim stewards who serve not-unappealing cold cuts and a very unappealing juice made from carrots, oranges, and apricots. Life jackets are under seats. That several passengers are reading Orwell's *1984* was entirely coincidental.

There isn't a no-smoking section anywhere, on the plane, in the country. The national anthem isn't sung, it's coughed.

Sarajevo, or "field around the palace," is filled with haze, pictures of the late Marshal Tito, and posters of Vucko, the Disney-like cartoon symbol of the Games. Big Brother isn't watching, but Tito and Vucko are.

They must like what they see. Faith may not move mountains, but the workers can. When the men's downhill course on Mount Bjelasnica (Byel-ASHE-nee-tza) lacked twenty-five feet of the minimum 800 meters, a restaurant with a twenty-five-foot ramp was built atop the peak.

Nature couldn't halt the Sarajevo plan. Rain or controversy won't either. Let the Games begin.

COLD, COLDER, COLDEST

FEBRUARY 10, 1988

CALGARY—Well, you don't have to worry about the snow melting. Only your nose freezing and falling off. Welcome to the *Wi-Wi-Winter Olympics.*

Hand warmers are optional.

The Great White North they call this place. I landed and expected to see Sergeant Preston; instead, I saw people running for cover. It was minus twenty-five degrees Celsius, which is about minus seventeen Fahrenheit. Why can't they hold bobsled races in Bermuda?

Everyone around here seems worried about the chinook, which isn't a Yiddish word for a wimp but a Blackfoot Indian word for a warm wind. "Snow eater" is the translation, because the temperature climbs as fast as Bobby Knight's blood pressure.

In Texas they tell Aggie stories. In England they tell Irish stories. In Calgary they tell chinook stories.

The best one is about the cowboy who on a snowy day tied his horse to a post and went in for a sarsaparilla. A chinook swept down from the Canadian Rockies, and when the cowboy walked outside, he found his horse hanging from the top of a church steeple.

In truth, the chinook can alter temperatures in remarkable fashion. In December 1983, it was three degrees at 7 P.M., thirty-seven degrees at 8:30 P.M., forty-three degrees at midnight, and after the wind blew on, five degrees at 2 A.M.

They're terrified of the chinook, the way pedestrians in New York worry about muggers. "The wind's coming in Wednesday," a bus driver warned. "It'll be up past freezing. Maybe for the opening ceremonies Saturday it could be forty degrees."

A year ago, when the pre-Olympic meet was held at Nakiska, some sixty miles southwest of Calgary, a chinook swept in and turned the runs to mud. "Mount Slushmore," it was nicknamed. I don't know about Jean-Claude Killy, but Mark Spitz could have done a hell of a job in the men's downhill.

Calgary was founded in 1877 by a band of men from the Northwest Mounted Police. They were trying to stop the settlers from trading whiskey to Indians at a place known as Fort Whoop-em Up. Now it's known as Fort Freeze-em Down.

Founded at the confluence of the Bow and Elbow rivers, Calgary was named for Calgary Bay off the Isle of Mull near Scotland. It began as a cattle and farming town and is now dependent on oil and natural gas.

Canadians have always been ingenious, eh? The writer Pierre Berton offers a definition of a Canadian: "Someone who could make love in a canoe." Or in a blizzard, whichever is easier.

Calgary and Edmonton are the two primary cities of the Province of Alberta. They say the roughnecks and field hands live in Edmonton, while Calgary, headquarters for hundreds of petroleum corporations, is a white-collar community. Sure. That's because the collars are covered with frost.

Winter Olympics are usually held in tiny alpine towns where cheese fondue is as popular as the giant slalom. Calgary, however, has a population of 647,000, give or take a few moose.

What's tiny here are the rooms for the press at Lincoln Park Village. Look, I'm not complaining, but to get your credential you had to be under six feet and weigh less than 160 pounds. Sleeping here is going to be an exhibition sport.

Calgary made four bids to get a Winter Olympics and was finally successful. The rumor is the contractor of the press village made one bid and was chosen. I'd hate to see some of the losers.

But the good news is this is one of the few places on the planet earth the American dollar hasn't gone downhill faster than Pirmin Zurbriggen. You get roughly 25 percent more for each U.S. dollar. What a deal.

Down there they call Calgary a "cow town." "We like our image," said Mayor Ralph Klein. "We don't want to forget our roots."

Their roots are buried beneath several inches of snow, which may be the safest place to be, not to mention the warmest.

I wonder. Is there a gold medal for frostbite?

DRIVING A REAL SPORT IN EUROPE

JULY 18, 1982

FLORENCE, Italy—The great thing about Europe is the cars go fast but time does not. No matter what it says on the calendar, on the continent it's still the nineteenth century.

Priorities differ. Europeans are unconcerned if the beds are too soft or the apricots too hard. Road signs out of Hans Christian Andersen leave them unperturbed. No one worries if it takes longer to place a phone call than it does to eat lunch. And stop complaining because the temperature is ninety-two degrees. The Medici family never had air-conditioning.

Italy has electricity, but that's no reason to put large light bulbs in hotel rooms. A bidet is more impressive. And there's an excellent reason bathtubs do not have shower curtains even if they have a shower. At the moment, however, nobody can offer a justifiable explanation.

Travel, it has been said, is broadening. Sportswriters, it has been said, are gripers. The deduction then is that traveling sportswriters gripe broadly. A germ of truth exists, but too many journeys to Cleveland or Cincinnati have an effect. Jaded, the journalist looks at the Arno and sees only the Ohio.

Observations must be made. The majority of citizens are wonderful. The cuisine is excellent. The lifestyle is unnerving. Everything closes from 1 P.M. to 3 P.M., except Parliament. That hasn't opened in years.

Not to worry. Italy has won the World Cup soccer championship. That and some fresh pasta will provide contentment. And if an additional outlet is required, always there is driving, Europe's most dangerous game. A narrow alley through Florence offers more excitement than the first lap at Indy, or even a 49ers highlight film.

Naiveté persists in the United States. Erroneously, Americans approach the automobile as a means of transportation, a method of moving conveniently from, say, Redwood City to Hayward. Our ignorance is appalling.

In Europe the car does more than transport people from point A to point B. The American male can purge his feelings of violence by watching NFL telecasts. No such vicarious manner exists here. With the Crusades long over and Savonarola long gone, other substitutes were necessary. Primary is the motorcar.

The idea in Europe is to drive as fast as possible as frequently as possible and never, repeat never, concede one portion of the road to another driver. After all, the entire Autostrada del Sole, from Milan to Naples, was constructed for your benefit. Others are simply invaders, infidels as it were.

Driving in the United States is relatively relaxed, mainly because a motorist selects a lane and keeps it, and mainly because some guy in a black-and-white California Highway Patrol car is liable to come zooming out of nowhere with a red light and a big grin.

But they don't have speed limits in Europe, not the type that are enforced at least. And as you are reminded on roads from Finland to Greece, you drive on the right and pass on the left. This makes for a ride comparable to that on the roller coaster at Santa Cruz. You hold your breath, shut your eyes, and pray.

Prosperity has blessed Europe the past few years. Expensive, powerful cars are everywhere. You see almost as many Mercedes-Benzes in Germany as you do in California. And nobody buys a Mercedes or BMW or Citroen to drive in the right lane. That's for the two-cylinder Fiat 500s. The idea is to show who's boss.

Swinging around some overweighted semi, an American driver pulls into the left lane. A horn that can be heard to Greenland blasts. You look in the rearview mirror. You shudder. Three inches off the rear bumper is a two-litre Alfa, three sets of lights flashing. You swerve back to the right. He roars past, traveling at least 100 miles an hour. Please, no remarks about life in the fast lane.

Even in the parking lanes, the food and refueling stops, the contest continues. Because the motorways are toll roads, a driver does not simply leave on the next off ramp to find a Union 76 station or a Denny's. Instead, every so often, about fifty kilometers or 30 miles, he comes upon an area that has gas pumps, a market, a restaurant, and, in certain places in Italy, guys peddling jewelry out of their pockets.

You pull into an area the way Bobby Unser might pull in for a pit stop, avoiding the trucks and cars trying to get back on the racetrack. You park and notice a sign in four languages— Italian, German, French, English—warning against people hustling goods. You watch with amusement as some guy pulls a garbage can in front of the sign and then wanders over to sell you a watch. The Marx Brothers would have loved it.

Perhaps Mark Twain would have too. More than a century ago, Twain sailed for Europe, later detailing his misadventures in the *Innocents Abroad.* He had to endure various hardships in the journey but was not subjected to motorway rest-stop salesmen.

Still, a guy has to make a buck, or a couple of thousand lire. Why should he be cheated out of the thrill of being overtaken by a car going 100? Doesn't he deserve to stay in a room that hasn't been dusted since Michelangelo was a guest?

But there I go, comparing, which is unequivocally unfair. If you want color TV, you stay home. If you want adventure and a return to the time of Garibaldi and the Hapsburgs, you come to Europe. To borrow an old political campaign line, you receive a choice, not an echo.

And you also learn why they had the Dark Ages. No one ever used a decent-sized light bulb in a hotel room.

IN SEARCH
OF A BOX SCORE

JULY 25, 1982

ROCAMADOUR, France—Habits remain naggingly persistent. Even in Quercy, the France of limestone cliffs and truffle soup, there is a frivolous yearning to know whether the A's have gained respectability or the Giants have gained in the pennant race.

Throughout the year, sportswriters gather seemingly for the sole purpose of complaining. At 2:30 A.M., after a World Series game in Yankee Stadium, oaths are merged with plaintive requests to get away from it all. Oh, to be transported to Kapalua, on the shore of Maui, or to some location deep in Europe where they don't know Tom Lasorda from Tom Thumb.

The opportunity arises. Is the journalist content? Of course not. The urge for information is too great, the affair with sport too emotional.

As perceptive as he is clever, Leigh Montville, sports columnist of the *Boston Globe,* expressed this weakness inherent in the breed. On a lovely afternoon at a resort in Florida he inexplicably was captured by a week-old, meaningless boxing match on cable TV.

Outside, svelte ladies sat by the pool. Inside, Montville, against his better judgment, sat in a darkened room for the poorest of reasons. Forgive us, for we know not what we do.

Getting information becomes extremely difficult on this side of the Atlantic. Fluency in languages besides English is rarely accomplished. And even the individual competent enough to hold a telephone conversation with a reservations clerk in Les Eyzies-de-Tayac may feel intimidated in Germany, Italy, or the Netherlands.

Nor is a thorough understanding of, say, French, entirely beneficial. The ability to read *L'Equipe* offers tremendous insight into the sixty-ninth Tour de France bicycle marathon, sweeping out of the Alps toward conclusion in Paris. Page after page of details and statistics are offered, which is not unexpected, because details and statistics are offered, which is not unexpected, because the publication serves as primary sponsor of the race.

The results of the British Grand Prix, rugby and soccer matches and even a feature on U.S. pole-vaulter Dave Volz (*le Yankee sans peur*) are available to those determined to search through the sports daily. But Dave Volz isn't Dave Concepcion. And the struggle to translate produces little satisfaction.

Nor are the papers from England much better, although, heaven knows, they are considerably easier to read than *Le Figaro* or *Die Zeitung*.

The week of the British Open, certainly, was not unrewarding. Stories by competent journalists, many of whom are old friends, on the oldest of golfing championships, fascinated and entertained. Nobody writes about golf, especially British golf, with the obsession and rectitude of the British. Tradition is benevolent.

Baseball results? *The Times* condescends to print them, in the most economical method, sparing perhaps an inch of small type. Strung together in paragraph form, the scores are invariably incomplete and incessantly irritating.

No standings are printed. No references are made. Has Fernando Valenzuela been elected president of Mexico? Has John McNamara been fired by the Cincinnati Reds? (I just learned he has.) Maybe *The Times* is getting even for the way American dailies run English soccer results.

Difficult as this is to admit, in the United States it is possible to survive without a newspaper. We are bombarded by radio and television reports. *Film at eleven!* Next report on the hour; next news when it happens. Stations seem to number in the billions.

TV hasn't overwhelmed Europe. Many homes do not have one set, much less two. During telecasts of World Cup soccer matches, crowds would gather around sets in storefront windows, as did Americans three decades past to watch the World Series or Milton Berle.

Radio stations are plentiful enough, but broadcast bands are different from those in the United States. And once again the language barrier exists. The guy who did the radio play-by-play of the Italy-Brazil cup match made Bill King sound like the slowest talker in the world. But his skill was wasted on at least one columnist who had to ask the hotel concierge which team won.

Where does this leave a U.S. traveler who wants to find out about the Roman influence in Arles and also wants to find out whether the Raiders at least have shifted to Los Angeles? It leaves him eternally grateful for two publications, the *Rome Daily American* and, most of all, the *International Herald-Tribune,* formerly known as the *Paris Herald-Tribune.*

Perhaps it is gauche to sit at a sidewalk cafe in Pauillac, the commune north of Bordeaux where Lafite Rothschild is produced, and study the American League pennant race, but no apologies will be given. Besides, I'd already crawled through seventeen pieces on Tour stage winner Beat Breu, none of which I could comprehend. What I do know is if Beat Breu played baseball, his name alone would be worth a couple of outside contracts.

As the competing papers aimed at tourists and expatriates, the *Daily American* and *Herald-Tribune* do frequent battle. The other day, the *Trib* ripped members of the Italian championship soccer team for dirty play, so the following day the *Daily American* ripped the *Herald-Trib.* Joseph Pulitzer would have loved it.

Trains run late. Airplanes are missed. In tiny stone-building towns such as Gramat, France, the *journaux* dealer does not even carry the paper. An emptiness is felt.

A two-day-old edition is obtained. Happily you learn Tom Weiskopf won the Western Open. Sadly you note the great Jackie Jensen has died, much too young. Baseball goes forward. The NFL labor talks go nowhere.

Who cares? At least one individual, and obviously a great many more. Strange, isn't it?

No one likes the news until he has to do without it.

THE PERFECT OPEN TOWN

JUNE 15, 1987

This is U.S. Open week in San Francisco, where each summer we put our best fog forward and a smart pro never tries to get out of a tourist trap with a five-iron or even a sand wedge. We're forty-nine square miles of people going in circles, wits and wags, crooks and crusaders; it's permissible to say we're crazy, but please don't call us Frisco.

This is the place where Steve McQueen drove down the main thoroughfares in *Bullitt,* and Billy Casper drove down the fairways at Olympic Club, a town of shallowness—as opposed to flatness, sybarites, and Siberian conditions.

Mark Twain may not have actually composed the quintessential remark about weather, to wit, "The coldest winter I ever spent was a summer in San Francisco." But no matter who gets the discredit, we all get the chills.

Somewhere the sun is shining and somewhere children shout, but west of Twin Peaks, whenever people strike out on a journey, they're swaddled in wool and narcissism.

More times than anyone knows, San Francisco has been described as "the cool, gray city of love," which makes it sound like we can't get any forehands in against Ivan Lendl. But we are capable of holding serve against all deprecation except our own.

Mike Royko slashes away like a fourteen-handicapper. "Chicago," he wrote of his own residence, "is a city of big shoulders. San Francisco is a city of swivel hips." Royko rooted against the 49ers in Super Bowl XIX "because many of the male fans view the quarterback standing behind center as an erotic experience."

That sort of derision just bounces off our egos the way a tee shot will ricochet off the zillion trees at Olympic.

Hell, we've even been ripped by Rudyard Kipling, who was

sort of a pith-helmeted Royko. "San Francisco," wrote Kipling "is a mad city inhabited for the most part by perfectly insane people." That was a compliment. We are not often called perfect.

When the Giants moved here from New York in 1958, the fans didn't think Willie Mays was perfect. On the other hand, when a premier of the Soviet Union showed up the following year, he received an unprecedented welcome. "What a town," griped Frank Coniff, a Hearst editor. "They boo Willie Mays and cheer Nikita Khrushchev."

What else would you expect from a town that used to be first in suicides, first in cirrhosis, and last in the National League— before Roger Craig got the Giants to start playing and management got the spectators to stop drinking. Beer is no longer peddled in the stands at Candlestick Park. You've got to make a concession to get food and drink.

"Disneyland for Drunks," we've been labeled, but nobody sells you a ticket to see Snow White, just large-bosomed dancers. We have water to the west, water to the north, water to the east, and Silicon Valley to the south—as opposed to the silicon hills in the topless joints in North Beach.

We also have everyone's favorite fault, the San Andreas. It runs under the first and second holes at Olympic. Who needs water hazards when you can have earthquakes? Par on the Richter scale is 6.8.

If the Big One hits during the tournament, don't worry. You can escape across the Golden Gate Bridge to Mill Valium. If the bridge can hold up 300,000 people, a quake will be inconsequential.

The Bay Bridge heads east, to such bedroom communities as Berserkley and Cokeland. It's usually bumper to bumper, but just yell "fore" and people will back away. One caveat: Don't be behind the "Dykes on Bikes" motorcycle club at the time.

San Francisco is like any other white-wine-sipping region in the United States. Unless you listen to Randy Cross, who's a member of the 49ers football team.

Last fall, when the fans weren't inebriated enough to cheer, he knocked their choice of beverages. Wanted claret instead of Chardonnay.

Years ago the 49ers wanted to get out of Kezar Stadium and into Candlestick. Voted by the pro football writers as the worst in America seven years running, Kezar had a press box open to the cold and wind—and practically every minor politician in the city. "It's the only press box I know," complained Jim Murray, "where you have to get elected to get in."

If you elect to go to the Olympic Club, bring your parka. It's going to be a week of excitement and cold weather—for San Francisco, nothing out of the ordinary.

Getting Back to Basics

BASEBALL'S TUMULTUOUS EXIT

OCTOBER 24, 1980

So now, for another year, it is over. The baseball season, the long season, has fled into the early darkness of an approaching winter, leaving behind the memories that are as permanent as an umpire's decision.

How enjoyable it all was, from the first days of spring training when optimism soared in the breeze to the ultimate out, when a bewildered young man named Willie Wilson swung fruitlessly at the last pitch of the World Series.

Day after day, week after week, men hit and threw and caught. On and on went the games, practically forever. April, May, June, July. Would they end, you wondered, would there finally be days without box scores and batting averages and play-by-play broadcasts? Yes, there would. They now have arrived.

Not for long, of course. In a short while, January will be evolving into February. And in places like St. Petersburg and Phoenix, practice will start once more. But now the diamonds are empty, the bats silent. Now it is time to look back, to recall, to muse.

Baseball, certainly, is as much a game of the mind as it is of the body, a game to be analyzed and argued as well as to be played. A small island of action in a great ocean of statistics is the way someone once described baseball. But instead of detracting from the sport, the statistics, the numbers provide a unique advantage.

Admittedly, those involved with the game utilize numbers to excess. Indeed, each time some obscure record was relayed to the press box during the World Series, the announcement would be met with cynical derision. Another worthless stat, we concurred.

But later, that worthless stat, that obscure record would find its way into a story, into a broadcast, into a conversation. And once more we linked progeny to parent, present to past. Once more we had a relationship with history.

In baseball, no one stands alone, in achievement or failure. Someone's always had a day almost as successful, or almost as miserable. There is always comparison, for consolation or for congratulations.

Yes, Willie Wilson of the Kansas City Royals had a terrible World Series, striking out a record twelve times. He was angered and frustrated, not without reason. But in 1952, Gil Hodges of the Brooklyn Dodgers, the great Gil Hodges, went hitless in twenty-one at-bats against the Yankees. And in 1966, Willie Davis of the Los Angeles Dodgers made three errors in one inning. In his disappointment, Willie Wilson has plenty of company— company of quality.

Baseball is blessed in that its last hurrah, its termination, is destined to be climactic. And—as this year's play-offs and World Series emphasized—it invariably is.

So much of baseball's excitement is attributable to tension rather than action. Acknowledging that a week or a series or a game, from out of the dozens and dozens of weeks and series and games that are played, is of special importance adds the ingredient that is lacking through much of the season.

Until recently, the Super Bowl, the overpublicized championship of professional football, generally has not met expectations. Having been flagellated by hype and hope, the public not surprisingly found itself unfulfilled at game's close. Descriptions included such words as *boring*.

You can call the World Series a great many things, but one of them will not be *boring*—even if the play demanded such a description. The pervading tension, the obligatory great plays, the statistics ad nauseam are enough to make us perceive excitement.

Maybe this year was better than most, maybe we had a glut of great baseball in concluding seasonal games, in play-offs, and in the World Series, baseball that left us ready to put a reassuring hand on our heart, the way Tug McGraw did in the ninth inning when Hal McCrae's apparent home run benevolently curved foul.

And yet, it's always that way, always so marvelous, that during the Series baseball, without question, is our national pastime, the Series baseball, without question, is our national pastime, the one focus of our attention. Even the editors of *The New York Times*, who normally treat sports with contempt, feel compelled to place at least one report of the World Series every day on the front page.

It's been said that the play-offs—or, more formally, the League Championship Series—are more critical than the World Series, and thus more exciting. And undeniably, that five-game tournament between Houston and Philadelphia that came to a tumultuous finish was laced with emotion.

But there was no letdown for the World Series, no tailing off. If anything, the Series was better than the play-offs, given the matchups and the style and the drama provided by fans who had never been gifted with a World Series or fans who had been three decades without one.

The Royals were favored, the Phillies won. Mike Schmidt and Pete Rose and George Brett were all we anticipated. Willie Aikens and Del Unser and Tug McGraw were more. There were heroes, there were bums. There were bonehead plays—why didn't Darrell Porter slide home that first game instead of tippy-toeing?—and there were great plays.

And most of all, there were memories, memories that will survive through the fall and winter, memories that keep the game alive from the time of the final out in the World Series until the first pitch of next spring.

CASEY'S K TURNS INTO HIT

JUNE 3, 1988

For a hundred years there's been no joy in Mudville. But plenty everywhere else.

A hundred years of leaving men on second and third. Of striking out on three straight pitches. Of becoming a metaphor for failing in the clutch.

"Casey at the Bat" was the second poem most of us learned, right after "Wynken, Blinken and Nod," which is one of the few rhymes, besides "Tinker-to-Evers-to-Chance" with three proper names in a single line.

Baseball. "The whole history of baseball," said the author Bernard Malamud, among whose works is *The Natural,* "has the quality of mythology."

Is there a greater American myth than Casey, standing there pounding with cruel violence his bat upon the plate? And then shattering the air—and our dreams of success.

"Our sweetest songs are those that tell of saddest thought," wrote another poet, Percy Bysshe Shelley.

Indeed. Had Casey responded to that hope which springs eternal, had he homered to win the game for the Mudville nine, or at least singled to drive home Flynn and Blake to tie the score at 4-4, we would never have been so captivated.

In 1988, Casey would have hit the 0-2 pitch into the left-field seats. And been interviewed by Al Michaels and Jim Palmer. And signed a contract, like Dale Murphy, to endorse Canon cameras. Or maybe cannonballs. Or at least Dyan Cannon.

But in 1888, not every ending was a happy one. Certainly not that of the home team.

When I think of the large body of baseball literature, I think of three disparate lines:

"Who's on first?"

"Buy me some peanuts and Cracker Jack, I don't care if I ever get back."

"But there is no joy in Mudville—mighty Casey has struck out."

As we all have now and then.

The protagonist, like the Greek gods, was not perfect, but the poem, written by a man who had studied the classics at Harvard, is very close to perfection. Maybe about the distance between bat and ball on Casey's last swing.

Ernest Lawrence Thayer created "Casey" in a few hours, basically to fill space.

In the *San Francisco Examiner* of June 3, 1888, the poem follows a story about the Republican National Convention, which would nominate Benjamin Harrison, and precedes an acerbic verse by Ambrose Bierce.

If any mistake was made, besides that by the mighty Casey, it was Thayer signing the poem with the pseudonym "Phin," which was short for Phinney. And thus, over the decades, numerous individuals claimed to be the author.

As opposed to the numerous individuals who claimed to be the subject, old Casey himself.

As opposed to the several communities that claimed to be Mudville.

Thayer majored in philosophy under Henry James at Harvard, edited the *Lampoon*—the business manager of which was one William Randolph Hearst, soon to become *Examiner* publisher—made Phi Beta Kappa, and, after refusing a job in the family woolen mill in Massachusetts, drifted to Paris.

Hearst cabled him there to come to San Francisco and write humor. Or is that a redundancy?

One of the names in the original poem is hardly redundant. It is confusing. As we're being set up for the great fall, Thayer tells us: "But Flynn preceded Casey, as did also Jimmy Blake/ And the former was a lulu, and the latter was a cake."

Yet Flynn singled and Blake, the much despised, tore the cover off the ball.

"And there was Johnnie safe at second and Flynn a-hugging third."

How did Jimmy become Johnnie in a few short lines? Why

in the modern version was "lulu" changed to "hoodoo"? Will Billy Martin make it through the season? What's going to happen to Larry Bowa and Lou Piniella?

The sportswriter Arthur Robinson called Thayer a great poet and a lousy reporter. Who was the opposing team? wonders Robinson. And the pitcher who struck out Casey?

And was there ever a Casey? Or a Mudville?

There was an Ernest Thayer. He died in 1940 in Santa Barbara, taking to his grave enough secrets to tantalize generations of Americans.

"There must have been times in his life," the baseball historian Lee Allen wrote of Thayer, "when he wished he had never written 'Casey' as a harmless filler for the *San Francisco Examiner.* He had no idea he was to become the center of a storm of controversy that would rage for more than half a century.

"A shy, cultured gentleman of unusual sensitivity and intelligence, he was destined to spend his life warding off the spurious claims of frauds who maintained either they had written the poem themselves or inspired the character of Casey."

Thayer long contended the poem had no basis in fact. But ninety miles east of San Francisco, in Stockton, once known as Mudville, there was a California League team in 1888. And in the league there were players named Barrows, Flynn, and Cooney, like the batters in the verse.

The arguments are frivolous. The poem is marvelous.

As long as it's read or recited, somewhere men will be laughing and somewhere children will shout.

And we'll all forever wonder why Casey went after that 0-2 pitch. What a bum!

THE COWBOY SURVIVES

"Momma, don't let your babies grow up to be cowboys . . . . "

He used to be disdained, belittled. He used to be scorned by the white-collar set, the dry-martini crowd. He was a country bumpkin, the cowboy was, in blue jeans and checkered shirt, a man out of bowlegged step with the times.

But now he's our last hope, our American hero. Now we're all buying ten-gallon hats and Nocona boots, all showing up in straight-legged Levi's, all listening to Willie Nelson records. Now we all wish our mommas had ignored the advice of Ed and Patsy Bruce, who wrote the song that Willie has made famous, and let us grow up to be cowboys.

Now we all wish we could prove our virility, our courage, the way Lyle Sankey does on, no, not a mechanical bull, but on the genuine ungulate creature in the rodeo ring.

"They never stay home and they're always alone . . . . "

It's true that Sankey, now breaking broncos and riding Brahmas during the Grand National at the Cow Palace, rarely stays at his home in Branson, Missouri. For more than half the year he's on the road. But alone? Not this cowboy, this professional performer.

Lyle Sankey is rugged, though. But he's no individualist. You won't find him on the old north forty or branding calves at Line Camp Three. Lyle Sankey doesn't bring in the herd. He brings in the cash.

One of the very few rodeo cowboys to compete in all three rough stock events—saddle bronc, bareback bronc, and bull riding—Sankey has earned more than $60,000 this year, a salary impressive even for a junior exec in some midtown Manhattan corporation. And Sankey doesn't have to wear Brooks Brothers suits.

His working clothes consist of Wrangler jeans—"Most of the

rodeo cowboys think they fit better than Levi's," said Sankey—Laramie boots, a long-sleeved shirt, and a championship silver belt buckle not much smaller than a hubcap. In other words, these days Sankey's on-the-job attire is about the same as everyone else wears off the job.

"But we have a saying," laughed the twenty-six-year-old Sankey. "It takes more than boots and a hat to make a cowboy." That it does. To make a rodeo cowboy, it takes skill—and daring. In other words, it takes the same things it takes to make a pro football player.

" . . . He's not wrong he's just different, but his pride won't let him do things to make you think he's right."

As a teenager growing up in Augusta, Kansas, some fifteen miles from Wichita, Sankey entered a junior rodeo—and was embarrassed. Having ridden horses practically from the time he could walk, Sankey simply couldn't comprehend why he was tossed seconds after climbing aboard a bucking bronc.

"I wouldn't allow myself to believe I couldn't stay on," said Sankey. "I had done so badly I had to prove I could do it."

He proved it, after a fashion. At Rose Hill High he was a football player, for a while. "I weighed 165 pounds and played right tackle. I was the second-lightest tackle in the league. The lightest was our left tackle."

Acknowledging that he would never make the NFL, Sankey shifted his body and his thoughts to rodeo, competing in junior and amateur events and attending classes in the fine art of keeping 1,200 pounds of irate equine from sending him Stetson over heels.

Among the curricula were sessions on a mechanical bull, similar to the type that has sent would-be cowpokes into potential orbit at Gilley's famous honky-tonk outside Houston. It was Gilley's that served as the setting for Aaron Latham's 1978 *Esquire* article on grown-ups playing cowboy. That story was corrupted by Hollywood into sort of a western version of *Saturday Night Fever.*

Sankey saw that film, *Urban Cowboy,* watched with skepticism when John Travolta climbed aboard the piston-driven mechanical bull. Lyle's feelings echoed those of the critics.

"The movie was accurate," said Sankey, "but it wasn't very good. It was a lousy movie."

"Don't let 'em pick guitars and drive them old trucks, make 'em be doctors and lawyers and such . . . "

Lyle rode enough mechanical bulls and live horses to earn

a rodeo scholarship to Fort Hays State College in Kansas. He was going to be a doctor, a veterinarian. But after a couple of years in school, Sankey figured his future was in riding animals, not helping them. He quit college and joined the rodeo circuit. It hasn't been dull.

"There's a parallel between rodeo contestants, especially those who ride stock, and pro football players," said Sankey. "We get banged up, and our careers last about the same. Like football, usually someone burns out emotionally quicker than he does physically. All that traveling—some people will compete in 150 rodeos in one year—and all that getting banged around wear you down."

A bronc or bull rider must stay on board for eight seconds, trying to display some semblance of control—of himself and the animal. Yes, there's fear. And there are a multitude of injuries. Even now, Sankey has cracked this and crushed that. Pain? It's as much a part of rodeo riders as determination.

"Why do I do it?" Sankey asked rhetorically. "Well, some people say it isn't what you accomplish in life that means something, it's the obstacles you overcome to reach success."

The cowboy has overcome a great many obstacles. He's now a hero, a man to be admired. How the times—and the fashions—have changed.

BASEBALL'S GENTLE SPRING

MARCH 17, 1985

PHOENIX—Spring training is a time when young men chase fly balls and old men chase dreams.

Spring training is when we no longer must wait 'til next year, when baseball is a game instead of a business, when again there is joy in Mudville.

Clichés, calisthenics, chaws of tobacco, and a cause of celebration. Dick Williams hanging on the screen behind home plate. Rookies hanging on Williams's every word. Sunshine supermen who in afternoon's warmth have a tendency to act like mere mortals.

Atlee Hammaker jogs from dugout to bull pen, accompanied by appreciative applause and myriad requests for autographs.

Dusty Baker stands nearly hidden behind layers of netting in a batting cage and lashes out at balls flung from the lean steel arm of a mechanical pitcher.

Ruben Amaro, a Cubs coach, leans on a dugout railing and muses about seasons in the sun and experiences yet to come. "Hey," he advises, "you go ask Manny Trillo if he plans to play more than sixty games this year." The final punctuation mark is a smug grin.

This is spring training, less a program of exercise than a state of mind. The players may be working on fundamentals, but we're all working on imagination.

Jim Brosnan, in his baseball classic, *The Long Season,* alludes to the obligatory pep talk for a manager on the opening day of spring training. "Wanna welcome all you fellows. Wanna impress on you that you each got a chance to make this ballclub. We got a job to do, and with a couple of breaks, I think we can win the pennant. Let's go get 'em."

Let's go. Let's talk about what might happen but probably won't. Let's laugh about what shouldn't happen but invariably will.

The Boston writer Melvin Maddocks described baseball in the spring as America's last communal value. The game is as much fun for the kibitzers as it is for the players.

"When I was young," said Nolan Ryan, the pitcher, "I looked upon spring training as a drudgery. It was so boring I thought I was being punished. Now, I enjoy it. I can go about things at my own pace. There's no pressure."

Those are magic words: No pressure. In a hectic, helter-skelter world, spring training offers a peaceful respite, a return to the good old days. The ballparks are small, but our vision is unlimited.

In the seats behind home plate, scouts, nearly every one wearing a broad Panama hat, sit and gossip. They are there to study the talent. But they spend as much time chuckling about the past as planning for the future.

An egalitarian concept guides spring training. For a few weeks, superstar and nonroster player are equal, sharing crowded conditions, ramshackle stadia, and threadbare uniforms.

Steve Garvey may someday reside in the Hall of Fame, but that does not excuse him from collecting balls around home plate.

Spring training is teenagers without shirts and senior citizens clad in nostalgia. That Gonzales is a good one, somebody will suggest, but he'll never be another Honus Wagner. People get old, but baseball never ages.

During the bottom half of the seventh at the A's-Padres game the other day, several fans sang an *a cappella* version of "Take Me Out to the Ball Game." The voices were strained, the intent was pure. Give them some peanuts and Cracker Jack. They don't care if they ever get back.

Spring training is a shared love of the game by athlete and spectator, who for these few weeks are in close proximity, physically as well as mentally.

Scottsdale Stadium, where the Giants play, has a board front that resembles the Last Chance Saloon. From Phoenix Stadium, the spring home of the A's, you literally can see saguaro cactus growing beyond the outfield fences.

Throughout Arizona and Florida, men run on real grass in jewel-box ballparks. No AstroTurf, no domes, no complications. That's spring training. And it's delightful.

WHY NOT SENTIMENT?

DECEMBER 28, 1986

> *It's a sobering thought that when Mozart was my age he had been dead for two years.*
>
> —Tom Lehrer, pundit

The great thing about getting old is nobody expects you to remember, and you expect never to forget.

Well, here's to auld acquaintance and new memories. Any year in which Reggie Jackson and Chris Speier come home has to be looked upon as a fine one. I don't know if the past will be prelude, but it was wonderful.

The Rockies may crumble and Gibraltar may tumble, they're only made of clay—as opposed to Muhammad Ali. But our heroes are here to stay.

Sentiment. "We're not bringing Reggie Jackson back simply because of sentiment," A's president Roy Eisenhardt told us. Why not? Let's take a sentimental journey. Put our minds at ease.

Deep in December, a man lyricized, it's nice to remember: Reggie in green and gold. Speier gliding over the Candlestick AstroTurf. They've come full circle, which means we have, too.

No place like home? Ask Pete Rose, who came back to the Reds. Willie Mays and Willie McCovey, returning to the Giants. Nate Thurmond to the Warriors. It's good to have them back where they belong.

Once in a while, we've got to think sports isn't a business—even if it is. Loyalty and nostalgia have to glisten brighter than a dollar sign. Old friends.

It's almost as difficult to strike the right note about sports as it is about humor; take either one seriously and you're accused of missing the point, which is their willful unseriousness.

We're all a few years younger this holiday season. It's 1973 once more. Reggie is hitting homers into the left-field seats at the Coliseum. Chris is beating the Padres in the Giants' home opener at Candlestick, and the message board is flashing: "Speier. Who Else?"

Who else? What else? Familiarity. In sport it brings not contempt but reassurance. We're having our class reunion. A reunion with a lot of class.

What if Reggie never had left the A's? Or Speier never had been dispatched from the Giants? The players prospered in their new environments, but the local franchises faltered.

More than anything, sport lacks stability. Players come and go. Teams are moved about like chess pieces on the board. There is no sense of community or continuity, no identification.

Joe DiMaggio was a lucky one. So were Yastrzemski and Musial. From start to finish their address was the same. "Getting traded for the first time," former pitcher John Curtis reminded, "is like being thrown out of your own home."

Jackson and Speier have been invited back. The front door is reopened. Their careers will end with the teams with which they were started. Too few are the athletes who have that opportunity.

The men running baseball on either side of San Francisco Bay are businessmen, but businessmen with a heart. And soul. "What really swayed Reggie about coming back," said his attorney, Steve Kay, "was when Wally Haas [the A's executive] called him and told him they really wanted him."

That's what happens when you have people who care. Wally Haas grew up in the Bay Area. He's about the same age as Reggie. He recalls the glory days. He knows what Jackson meant to the A's and what he will mean to the A's.

Al Rosen, the Giants president, sought a veteran utility infielder. He spoke about a trade. None was needed. Speier was a free agent and a remarkably logical choice.

Jackson played for the last A's team to win a pennant. Speier played for the last Giants team to win a division. Tradition.

"What I want to do is make the team better and make the fans and front-office people glad I'm here," Reggie told us at the Christmas Eve press conference.

We're glad you're here, Reggie. And you too, Chris. You've brought back some of what we lost.

The reference is not to the standings. It's to the emotions.

You're never too old to remember the joy of being young.

USF RELIVES GLORY

NOVEMBER 22, 1985

Bill Russell, gray in mustache and mellow in mood, squinted into a spotlight and tried to peer into the past.

"Who are all those old people sitting next to me?" he asked in mock surprise. A muffled laugh carried through the room. Sweet nostalgia brings with it frightening realizations.

Thirty years had flown since that first championship season. Who knows where the time goes?

Yesterday, when we were young, these men had carried the University of San Francisco to consecutive NCAA basketball titles. Now there were bald heads, potbellies, and delicious memories.

Their accomplishments continued after graduation. "One judge and several lawyers," advised Phil Woolpert, coach of those USF teams. "These men have been successful."

How reassuring in this era of college scandals to know these gentlemen—Hal Perry, Carl Boldt, Gene Brown, Rudy Zannini, and, of course, the nonpareil, the great Bill Russell himself—had learned more at USF than just how to dribble a ball.

This is what intercollegiate sport was meant to be, an activity that was beneficial not destructive, that provided direction not embarrassment.

USF has known it all—the heights, the depths. And now it is going to try once more, is going to resurrect a program that was too full of violations and too lacking in responsibility. What better way to start again than to align with tradition? The hope is that someday the past will be present.

So USF hung a big green-and-gold banner in the ballroom of the San Francisco Hilton and shook down the echoes. Then they called on the old coach and his aging star to lead everyone back to glory. The journey was fascinating.

"Isn't it great to be back together on an occasion like this?" shouted Woolpert, a sprightly sixty-nine. His response was thunderous applause, as he knew it would be. Who can resist an opportunity to recall glory days?

In 1955 and 1956, the best undergraduate basketball team in the land came from a hilltop in San Francisco. It had a spindly, remarkable center in Russell, who would go on to lead the Boston Celtics to repeated championships, and a group of other skilled players.

They all returned, save two. "K.C. Jones is working in Massachusetts," reminded Woolpert in an allusion to the Boston Celtics coach.

Another could not make it. Jerry Mullen died eight years ago of a heart attack. "A great player," said Woolpert. At the head table, Mullen's brother, Monsignor William J. Mullen, could only nod in agreement.

But this was a night for laughter not sorrow. A night for standing ovations. A night for Woolpert, now living in relative obscurity in the state of Washington, and his players.

"I may sound immodest," said Woolpert, "but I firmly believe these two teams were as great as any in college basketball."

They certainly rank near that zenith, along with the UCLA clubs of Walton and Alcindor, the Indiana team of 1976, and the Georgetown team of 1984.

"In 1956," said Woolpert, "we beat everyone by seven points or more."

They did it primarily because of Russell, an insecure, late-developing teenager from McClymonds High in Oakland.

"An athlete," contended Woolpert, "who through his heart and his head became the most successful basketball player in the country."

But nobody dreamed of that possibility in January 1952, when Russell graduated from high school and took a job in a sheet-metal factory.

"I was at USF from 1950 to 1952," said the Reverend John LoSchiavo, now the university president, "then I went away to Alma College in Los Gatos to study theology the four years Bill was here.

"But before I left, I remember Phil Woolpert watching this kid in the gym. I asked, 'Who's that?' He said he was from Oakland and he was going to take a chance on him." It was the chance of a lifetime.

"When I got out of high school," Russell would quip, "most

of the kids in high school had never heard of me. I wish I knew what Phil saw in me."

Russell is appreciative now. A while back he claimed Woolpert and others at USF were racists. Feelings have been soothed.

"At this point in my life," Russell confessed, "I have thrown down some of my psychological baggage."

And picked up the gauntlet.

"I personally intend to support the new basketball program. I treasure the years I spent here."

Maybe college sport has some virtue after all.

ANOTHER FLAME

JULY 29, 1984

LOS ANGELES—The small memorial candles were not nearly as bright as the torch above the Coliseum. Yet they burned with a special fire that seared the heart and the mind.

The opening of the Olympic Games is a time for pageantry and joy—incredibly so last evening—a time for nations to gather in friendship and competition. For the small land of Israel it is also a time for grief, a time to remember the most heinous act of international sport.

It is twelve years now since hooded Palestinian terrorists broke into the Olympic Village at Munich and killed eleven members of the Israeli team. The International Olympic Committee tried hard to ignore the tragedy. Now, it seeks to forget entirely.

Israel asked the IOC for a moment of silence, a moment of reflection and sorrow in the unbridled pleasure that is an opening ceremony. Israel wanted the world to acknowledge the suffering yesterday. And then the dancing and cheering could go on.

But the IOC refused. No one would rain on its parade. "It might dampen the enthusiasm of the Games," a spokesman said. "It might offend certain Arab countries." What the IOC has offended is the common sense of peaceful men everywhere.

Jews have heard the word *no* before. They knew what to do. They held their own observance. Forty-eight hours before the 1984 Summer Games were officially opened, dozens of people of all religions gathered in the courtyard of the Simon Wiesenthal Center, a building dedicated to the memories of other martyrs, victims of the Holocaust.

There on a soft summer evening, cypress and olive trees standing in the glare of floodlights, stars glistening above, Mimi Weinberg, widow of the first man killed by the Munich terrorists, sought not retribution but only retrospection.

Moshe Weinberg was the Israeli wrestling coach. He answered

a knocking at the door of the team's quarters in the predawn hours to face armed men. Weinberg slammed the door shut, threw his bulk in front of it, and shouted at others to flee. He was machine-gunned down.

Ten others were to perish before the ordeal came to a bloody end at the Munich Airport. The dead were sent home along with the living. Accompanying the caskets was Shlomit Nir-Toor, Israel's best swimmer. She never competed again.

"I used to love to swim," said Nir-Toor, "but after the killing I could not find the desire. I do not think others should quit. I think the Olympic Games must go on and Israel must compete. Otherwise, the PLO has achieved its aim."

Nobody from the IOC attended the memorial service. Others were more thoughtful. Leo McCarthy, the lieutenant governor of California, was there. So was Jean Shiley Newhouse, a gold medal winner for the United States in the long jump in the 1932 Olympics. So was twelve-year-old Gouri Weinberg, Moshe's son.

Gouri was two weeks old when his father was killed. He is blue-eyed and lean. He plays soccer, basketball and baseball. He also plays the cello. He will not be a wrestler.

The solemnity of the evening was eased by Gouri Weinberg, who doesn't remember August 1972.

"I didn't know my father," he told the audience in almost flawless English. "Let us hope these Games will be friendly and safe. I wish my father were here today to take me to the Olympics and perhaps to the Michael Jackson show."

Midst tears there was laughter. That is only proper. Tradition demands a reaffirmation of life.

"Sportsmen of the world," pleaded Mimi Weinberg, "please try to understand each other."

Mimi Weinberg has made no attempt to understand the events of Munich. "They say it is good to talk," she would explain later, "but the first five years after it happened it was very hard.

"I used to love sports so much—tennis, wrestling. Now I hate what sport has done to my life. My husband loved wrestling more than he loved me. He was the best in Israel."

The eleven yahrzeit, or memorial, candles were extinguished, one by one. It was time to consign Munich 1972 to memory and think about Los Angeles 1984.

HERE'S LOOKING AT YOU, KIDS

DECEMBER 30, 1987

We lurch toward another new year wondering about what will be, musing about what was. I hear the bell-like voice of Judy Collins singing, "Who knows where the time goes . . . . " And no one can provide an answer.

Memories. The Warriors in the play-offs, the Giants in the play-offs, the 49ers advancing to the play-offs. Could any region be more satisfied with the results of its major sporting franchises in the last twelve months?

We approach 1988, when Willie McCovey and Superman and I each turn fifty. And the men and women I watched play now sit and watch their sons and daughters play. And the seconds keep ticking. The game has only one ending.

You listen to a melody or glance at an old picture and the past comes hurtling back, teasing and taunting and giving you pause. "Was it all so simple then," Barbra Streisand lyricizes, "or has time rewritten every line?" How do you respond?

The funny thing about sport, and perhaps life, is that the moments once so important disappear into a swirl of insignificance. And the games go on, and another kid throws up another jump shot.

Where have you gone Joe DiMaggio? And Joe Namath? And Joe Morgan? And Joe Fulks?

And why is Barry Bonds in the outfield when it should be Bobby Bonds?

Walt Frazier's kid is playing basketball at Penn? Wasn't it only yesterday Walt was at Southern Illinois?

Reggie Jackson and Tom Seaver and Julius Erving retire, and we recall the big home runs and the frightening fastballs and the famous dunks.

It was Dr. J. who made the stuff shot an art form, the way

96

Reggie made the homer a Shakespearean production. But they have come and gone, and now the headlines belong to Mark McGwire and Michael Jordan.

The salaries escalate and the problems irritate and the prophets of doom keep predicting a sporting Armageddon, the end of fun and games as we know it.

Yet, kids keep going out to the sandlots and the playgrounds, with dreams and schemes and the patience to improve. And the stadiums always seem to be full. And the television set is always on.

Did you ever stop to consider what it would have been like if ESPN existed in the 1950s? Would any American boy have done his homework? Does any American boy do his homework now? Or does he simply study the phrases of Chris Berman or Dick Vitale?

There are too many teams in too many sports, and all the owners ever talk about is expansion. Soon we'll have pro basketball in Orlando, and, I suppose, pro hockey in San Jose. And more names to digest.

Was it all so simple then? All we had to learn were sixteen major-league managers. And teams stayed put, like an oak tree in the back yard. The Dodgers? Brooklyn. Every World War II movie made that point. Then came confusion. And expansion. And imbalance.

The more things change, Alphonse Karr, a Frenchman, told us, the more they stay the same. You can interpret that any way you wish.

Television is always showing us the Dodgers or Mets or New York Giants because New York and L.A. are not only the two largest cities in the land but the media centers as well, and the producers and directors, who are Mets and Dodgers fans, impose their ideas on the whole country.

Return with us now to the stirring days of yesteryear, one of the Lone Ranger on radio and *Sport* magazine on monthly mailing lists. It is the late 1940s and early 1950s. And since *Sport* is based in New York, the covers feature Mickey Mantle or Duke Snider or Willie Mays.

But now the joke's on them. In 1987, no baseball or football team from New York or the Los Angeles area advances to the play-offs. And America survives quite well, thank you.

When Mark McGwire started sending balls over fences, we

wouldn't appreciate him for what he was doing, only what he might do.

We make Mount Shastas out of anthills, gazing out to center field when we should be focused on home plate.

The days go by and the athletes go by. Soon it is tomorrow, and we've hardly concentrated on today.

Michael Jordan and Mark McGwire will be retiring all too quickly. Who knows where the time goes?

NOT FIT
FOR A KING

MARCH 6, 1986

MESA, Arizona—King Carl he was called, but this glorious day he was only a commoner, an old man at rest watching young men at play.

On a summer afternoon more than fifty years ago, Carl Hubbell gained a place in baseball legend.

In the 1934 All-Star Game at the Polo Grounds, Hubbell struck out, in order, the five best hitters in the American League: Babe Ruth, Lou Gehrig, Jimmie Foxx, Al Simmons, and Joe Cronin.

The batters are all dead now. Hubbell survives. Barely. He is eighty-two, a widower with leathery skin and gnarled bones, who they say has financial problems. He definitely has physical ones.

At the Chicago Cubs training site yesterday, Hubbell sat on a folding beach chair. He peered through a cyclone fence near the right-field foul pole, unrecognized, unappreciated.

The entrance to the three-field complex is beyond the center-field fence. Hubbell intended to walk to the stands behind home plate. "But," he sighed, "this is about as far as I can go."

Baseball obviously hasn't gone far enough for Carl Hubbell, to permit this man with failing eyesight and shaky legs to slip away from the protection of the game.

The dozens of other spectators, many adorned in Cubs paraphernalia, passed by without a clue. You don't have to be out of sight to be out of mind.

Hubbell has lived in Mesa since 1977, when the only major-league team with which he was affiliated, the Giants, "retired" him after a stroke. Baseball was his life. Now it's his love.

"Hey, is that Durham at bat?" a young man asked nobody in particular. Hubbell lifted his head and stared through prescription sunglasses. "No," he said. "Can't be. Durham's left-handed. That batter's right-handed."

Right-handed or left-handed, Hubbell got them out in his

sixteen-year career with the New York Giants. Twice, 1933 and 1936, he won the National League Most Valuable Player award. He ended up in the Hall of Fame, as did the five batters he struck out in the All-Star Game.

A left-handed thrower, Hubbell is known as the father of the screwball, a pitch that in the subsequent years Fernando Valenzuela of the Dodgers has utilized with similar success.

"I never claimed to have invented it," Hubbell said a few years ago. "Baseball had been played for many years before I tried it, but I did develop it in the 1920s after watching a left-hander throw a sinking fastball in the minors."

And he did name it. "It reminded me of a turning screw."

The screwball is a reverse curve, breaking away from a right-handed hitter when thrown by a left-hander. There are so few screwball pitchers because it is almost anatomically impossible for human beings to throw screwballs.

"Nature," said Hubbell, who retains his mental sharpness, "never intended a man to turn his hand over that way throwing rocks at a bear.

"All those years of evolution developed a body construction that encourages you to throw fastballs when something is coming after you."

Hubbell had what he calls "loose wrists." So does Valenzuela.

"Others have thrown the screwball, Tug McGraw, Mike Marshall, but I've never seen anybody except Valenzuela do it the way I did it, with exactly the same delivery over the top for the fastball, slider, and screwball.

"That's the key. To make the batters think you are throwing something else. Then the screwball comes in and breaks away. They're not ready for it."

Neither is Hubbell ready for what passes as baseball in the 1980s.

"They still use a bat and ball, but the ball is wound so tight. It's a lot livelier. TV has made the players actors. They don't seem to worry about doing the job.

"We had to concentrate. In the 1930s, we had the Depression, and you sure as hell didn't want anybody to get your job. There were millions of people in breadlines, and you didn't want to go back to that."

When Hubbell arrived in baseball, off an Oklahoma farm, uniforms didn't even have numbers on the back.

"That started in 1933. Before that you'd go to a game, and before the game a guy with a megaphone would announce the pitchers and catchers and then he would announce each batter as he came out of the dugout."

Nobody is around any longer to announce the presence of Carl Hubbell. He carries his folding chair and goes about practically unnoticed.

Is that any way to treat a king?

A HAND FOR BASEBALL GLOVES

MAY 24, 1981

The true joy of baseball, it has been said, is that it enables the generations to talk to each other. If that be true, then one of the primary languages is that of the glove.

Is there a more magical, more meaningful bit of athletic equipment? Nothing else in the world of sport seems to have such a positive force, an ability to free us from reality.

A baseball glove is a boy's first step toward manhood, a man's lingering reminder of his youth. A baseball glove is at the same time a promise and a memory.

A baseball glove united Babe Ruth with George Brett, Willie Keeler with Willie Mays, the big-league star with the kid down the block. To have a glove, your own glove, is to clutch the leathery fringes of fantasy.

I cannot walk into a sporting-goods store without wandering over to the rack where the gloves, richly odorous with the aroma of tanned hide, sit like sirens on an ageless rock.

Some mystical force persuades me to select one, any one, and put it on, and pop it a few times. In those few seconds the passage of time has been reversed.

I am backhanding smashes down the third-base line like Brooks Robinson, racing back to the center-field fence at the Polo Grounds like Willie Mays, running in desperation to grab a pop fly that will save the 1953 World Series like Billy Martin. It is to dream.

Your own glove. That's all you wanted as a boy. It was a symbol of accomplishment, of belonging, of growing up. Pretty soon, you were told in words that beguiled, you'll be old enough to have your own glove. Whether you could use it was inconsequential.

There remains something special about a father buying that first glove for his sons, or in my case—and here one can be grateful for the changes in society—my daughters. For a boy of seven or eight or nine, nothing will be selected with so much care or intent until, many years in the future, he takes a bride.

It is no easy task, choosing that first glove. No woman purchasing a dress spends more time or effort. Not only do style and price have to be considered but so does the major leaguer whose cursive identification crosses the heel. Do you pick a model endorsed by Mark Belanger or by Mike Schmidt?

Gloves are cherished, become keepsakes. Bats splinter, balls unravel. But gloves last, if not forever, then long enough to grasp the excitement of days gone by.

Three decades past, the glove everybody wanted was a Marty Marion "Mr. Shortstop," one of the first in which the fingers were laced together at the tips. I never had one. My glove was a trapper, a first baseman's that somehow disappeared.

But a few years later, older and presumably wiser, but no less a romantic, I purchased a Dick Groat model fielder's glove. Now, nearly a quarter-century distant, that glove remains a flexible beauty, to be hauled out of the closet on appropriate occasions.

Kids used to walk to school with gloves attached to their belt, between the first and second loops, like sheaths on the hips of a Dumas swashbuckler. Or they would hang them over the handlebars of their bikes. Nowadays the gloves seem to disappear into the backpacks that are as obligatory as running shoes, hidden until required. How unfortunate.

Another difference, of course, is cost. In the 1950s, $20 would acquire a quality glove, and for $30 you could buy one of the top-of-the-line models, exactly like Mickey Mantle or Duke Snider wore. Not that this would provide insurance against the misplays that forever proved embarrassing.

Buying the mitt was one thing, a big thing. Preparing it was something else. Oh, if only such care were displayed with other possessions.

You rubbed the new glove with saddle soap or neat's-foot oil, jammed a baseball or two into the middle to form a pocket, and then stuck it under your mattress, the better to stay near through the night.

Modern gloves are not only more expensive, they come in such pastel shades as blue and green—imagine walking out on a sandlot with a blue glove—and are made in such incongruous locales as Japan and Korea. Well, I guess if we can drive Toyotas and Datsuns, we can catch baseballs with Mizunos.

Until slightly more than a century ago, we caught them with our skin, our palms and fingers. If you think that it was difficult and uncomfortable, well, it was.

"When it is recalled that every ball pitched had to be returned," wrote Albert Spalding of Boston in 1870, "and that every swift one coming my way, from infielders, outfielders, or hot off the bat, must be caught or stopped, some idea may be gained of the punishment received."

A few years later, despite the possibility of abuse from fans and teammates, Spalding began wearing a vented glove that wasn't much more than the type a foundry worker might use in his job. Others also adopted the glove, but in 1894, one Boston player, Harry Schaefer, said the game was being spoiled by "allowing players to wear those abominations known as mitts."

Fortunately, no one paid much attention to Harry Schaefer. Gloves came to be worn and to be treasured.

A glove is dreams, heroics, and sportsmanship. A glove is something in which to pound a fist or snare a liner. A glove is a promise for the young and a memory for those not so young.

A baseball, and baseball, it has been said, enables the generations to talk to each other.

IT WAS THIRTY YEARS AGO TODAY

APRIL 15, 1988

We always had borrowed our major-league baseball from another state, first through radio re-creations, then in the early 1950s on small black-and-white TV screens.

California had midwifed the careers of so many of the game's great players, Ted Williams, Joe DiMaggio, Jackie Robinson, Duke Snider, but their reputations were earned east of Eden, on the far side of the Sierra.

Their fields of play, Fenway, Yankee Stadium, Ebbets, literally were beyond our field of vision.

And then thirty years ago, April 15, 1958, big-league ball truly became our national pastime. It was opening day, not only of a new season but a new era.

The Los Angeles Dodgers and San Francisco Giants would play at Seals Stadium, changing forever the structure of sport in America. The Giants would win, 8-0, with Ruben Gomez pitching nine innings and defeating Don Drysdale.

And a certain UCLA sophomore who once had watched Drysdale pitch for Van Nuys High—yes, he was another Californian—would listen to someone named Vin Scully and share those historic hours.

How long ago it seems. How near it seems. Only yesterday, three decades. Before Vietnam. Before the assassinations. Before our loss of innocence.

We wore chinos with a belt in the back. Ivy League was a designation of style more than of schooling. We danced to "Twilight Time" by the Platters and "Sweet Little Sixteen" by Chuck Berry. And on April 15, 1958, we became major league.

"God, was it thirty years ago?" Lon Simmons asked rhetorically. "Unbelievable."

Lon was announcing a major-league game for the first time. He was the #2 man to Russ Hodges, who had moved west with the Giants from New York after 1957. He remembers Hodges' encouragement. He doesn't remember much about opening day.

"I can tell you things about the doubleheader against the Dodgers in 1959," said Simmons, who now works across the Bay, doing A's games.

"About the way Russ told me to keep going—even though it was his turn—when Juan Marichal was pitching a no-hitter in 1960 on my birthday.

"But the first day was almost surrealistic. I didn't know what I was doing or what to expect."

If you studied the papers on April 15, 1958, you found in the agate type the name of a USC junior batting .318. Ron Fairly would work his way to the majors and, ironically, to the position once held by Simmons as the Giants' announcer.

Hank Sauer's name was writ large. He would start in left field for the Giants, at least that's what the *Examiner* and *Chronicle* promised. The promise was broken. Bill Rigney, the Giants' manager, had a change of mind.

In Bay Area barrooms, when guys put down a glass and pick up the gauntlet, the two most-asked trivia questions through the years were these:

What was the halftime score of the 1957 49ers-Lions play-off game? Answer: 49ers 24, Lions 7. San Francisco made it 27-7 early in the third quarter, then lost, 31-27.

Who started in left field for the Giants in their first game? Answer: Jim King. We shall let one William Rigney, Bay Area native and Giants manager that season, tell us the reason: "It's 8:30 or 9 o'clock in the morning and I'm driving from my home in Walnut Creek," recalled Rigney. He is sixty-nine now and, like Simmons, interestingly enough, also working with the A's.

"I've got butterflies," said Rigney. "I'm coming back to the place I was born to manage the first major-league game. My father and mother were both born in San Francisco, before the fire and quake. I really want to win.

"I park the car, and I look at the flags at the ballpark, and they're blowing to right field. And with Drysdale, a right-hander, pitching, I'm thinking, 'Will we have our best lineup in there? Will Sauer be overmatched?'

"So I switched to King, a left-hander. He goes 2-for-3, a couple of doubles. But when I tell Sauer before the game, his face drops a foot and a half. And he won't speak to me for two and a half weeks."

Sauer speaks considerably these days. He is a Giants scout and before games at Candlestick Park, like one the other night against Cincinnati, can be seen chatting with Yankee scout Charlie Silvera and Phillies scout—and onetime Giants teammate—Jim Davenport.

San Francisco's first major league game was Davenport's first major league game. Davvy, Orlando Cepeda and Willie Kirkland were the three rookies who made the Giants' starting lineup.

"I struck out the first time against Drysdale," said Davenport. But he ended up 2-for-4. "I wish my average would always have stayed at .500," he laughed.

Gino Cimoli, a San Francisco native playing center field for the Dodgers, was the game's first batter. He now lives in Tiburon and works for United Parcel Service in San Francisco. Gomez, the Giants' pitcher, is sixty and back in Puerto Rico, selling insurance and playing golf.

Drysdale, fifty-one, is back with the Dodgers, as #2 announcer to the indefatigable Scully.

"Outside of getting beat, 8-0," said Don, "I don't remember very much about that first game. I couldn't worry about the pageantry. I had to pitch.

"Oh, I do remember looking up at the big Hamm's beer glass on the brewery next to Seals Stadium and watching it filling up again and again. I was kind of intrigued by it. After the game I had, I could really have used a beer."

The rest of us need only our memories. California went big league thirty years ago. Who knows where the time goes?

Nothing Exceeds Like Success

KAPP AND THE CAPPER

NOVEMBER 23, 1986

The evening was properly bittersweet for Joe Kapp, a man who could never understand criticism and was unable to accept reality. He rode the backs of his players late on this remarkable autumn afternoon as earlier they had ridden a wave of emotion to surely the greatest upset in Big Game history.

In Kapp's last game as head coach, the University of California, an eighteen-point underdog, defeated rival Stanford, 17-11, at Memorial Stadium. The improbability of sport will never cease to amaze.

What Kapp would later call a nightmare season would peak with a dream performance, Cal saving a bit of respectability even though there was no chance to save Kapp's position.

His years of living dangerously are finished. No longer will he hold the only job he ever wanted, football coach at his alma mater. He had been fired three weeks ago. This was a last hurrah. And a memorable one.

This was the stuff of cinematic whimsy. Of fictional charm. This was revenge against those of little faith and great impatience.

This was a chance for Joe Kapp to smile. But, true to form, he did not. Instead, Kapp cried as he was carried above the mass of humanity that had flooded the artificial turf. Those hardly were tears of joy.

"We want Kapp . . . . We want Kapp," the Cal rooting section chanted in the final glowing moments after the Golden Bears had squelched the ultimate Stanford drive.

But they will have him no more. After five seasons, Joe Kapp is history. His record this year was 2-9. His record for five years was 20-34-1. Parting is not such sweet sorrow.

Kapp is a rough man whose edges were smoothed as a Cal undergrad, a kid from the streets who clawed and scratched his way to a diploma and pro football. He has the exterior of a rhinoceros and, despite years of culture, occasionally the disposition of one.

His sense of humor is harsh, a cover-up for a sense of honor. He offers a sneer instead of a grin. He takes games seriously. When you're growing up poor and insecure, you have to.

The human quality Joe Kapp treasures most is loyalty. You're either for him or against him, a teammate or an opponent, one of "us" or one of "them."

In a gray world, Joe is a black-or-white kind of guy. Cal was his school, and he would do anything for it. He never realized the day would arrive when his loyalty would be repulsed, when he would be fired.

The Cal locker room is under the north end zone of the stadium. For his final press conference, Kapp stood in a large area where team meetings transpire.

The sounds of victory could be heard out the window, repetitive cheering from lingering alumni and students. But Joe was decidedly cheerless. He spoke slowly, words arriving with the dull thud of a hammer.

"It has been a privilege and honor to coach the Golden Bears," said Kapp. "Like all Bears, in some way they fall in love with the place. It happened to me in the eighth grade. It was a boyhood dream to become coach of this team.

"This has been a nightmare season. I never believed the earthquake was going to hit out here. But I can't think of many things more that could have happened to hurt our team than happened this year."

The man was hurt more than the team. When a writer Kapp felt had been knocking him through the season asked whether Kapp was crying at game's end, he bristled.

"None of your business," Kapp answered. "Why should I respond to a man who's been knocking me forever? But I will. I'm a big person. Yes, I was emotional."

Emotion was why Joe Kapp was hired in December 1981 to lead Cal. He had no coaching experience. But he had won as a player, on guts and verve.

The Bears won his first season, 1982, but they sank in subsequent seasons. And strangely, Cal played without emotion. And the carping began. And Kapp's enthusiasm turned to anger.

"I'm not saying anything," Kapp had growled a few nights

ago, when asked to summarize his years at Cal. "You write what you want. Don't you have a sense of what I feel?"

Yes, we do. Joe feels abandoned.

The people who once gave him support, the Cal athletic director, the sports columnist, turned on him.

The guys who wanted him hired were now the ones who wanted him fired. This was the ultimate in rejection.

Right and wrong were not the issues. Winning and losing were not the factors. The people in whom Joe Kapp believed no longer believed in him. A code of conduct had been broken. A man had gone back on his word. To Joe Kapp, there was nothing worse.

Kapp tried to mask the hurt with flippant comments. The mask would slip.

"I thought mercy was an Irishman," he said in that bellow of a conversational voice. "Why didn't he leave this poor Mexican boy alone?

"I've had a season one of us Bears wouldn't wish on any other Bear."

There it is, his philosophy in blue and gold, which, of course, are the Cal colors. He could wish it on a Stanford coach, a UCLA coach. But never on anyone associated with his school, Cal.

Nobody wished this year on Joe Kapp. But it happened. The Bears had a schedule full of bowl teams and a roster full of unprepared kids. Soon they'll have a new coach.

This one, at least, departed riding high.

FROM "ON THE BRINK" TO "AT THE TOP"

MARCH 31, 1987

NEW ORLEANS—You can throw away the book on Bobby Knight. He's gone from a season on the brink to an ending on a cloud.

Indiana is the NCAA basketball champion again, and the irony is as thick as the gumbo down at K-Paul's. Some guys have all the luck. And the brains.

The man is a winner. What else can you say? He makes lemonade out of lemons and winners out of anybody. He isn't so much an intimidator as a creator. He may not like what he's got, but that won't stop him from taking advantage of it.

Bobby Knight never believed in recruiting junior-college players. But he changed his opinion. It was a former junior-college player, Keith Smart, whose jumper with five seconds left gave the Hoosiers the 74-73 victory Monday night over Syracuse.

Bobby Knight still doesn't believe in the three-point basket. He talks about it going the way of the Edsel. It was seven three-point baskets by Steve Alford that enabled Indiana to keep from being chased out of the Superdome.

This was another of those wonderful games full of chances and challenges that make you wish forty minutes would last forty years. It left you with more questions than answers and two teams separated by a mere point.

It's the type of game guys like Bobby Knight—and Vince Lombardi and Ted Williams, two of Knight's heroes—invariably win.

It doesn't matter whether he does it with mirrors or persistence, Knight finds a way.

One of the reasons is that a year ago he found Keith Smart

playing JC basketball in Garden City, Kansas. Smart was a guy who kept breaking his wrist. But Knight gets him, and Smart breaks Syracuse's heart.

Smart is a kid from Baton Rouge, ninety miles up the Mississippi from New Orleans. Born on the bayou. Not long ago he was earning $3.25 an hour flipping hamburgers at a McDonald's. When last seen, he was responding to the roars of the Indiana fans by grabbing a large school banner and waving it like one of Napoleon's troops.

Remember that song by Tony Bennett? I want to be around to pick up the pieces. Knight has put Humpty-Dumpty together again. He didn't use Magic Glue, he used his ingenuity.

Two years ago the world thought volatile Bobby Knight had gone over the precipice from which he'd been hanging. He benched some of his starters. He threw a chair at an official. Some people thought Knight needed a new center. Some thought he needed a straitjacket.

Last year, Bobby permitted journalist John Feinstein to spend six months with the Hoosiers. We got a book, *A Season on the Brink*. Bobby got a change of heart. He brought in two JC players, Dean Garrett from City College of San Francisco, and Smart.

"I think Keith is one of the great all-time stories I know about," said Knight. Once again, Knight is right.

At McKinley High in Baton Rouge, Smart was a Munchkin, an accident-prone one at that.

"I was five-foot-three as a junior," said Smart, "and only about five-foot-seven as a senior. And three games into my senior year I broke my left wrist when I fell in a game."

Smart is right-handed, as Syracuse will verify from that winning shot, but he still missed the rest of his final prep season.

"We got two schools in Baton Rouge," he sighed, "LSU and Southern, and they didn't want me. Nobody wanted me. The only school that wanted me was William Penn College in Iowa."

And that didn't last that long. The summer after graduation, Smart, then five-feet-nine, was given a motorcycle, a Yamaha 250, by his parents. "I was riding home from McDonald's, a friend yelled at me, I turned around, ran up a curve, and turned the cycle over."

His left wrist was broken a second time. William Penn withdrew the offer.

"Best thing that ever happened to me," said Smart.

When the wrist healed once more, Smart joined the pickup games at Baton Rouge Sports Academy and impressed recreation worker Lester Roberts. Roberts sent him off to Kansas. Where Smart broke the wrist again.

Medicare liked him. Knight did also. He got an envelope from Indiana. "I threw it in the wastebasket." Swish. Probably just warming up for the closing moments of the NCAA final.

Knight persisted. Smart consented. The rest is now history, however recent.

"We thought Steve Alford would take the last shot," conceded Syracuse coach Jim Boeheim. "We didn't want Alford to beat us."

So Smart beat them. Keith scored twelve of the final fifteen points for Indiana, and finished with twenty-one.

"He was the only guy," growled Boeheim, "who did anything."

And that will enable Indiana's Daryl Thomas to do something else.

"I'm going home now," chortled Thomas, "and read that book about us and Coach Knight. Then I'm going to close the book . . . and write one of my own."

At the least, Keith Smart deserves a chapter.

COMMONER TO KING

APRIL 20, 1986

ALBANY—The sport of kings. And of commoners. Serfing U.S.A. Little people with big dreams. Uneasy riders who begin by cleaning stalls and occasionally finish by cleaning up, as in big bucks.

There are no college scholarships for jockeys. You make the grade by making the weight and then making a horse leave his competition and your past behind.

You start small, and hope to stay that way. Otherwise, you might lose a mount because you've gained weight.

It's a world where the rich get richer and the poor get pushed wide on the far turn. Tack rooms and tacky motels. Dark days inside stables hoping the reins will come and wash away the smell of duress.

Eddie Delahoussaye, thirty-four, is the son of a street commissioner in New Iberia, Louisiana, where they create McIlhenny Tabasco sauce. There were few hot times in Eddie's old town. He started slowly and lowly. So much for the spice of life.

At age sixteen, after experience on quarter horses, he became a Thoroughbred apprentice, or bug boy for the asterisk first-year riders carry in the program. It was a year nearly without end, amen, and without a victory. Talk about being bugged. Boy!

But the man from Cajun Country, who yesterday guided the favored Vernon Castle to a win in the seventy-first running of the California Derby at Golden Gate Fields, stopped learning and started earning.

When trainers learned about him, Eddie went from also-ran to very grand.

"Put me on good stock," Delahoussaye (Della-WHO-say) said a while ago, "and I'm as good a rider as anybody else."

Perhaps he's better. With victories aboard Gato del Sol in 1982 and Sunny's Halo in 1983, Eddie became only the fourth jockey ever to win the Kentucky Derby back-to-back.

Both horses had a nominal relationship to the star around which the solar system revolves. Delahoussaye, indeed, found sunshine in his life.

Which horse he'll find himself aboard in Kentucky Derby #112 on May 3, should be decided before long. Eddie will have a choice of either Vernon Castle or Icy Groom.

"I'll wait until Icy Groom runs in the Bluegrass Stakes at Keeneland," said Delahoussaye, "and we'll see what happens there. It will be nice to have an option. You always want to get a ride in the Derby."

Delahoussaye always wants to get a ride anywhere.

Eddie flew in from Southern California inherently just to make certain Vernon Castle became the first favorite in eleven years to win the Cal Derby. But he also took five other mounts during the day.

"You want to keep in shape," Delahoussaye insisted. "Otherwise, I sit around and get bored."

Instead, he sat on horses and got an idea of what was happening.

In the second race, Delahoussaye rode Tablor, one of the choices. When it became obvious Tablor was terrible, Eddie pulled him up in the stretch. The tactic apparently permitted the jockey to get the feel of the track.

"I always study the track I'm riding on," he conceded. "That's why I try to ride a few races besides the big one and why I go back to the Kentucky Derby a day early. You don't want to be surprised."

The best surprise, they used to advertise at Holiday Inn, is no surprise. Yet Vernon Castle might be a pleasant surprise.

"He got a little tired in the stretch," said the jockey, "but this is only his second race this year. He's well bred, got a hell of a stride. He really impressed me."

To impress the average American, the guy who doesn't know a fetlock from a hammerlock, a horseman and a horse have to make it to Kentucky the first Saturday in May. Then, they've got to win.

Delahoussaye has done it. Could Vernon Castle do it? What does the rider say to the trainer and the owner?

"It's hard to tell people what to do," said Delahoussaye. "My opinion doesn't matter. He's a young horse with only a few races. Every owner and trainer wants to get to the Derby. Every jockey, too.

"If Vernon Castle runs in the Derby, he's going to have a lot more tough horses to face. But you never know what will happen in the Kentucky Derby. And this horse has a hell of a future."

Delahoussaye has a great future and a great past.

"I didn't set any goals after my first Derby win. The thing I'm concerned about is that my horses keep running. Then I know I'm doing all right."

Eddie Delahoussaye's doing fine. He's gone from commoner to king.

YANKEE DOODLE DANDIES

FEBRUARY 23, 1980

LAKE PLACID—It had been an hour since that ecstatic moment. An hour since the green numbers on the game clock at last had fixed themselves at 0:00. An hour since their team, America's team, the U. S. Olympic hockey team, had completed a 4-3 victory over a Soviet Union squad that no one is supposed to beat.

In that hour there had been bedlam on the ice, sticks and gloves being hurled toward the rafters. And there had been singing in the locker room, "God Bless America," only proper since Kate Smith lives just a few blocks away. And there had been a phone call from Jimmy Carter.

There had been plenty of time, sixty minutes, for life to return to some semblance of normality in Lake Placid. But life had not. Main Street was still packed with people, some waving American flags, some chanting "U.S.A., U.S.A." some singing— honestly—"The Star-Spangled Banner." Who says Americans aren't nationalistic?

They certainly were last night. Maybe it was because the U.S. hockey team supposedly had no chance against the Soviets. Maybe it was because tickets were as dear as gold, scalpers asking as much as $160.

Remember those scenes of the Allied Forces liberating France? Well, that's what Lake Placid looked like last night. You didn't see any beautiful young ladies leaping on armored trucks to kiss soldiers. But that was the only thing missing.

For the 1980 U. S. Olympic team, almost nothing was missing. And goalie Jim Craig missed almost nothing. Despite the final score, the Soviets dominated this game. They had great passing.

They took thirty-nine shots, as compared to sixteen for the United States. But they didn't win.

Jim Craig was a major reason. A graduate of Boston University who's been drafted by Atlanta of the NHL, Craig—with help from his teammates, of course—kept the Soviets scoreless for the final thirty-six minutes. Hell, against Canada the Russians got three goals in less than two minutes.

"Jim Craig," said U.S. coach Herb Brooks in an understatement, "was a tower of strength tonight." Said Soviet coach Victor Tikhonov, "Their goalie was fantastic."

The same could not be said about the Russian goalies, Vladislav Tretjak—whom some rank as merely the best in the world— and Vladimir Myshkin. Tretjak started because, according to Tikhonov, Myshkin was nervous. Tretjak was only porous, allowing two goals before coming out with one second to play in the first period.

Myshkin wasn't terribly impressive himself. With the United States trailing, 3-2, in the third period, Mark Johnson picked the puck off a Soviet player's stick and scored on a power play with 8:39 gone. And then Mike Eruzione, like Craig from Boston University, beat Myshkin with ten minutes gone for the goal that defeated the Soviets.

Among the standing-room-only crowd of more than 8,000 in the Olympic Fieldhouse were Mike's parents, Gene and Helen Eruzione. They're common folk from Winthrop, Massachusetts, just north of Boston, and Gene works two jobs, as a bartender and a maintenance man, to make ends meet.

And that winning goal by their son was something special to Gene and Helen Eruzione—even more so than to other Americans. "Hey," said Gene Eruzione, now sharing the limelight with his son, "I told my wife when it was tied, Mike is going to get something. He always comes through."

Come through. These days that's a slogan for Connecticut General Insurance. It used to be something you could depend on all Americans to do. That's when we were tough and jingoistic and of the opinion that we were the world's best and brightest.

But a lot of things have happened over the years. The best cars come from Germany. The best cameras come from Japan. The best hockey comes from, yes, admit it, the Soviet Union. No wonder the win last night, coming only two weeks after the same USSR team beat the same U.S. team, 10-3, was so reassuring.

So, troubled Jimmy Carter, feeling uplifted down there on Pennsylvania Avenue, grabbed a phone and called U. S. coach Herb Brooks. "He told us," said Brooks, "we made the American people happy tonight. He invited us to the White House for a couple of Cokes Monday."

The U.S. players drank champagne after the victory, but they are wary. They acknowledge the Soviets are still the best on the globe—but didn't play well last night. And the United States still has to beat Finland tomorrow to win the gold medal. In fact, if Finland beats the United States by two goals and the Soviets tie Sweden, the United States won't get any medal.

"I'm happy," said Mark Johnson, who got two goals. "But I'm not sure how we won. In fact, if we played them again in two days, I'm not so sure we could win."

But they won last night. And the memories came. It was twelve years since Russia lost a hockey game in the Olympics. That one to Czechoslovakia. It was twenty years ago in Squaw Valley when the United States last beat Russia in Olympic hockey. The guy who scored the winning goal in that 3-2 victory was Bill Christian. Last night Bill's twenty-year-old son, Dave, had an assist on Mark Johnson's first goal.

"Yeah," said Dave Christian, "as the clock ticked down tonight I thought about my dad and his team that beat the Russians."

And defenseman-forward Bob McClanahan thought about how incredible it all was, saying, "Russia is a great team, but they haven't played as well as they could. I'm not saying we're the best in the world. But we beat them."

And a lot of Americans on Main Street in Lake Placid—and across the country—didn't want to stop celebrating that joyous fact.

A WOMAN OF DESTINY

FEBRUARY 16, 1980

LAKE PLACID—She had her head tipped back as she listened to the question. And the look on her face was that of an angel, like those in the pictures on the walls of Schönbrunn Palace in her native country of Austria.

But behind that beatific look, behind those eyes as pale blue as the shadowed snow over which she had just skied, is a bundle of arrogance, determination, and skill that is more devil than angel.

That's because for Annemarie Moser-Proell, heaven can wait. But the gold medal could not. So on a morning when the icy wind chilled the hearts of the other competitors, she zoomed down the glazed steepness of Whiteface Mountain to win the women's downhill ski race of the 1980 Winter Olympics.

Moser-Proell—students of the German language know that there should be an umlaut over the "O" in her last name and the "E" should be dropped—was an impressive winner. In a sport where hundredths of a second can make the difference between triumph and frustration, Annemarie yesterday finished first by seven-tenths of a second.

She covered the 2,698-meter course in one minute 37.52 seconds, while Hanni Wenzel of Liechtenstein was runnerup in 1:38.22. Marie-Therese Nadig of Switzerland, expected to give Moser-Proell her biggest challenge, came in third in 1:38.36.

The good ol' U.S.A.? Well, eighteen-year-old Heidi Preuss surprised everyone by finishing fourth—although with that name, she could just as well have come from the Alps as New Hampshire.

Cindy Nelson, who was supposed to have a good chance for a medal? "I know I'm one of the best in the world," said Nelson, who was eighth, "but today I didn't ski like one of the best."

Annemarie Moser-Proell did. Annemarie Moser-Proell usually does. "She's in a class by herself," said Irene Epple of East

Germany. "The only way anyone else can win in the downhill is if she falls."

Annemarie didn't fall and didn't fail. She came hurtling down the mountain toward destiny—and victory. And after she crossed the finish line and threw out the tails of her skis, spinning to a jet stop, a group of enthusiastic young men dressed alike in blue parkas with the white triple stripes of Adidas on the shoulders, didn't fail Annemarie.

They were from Moser-Proell's hometown, Kleinarl, some forty miles south of Salzburg, and they were members of what they said was the "Kleinarl Ski Club," but in fact was more of a rooting section than an athletic organization. And in the group was Herbert Moser, Annemarie's husband.

And when Annemarie Moser-Proell crossed the finish line and the electronic clock locked on her time that would hold up as the best, the Kleinarl Ski Club, including Moser, began their chanting: "Anna-ma-REE-ya . . . Anna-ma-REE-ya . . . Anna-ma-REE-ya . . . Aus-tree-ya." Again and again they sang, to the lady and the land.

Austria: Music and mountains, schnitzel and beer, Mozart and Strauss. Austria: The first of the psychiatrists, Sigmund Freud, the last of the Hapsburgs, Franz Joseph. Austria: The land that practically invented modern skiing, the sport being transported to other countries by instructions from the town of St. Anton in the Arlberg. The land that in this XIII Winter Olympics has locked up the only two medals awarded thus far in alpine events.

Thursday, unknown Herbert Stock, from the mountains near Innsbruck, won the men's downhill. Yesterday, well-known Annemarie Moser-Proell won the women's downhill.

And thus a marvelous skiing career was embellished. Since she started coming down runs in earnest in 1958, when she was fourteen, she had done almost everything—except win an Olympic gold. She had won sixty-two events in the World Cup. In 1973 she won eight consecutive races in the Cup. She owns a restaurant in Kleinarl, Café Annemarie. She owns several expensive cars. But not until yesterday did she win in the Olympics.

In 1972 in Sapporo, Japan, Annemarie was favored in both the downhill and the giant slalom. But she was upset in both by Nadig. And Proell—she didn't marry Herbert Moser until 1973—came back home with two silver medals, tears in her eyes, and more desire than ever to succeed. To the dashboard of her car she attached a small plaque reading, "NEVER FORGET SAPPORO."

She barely remembers Innsbruck, the Winter Olympiad of 1976, held not far from her home. That's because she had gone into semiretirement to become a housewife and to care for her ailing father. "I didn't even watch the races," she remarked yesterday about the previous Games. "My father was very ill, and I didn't think one bit about racing. I don't regret it one minute."

Her father, Joseph Proell, died a few weeks later. And by the end of that year, Moser-Proell, requiring money to pay off the loans for the restaurant—"amateurs" in skiing make as much as $200,000—returned to training.

Now when she was out against some mountain and her opponents, she kept a picture of Joseph Proell sewn into her uniform. He was the one who put her on skis when she was four. He was the one from whom she inherited her incredible drive.

Frau ohne Grenzen is what Austrians call her, "Woman without limits." She has strength and skill—and haughtiness. "I was confident I would win," said strong, skillful, haughty Annemarie. "Winning is normal for me. I race for myself. I win for myself. I am obliged to win."

And after she's won, to look like an angel—even though she's anything but.

IN THE BEGINNING . . .

APRIL 9, 1986

HOUSTON—The skeptics were right. Will Clark is going to find the major leagues different from the minors. In the minors, it took him five pitches to hit his first home run. In the majors, it took him three.

One moment Will the Thrill was standing at home plate in the Astrodome looking at Nolan Ryan, who's merely struck out more batters than any pitcher in history. The next moment the ball is sailing toward downtown - or was that Cooperstown?

It was a debut worthy of Pavarotti. Or Judy Garland. You can just hear the stage manager in *42nd Street* saying, "You're going out there a kid, but you're coming back a star."

Crack! The sound resonated through the Dome like summer thunder. The ball rose as if shot from a cannon. This wasn't happening. Not to a member of the Giants. Hello, doctor, I kept having these illusions, guys in gray uniforms running around the bases.

Clark came from Mississippi State University and the California League. He might as well have come from heaven. Did you ever see a dream walking? Or swinging?

So here's Ryan, who was already in the majors when Will Clark was four years old, who has five no-hitters, who has more than 4,000 strikeouts, winding and throwing. Strike. Again. Ball. Again. Boom. History.

"I'm watching it," said Roger Craig, the Giants manager, "and I'm not sure I believe it. I'm thinking, 'Just keep going, just keep going.' And then I tell myself, 'That ball is out of here.' What a thrill."

What a Will the Thrill. For the fifty-third time in major-league annals, a player has hit a home run in his first at-bat. The rookie is a cookie. Nearly two and a half hours later, the Giants are winners, 8-3, over the Houston Astros.

And in a locker room as raucous as a fraternity-house party,

125

the Giants are standing around in various stages of undress and disbelief.

Except for Will Clark. He's trying to remind everyone that there are 161 left to play. True. But there'll never be another like this.

Another opening, perhaps, another show. But not another performance of this magnitude. You only go around once in life. "Will Clark," chortled Roger Craig, "will never forget this night."

He won't be alone. "The stuff of legends," shouted winning pitcher Mike Krukow, waving a victory cigar about half as long as Clark's bat.

"A gamer," said Chili Davis. "The Thrill wasn't going to let us down. What a way to start. All that pressure on him, and then he opens with a homer. I can't wait to get back to watch the highlights on TV."

Clark had seen it all before, in a manner of speaking. His first professional at-bat, last June 21, he also homered with his first swing. But that was against Visalia. This was against Nolan Ryan.

"He got hold of a bad pitch," sighed Ryan, "but I did strike him out the next time."

Sure. And the Trojans never accepted another wooden horse after the one the Greeks brought.

The Astrodome is supposed to be a dungeon, the place where fly balls go to die. The fences are farther away than the Dallas city limits. The air inside is heavy.

Which is the reason that Clark, Jeffrey Leonard, Bob Brenly, and the Astros' Glenn Davis hit home runs. What did they put in the air-conditioning system? Or the baseballs?

Clark was #2 in the order, after batting sixth most of the spring. "I decided he would see more good pitches in the second spot," said Craig. The first one Will saw from Ryan was good, the second bad. "I was hoping he'd throw me a fastball," said Clark. He did. Adios.

A few rows behind the third-base dugout, Bill and Letty Clark, Will's parents, were having a hoedown. They had driven six and a half hours from New Orleans to watch their oldest child in a major-league uniform.

"I'd rate it a 10," said Mrs. Clark. Make it a forty. That's how many Clark relatives and friends were at the Astrodome. They

"Sure, it was great," said Will, "but the first thing I thought of was it gave us a 1-0 lead. When I got to the dugout it all started to sink in."

Krukow watched Clark's journey around the bases.

"He got to the top step of the dugout," said the pitcher, "and smiled, and chills went through me. It was one of those moments that last forever."

Which is about the length of time the Giants have been waiting for a guy like Will Clark.

SAN FRANCISCO BECOMES A WINNER

JANUARY 25, 1982

DETROIT—Time no longer mattered. Not the few seconds that seemed frozen on the clock, not the decades that lurked in the past. Only the present counted.

There were fourteen seconds left, fourteen seconds between the 49ers and history, fourteen seconds that no one would ever remember. The players hoisted their diligent coach on their shoulders, and Bill Walsh lifted his arms in a gesture that lifted a curse. San Francisco was at last a winner.

Yes, the championship that so long had been denied, that was taken away by Bobby Richardson's catch in the bottom of the ninth of the 1962 World Series, that was squandered in the second half of the 1957 playoff against the Lions, that was dropped in 1972 in the final minute against the Cowboys, finally had been captured.

It was a time for cheers and tears, a time for memories, for raising a glass in salute the way Bill Walsh raised his arms in the symbol of triumph. It was time to forget about life's troubles, to laugh and cry and enjoy.

Only a game? Yes, undeniably that's true. The 49ers' 26-21 victory over the Cincinnati Bengals in Super Bowl XVI yesterday at the Silverdome was nothing more, and nothing less. No monarchies tumbled, no wars ended, no lives were saved. It was only a game.

But it was a game that brought a measure of joy to a great many people, a game that proved there is virtue in faith and hard work, a game that altered an image and destroyed a myth.

San Francisco, the town and the region, will be the same today as it was the day before, full of troubles, a mosaic of concrete and concepts, shattered citizens and broken pavement.

There still will be gays and hippies and kids in the Mission without hope or a job. There still will be talk about little cable cars and morning fog and Jeanette MacDonald melodiously insisting to open that Golden Gate. Everything will be the same. And yet everything will have changed.

The label as the "City of Losers" had been stripped away.

People still would drink too much at Perry's or the other Union Street haunts—indeed, the victory only offered yet another excuse—and BART still would run behind schedule and inflation still would be unchecked. But City of Losers, no way.

A major-league championship had been earned, earned in that most appealing of methods, by a team that arose from the garbage heap, by a team that wouldn't heed the admonitions, by a team that is almost the realization of the American Dream.

The 49ers are San Francisco's team, the Bay Area's team. Long before the arrival of the Giants and Raiders and Warriors and A's, the 49ers built a franchise and a following. From Fresno to Eureka, from San Rafael to Reno, if you weren't a 49er fan, well, you didn't have any choice.

You were trapped, ensnared in the fascination and frustration of a club that provided continual excitement but never a title. For thirty-five years the 49ers were tantalizing, tempting—and disappointing. For thirty-five years—until yesterday.

Then, with fourteen seconds remaining, the 49ers knew the agony was at an end. In the stands, the thousands of fans, the 49er Faithful, who had made the pilgrimage to the nation's snowy heartland, hundreds of thousands back in the Bay Area who gazed nervously at TV screens, also knew. San Francisco was now the city of at least one winner.

Oh, that locker room, filled not only with the expected euphoria but also with the very lively ghosts of the past, the heroes of yesterday. Bob St. Clair embraced Frankie Albert. O.J. Simpson shook dozens of hands. Why, almost no one even seemed to notice the figure in the overcoat standing to one side, Governor Jerry Brown, who obviously had come down with a case of 49er Fever.

O.J. was talking about the first time he managed to get into Kezar Stadium. It was that infamous December afternoon in 1957, when the 49ers took a 27-7 third-quarter lead over Detroit in the play-off for the NFL Western Division championship—and lost, 31-27.

"I remember that," said Pete Rozelle, now the super-mogul, the NFL commissioner, but then the general manager of the Los Angeles Rams. "It looked like the 49ers were going to do it that day. But they didn't."

They didn't that day, or any other day—until yesterday. And that's why St. Clair, the lineman-turned-politician, could insist, "It was tremendous. I feel tremendous." And why Albert, around at the founding in 1946 and ever since, could sigh, "It sounds corny, but this is the high point of my life."

"San Francisco," Bill Walsh claimed in his moment of glory, "is deserving of a world championship. It is the greatest city in the world, with the greatest people. I feel so fortunate to have coached at Stanford and with the 49ers. San Francisco is my home, and these are my people."

Those people now can celebrate. The football team that had tried for seasons finally succeeded. The years of waiting have been rewarded. For the 49ers and their fans, time no longer matters.

MONKEY OFF HIS BACK

MAY 6, 1984

LOUISVILLE—This time the frustration would end for Laffit Pincay. This time he would grab for roses while others grasped for answers. This time on a gray afternoon in the Bluegrass country he would have a horse under his saddle and a monkey off his back.

He had been called the finest jockey never to finish first in the Kentucky Derby. Bad mounts and bad breaks always left him back in the pack, picking up the dirt clods while somebody else, a Shoemaker, a Delahoussaye, picked up the accolades. He was Sam Snead in the U.S. Open, Ray Meyer in the NCAA basketball tournament. He couldn't win the Big One. Until yesterday.

Then, in marvelous control of Swale, a beautiful colt with a pedigree as impressive as the House of Tudor, Pincay arrived at horse racing's most cherished locale, the winner's circle at historic Churchill Downs. A mountain had been climbed.

Pincay, with millions in winnings, with the respect of his peers, said persistent failures in the Derby did not concern him. It was just a horse race, he suggested. Indeed. And the *Mona Lisa* is just a painting.

Hemingway said it isn't wise to want something too much. And wisely, Laffit tap-danced around the disappointment when his horses couldn't run quickly enough around the oval.

"A lot of people say it is a monkey on my back," Pincay would reassure, grinning in defense. "But I don't think so. Maybe I'm destined to run this race all my life and never win. I am prepared to accept that."

Acceptance is no longer required. Ten times he had come up short. Ride #11 took him into history. The best horse and best jockey made light work of the 110th Kentucky Derby and of the idea that a female horse could keep up with the boys. Swale is an offspring of 1977 Derby and Triple Crown winner

Seattle Slew. In the hyperbole of a normal prerace week, the horse was surprisingly ignored.

We had been told about the ladies, the favored filly Althea and her stablemate, Life's Magic. About Silent King, starting in the twentieth post position out there near Cincinnati. About Taylor's Special, trained by Bill Mott, who once slept in pig stalls in a barn. About Vanlandingham, ridden by local hero Pat Day. And, of course, about the horse that wasn't here, Devil's Bag, trained by the old man, Woody Stephens.

Stephens withdrew Devil's Bag on Tuesday. But he didn't weep. Instead, he predicted his other horse, Swale, would capture the Derby and a nation's fancy.

This was a marriage of fable: Swale, owned by famous Claiborne Farm, which had never won a Derby, ridden by Pincay, who had never won a Derby, saddled by Stephens, whose hopes seemed to be disintegrating. Swale, in post position 15, where horses get jostled like shoppers at a bargain-basement sale.

For Pincay, Swale might as well have been marked *Fragile*. Laffit brought the colt out quickly and smoothly, in front of the traffic and, as the pack thundered into the first turn and the crowd of 126,453 thundered its approval, alongside Althea.

What was a nice girl like that doing in a place like that? Trying to escape being trapped against the rail, having been assigned the difficult first post position, Althea was flying. Swale was breezing.

Pincay had been Althea's rider in previous races. He sensed what the filly could do and couldn't do. On the backstretch, drawing even with Swale, Pincay was filled with excitement.

"Coming into the stretch my horse pricked up his ears," said Pincay. "I showed him the whip, and he responded."

Althea, the betting choice, also responded. By giving up. Two fillies have won the Kentucky Derby. This year there would not be a third. As Pincay brought Swale into a lead that grew with each powerful stride, jockey Chris McCarron was reining in Althea.

She would finish nineteenth, and Pincay, her former rider, would sigh correctly, "I thought running a mile and a quarter with the boys would be tough for her, and especially from the #1 post."

The mile and a quarter on Swale was easy for Laffit. And rewarding.

SHOE PULLS
A NICKLAUS

MAY 4, 1986

LOUISVILLE—He came back again, back for the roses and the memories, back for the glory and, yes, the grief. Bill Shoemaker is a man time won't forget and racing will never regret.

He transcends his sport, as does Jack Nicklaus at golf, as did Muhammad Ali at boxing. He's the best ever, a champion, a celebrity, and, once more, a hero.

Thirty-one years ago, 1955, Shoemaker rode his first Kentucky Derby winner. Freeze frame. Yesterday, fifty-four-year-old Willie Shoemaker rode his fourth Kentucky Derby winner, bringing the long shot Ferdinand flying down the stretch.

The crowd was cheering. The Shoe was crying.

"I had a few tears in my eyes coming back to the winner's circle," said Shoemaker. "I knew earlier in the year I might have only one more chance to win the Derby and this might be it."

Shoemaker seized the time. The great ones produce when they must. Gamers. Reggie Jackson in the 1977 World Series. Jack Nicklaus in the 1986 Masters. Bill Shoemaker in the 1986 Kentucky Derby.

"I never felt more emotional after any other race," said Shoemaker. "I said to myself, 'Old Jack Nicklaus did it, and I did it.' "

That he did. A man must have a horse to ride. But then he must know how to ride that horse. Nobody knows more than Bill Shoemaker.

"What athlete is better at fifty-four?" asked Ferdinand's trainer, Charlie Whittingham. "Maybe Bill can't ride as he used to, but he knows where to put a horse. And he's been around this track so many times."

This last time was a wonderful time. A classic three-year-old horse, a skillful fifty-four-year-old jockey, and, in Whittingham, a shrewd seventy-three-year-old trainer. A combination for the ages.

For Whittingham it was an opportunity for fulfillment. In half a century of training, his horses had done everything. Except win a Derby.

"And for some people," said Whittingham, who like horse and jockey is based in Southern California, "there's no race but the Derby in the world."

There's never been a jockey like Shoemaker, now the oldest, by twelve years, ever to win a Derby.

He's been in commercials with Magic Johnson and on TV shows with Bob Hope.

He's made millions. He's made mistakes. Big mistakes.

Horses and courses. Victories and defeats. Greatness and disgrace. The more chances a man takes, the more chances he has for success. Or failure.

Four times now Shoemaker has ridden a winner in the Derby—Swaps in 1955; Tomy Lee in 1959; Lucky Debonair in 1965. Yet at Churchill Downs, that whitewashed relic of a racetrack, the Shoe is still remembered for the race he lost.

It was 1957. The baseball Giants were in New York, Eisenhower was in the White House, and Shoemaker was in the saddle on Gallant Man. He also should have been in the winner's circle.

"I blew it," recalled Shoemaker. Misjudgment. Shoe saw the one-sixteenth pole and thought it was the finish line. He stood up. He thought he was under the wire; he was only under the gun.

Iron Liege flashed by. Shoemaker dropped down again and went to the whip. A distance of 110 yards isn't much in a horse race. Iron Liege held on by a nose.

"It was all my fault," said Shoemaker. "But that wasn't the only time I did something like that."

To err is human. To win 8,537 races and $100 million in stakes is, well, not divine. Shall we say remarkable?

He rode his first winner on a damp winter's day in 1949 at Golden Gate Fields, across the Bay from San Francisco. He rode his 8,537th on a glorious afternoon in the land of the bluegrass.

"I first saw Ferdinand last summer at Del Mar," said Shoemaker. "Charlie showed him to me and said, 'We can have some fun with this one.' Early this year, I thought we'd have a chance in the Kentucky Derby with this colt."

They had more than a chance. They had a victory.

"Shoe and I," said Whittingham, "have won more stakes together than anyone."

They should win even more. Numerous wrinkles have impinged on the eyes above Shoemaker's high cheekbones. There are flecks of silver in the hair. Yet he keeps pulling on his size 2D boots and going to the track.

"You don't have to worry about Shoe," said Whittingham. "He's out there like the young guys early in the morning when I ask him. He rides any horse I ask him. He may be old in years, but he's not old."

Old or not, he's tremendous. Bill Shoemaker is a jockey for all reasons and this season. Roses, anyone?

THE GREAT LEVELER

JUNE 22, 1987

She's a feisty lady, the Olympic Club, a real San Franciscan who isn't impressed by reputations and laughs in the face of legends. Ben Hogan couldn't woo her. She kicked Arnold Palmer in the teeth. Now Tom Watson is the latest to know her fickle ways.

We kept hearing how U.S. Opens are not won but lost. But the 1987 U.S. Open, which came to a tumultuous finish on a Sunday of sunshine and tension, was damned sure won by Scott Simpson.

He beat Olympic. He beat Watson.

Somehow you knew it would happen this way. At Olympic it always has. Probably always will.

Hogan was sitting in the locker room when word arrived that, remarkably, Jack Fleck had tied him in 1955. Fleck won the play-off.

Palmer was strutting toward a U.S. Open record in 1966 when his game took off toward Sausalito and he was tied by Billy Casper. Casper won the playoff.

Watson was standing about one hundred yards from the sixteenth green Sunday when Simpson knocked in a birdie putt to take the lead and take the Open. Touché!

A long while ago, U.S. Open championships were reserved for people whose names were engraved on the back of golf clubs or the back of matchbook covers. They comprised golf's "Who's Who." But the times have changed, if not for the best.

This is the era of golf's "Who's He?" For every Ray Floyd or Jack Nicklaus, we have a Larry Nelson or, yes, Scott Simpson. We have someone who ignores all the predictions—not to mention the slick greens and narrow fairways.

That isn't to say Scott Simpson, who shot a three-under-par total of 227, is undeserving. While practically everyone about him was losing strokes, not to mention his head, Scott Simpson was flying down the final holes like O.J. Simpson. Birdie at fourteen, birdie at fifteen, birdie at sixteen. Your turn, Tom.

Watson responded like the champion he is. But the Olympic Club was not going to be his course—as it was not Hogan's course nor Palmer's course.

And in the end, Watson's forty-five-foot birdie putt on the seventy-second hole, the grand and glorious eighteenth at Olympic where a hill forms a natural amphitheatre and the crowd creates a din, was inches short. And the echoes were awakened once more.

Three Opens at Olympic, three remarkable finishes. Fleck making birdies to catch Hogan. Palmer making bogeys to fall to Casper. And Watson and Simpson, the famous against the unheralded, going at it *mano a mano,* wedge to wedge, putter against putter.

Olympic had battered Jack Nicklaus these final two rounds, but Jack went on ABC-TV as a commentator, watching the drama and the trauma. Like everyone else at Olympic, Nicklaus was impressed.

"That wasn't good golf those two guys played," said Nicklaus. "It was sensational golf. Top drawer."

It was golf of agony and ecstasy, of hoots and hollers, of "Go get 'em, Tommy" and "Hang in there, Scott."

It was golf that made memories and should make the U.S. Golf Association and the Olympic Club get together to bring the Open back to San Francisco as soon as possible, realistically another ten years.

Scott Simpson is from San Diego and USC, but he's played in Northern California for years.

Now he credits religion for giving him equanimity. But you recall a teenage Scott Simpson in the State Amateur at Pebble Beach beating on his golf bag with a sand wedge after leaving a ball in a trap.

Tom Watson is from Kansas City, but he attended Stanford and spent days on many of the Northern California courses.

He's always been a man of integrity. You recall in the 1968 San Francisco City Amateur, Watson calling a stroke on himself when he nudged a ball in the trees at Harding Park—across the Lake Merced reservoir from Olympic.

They say you find out a lot about a person by his actions

on a golf course. What we found out in the final round of the Open was that Scott Simpson could handle the pressure. And Tom Watson could handle defeat.

"Scotty just played better and beat me," said Watson.

That's golf, a game where there is no defense, a sport where Hogan, Palmer, and Watson were pummeled by destiny.

Seve Ballesteros, the Spaniard who finished third, was frustrated by poor putting and encouraged by great receptions. At times, Seve has been belittled by golf crowds. But not at Olympic.

"People were on my side here," said Ballesteros. "It hasn't always been this way. I think the people here made all the foreign players feel at home."

The spectators made everyone feel at home.

They contributed to a memorable Open at Olympic, the course that keeps embracing the underdog and exciting us all.

A PAGE FROM JOHNNY'S PAST

FEBRUARY 2, 1987

PEBBLE BEACH—So it's another day of tears and cheers, when sport becomes a joy and we all become younger. Music, please. Sinatra, of course: "Fairy tales can come true . . . . "

Johnny Miller creeps from our memories for a marvelous victory and, perhaps, a last hurrah. It is 1974 all over again, if only for a moment much too fleeting.

One week it was Jack Nicklaus turning back the clock at Augusta National. Another it was Willie Shoemaker turning for home at Churchill Downs. Ponce de Leon would have been surprised to learn the fountain of youth was really a bottle of Gatorade.

"Hey," an unspoken voice told Johnny Miller, "you can still do it." Miller was afraid to ask what "it" could be. Three months from his fortieth birthday, John was thinking about retirement, Now, the only thing he needs to retire are his fears.

It was agonizing out there on the cliffs above Carmel Bay, on that magnificent sporting stage called Pebble Beach Golf Links. Was fate teasing him, teasing all of us? What a cruel trick to tantalize and then disappoint.

"I'm too old for this," sighed Johnny's wife, Linda.

She meant for the drama, not for the outcome.

It had been four years since Miller won, two years since he had been a contender. Who would have suspected an afternoon's walk in the sun was about to become a stroll with fortune?

John was playing for destiny. Linda was thinking of respectability.

"All I want," Linda Miller whispered along the sixteenth fairway, "is for him to finish well."

John finished well, as well as anyone could want. John won the AT&T Pebble Beach Pro-Am Sunday. The improbable became the verifiable. John could only shake his head. Linda was able to cry.

"I'll tell you," she told us. "It was tough. It's hard to want something for somebody so much and know there's nothing you can do about it except pull for him.

"For him to win again, and to win in California, near his home, it's special."

Johnny Miller is special. He's the kid from San Francisco who as a boy of six smashed balls into a canvas backstop in his home and toyed with the idea of becoming a champion.

John was not afraid to work, taking lessons from first his father, Larry, who in retirement in Napa must this day be a very proud man, and then pro John Geertsen, Sr., who Sunday was in Miller's boisterous gallery.

John was not afraid to dream. "If there is one tournament I want to win," he advised us when still a teenager, "it is the U.S. Open."

In 1973, Miller would do just that, shooting the lowest round in seventy-three years of U.S. Opens, a sixty-three, and finishing first at Oakmont in the rolling suburbs of Pittsburgh.

And for the next two years, the PGA Tour would belong to Miller, who made the game seem so embarrassingly easy that you wondered why anyone else was even entered in tournaments.

In 1974, rumor had it, he didn't need to use Seventeen-Mile Drive to get to the first tee at Pebble Beach, he just walked across Monterey Bay.

It was about then that he provided a memorable remark. "Serenity," he said, "is knowing your worst shot still is going to be good."

Miller not only made the cover of *Sports Illustrated,* but also of *Newsweek.* "Golf's Golden Boy," he was labeled. Sears gave him his own line of clothing. Journalists gave him their appreciation. Nobody provided quotes that contained such charming hyperbole or refreshing candor.

In 1975, Nicklaus edged Miller and Tom Weiskopf by a stroke to win the Masters. Jack holed a mammoth putt on sixteen for a birdie and then leaped in the air. John was asked if he saw the birdie. "No," said John, "but I saw the bear tracks on the green."

In 1972, with a chance to win the Crosby, Miller hit a six-iron dead right for his second shot on sixteen. "I hit a perfect shank," he would say later, instead of choosing a euphemism for that most dreaded of golfing terms.

Miller was among the first boys whose fathers did not belong to the San Francisco Olympic Club permitted to join as a junior member.

He honed his game there. Olympic hosted the 1966 U.S. Open. Miller was a nineteen-year-old sophomore at BYU. He signed up to caddie, but never got the chance. That's because he qualified to play. One of his two partners in the first two rounds was a practically unknown pro who would finish fiftieth: Lee Trevino.

Miller would finish as low amateur, tied for eighth overall— and be unhappy. "I was so dumb and naive," he said years later. "I thought I should have won."

He would win, of course, in 1973, following the path of another San Francisco Lincoln High graduate, Ken Venturi, who did it in 1964—the year Miller won the U.S. Junior Amateur. Irony: Venturi was in the CBS-TV announcing booth behind the eighteenth green at Pebble Beach when Miller won the AT&T.

"I thought my days were over," Miller said over the public-address system during the awards ceremony. "You can't believe how exciting this is. This is my favorite tournament. This is sort of my home course."

He paused, glanced at the blue water pounding against the sea wall and the hazy outline of Point Lobos in the distance, then began once more: "This is the most beautiful place in America, right here."

The older you get, the better it looks.

SEVE SIZZLES

JULY 18, 1988

LYTHAM ST. ANNES, England—The tournament battered by the rain in Britain ended up being graced by the reign of Spain.

When the clouds finally moved away, the man some think is the world's best golfer moved in.

Severiano Ballesteros danced a flamenco in the sunshine and breeze along the Lancashire coast, tying a record and, alas, maybe breaking a heart.

The young man who learned to play by swatting rocks on a beach in his native Spain won a third British Open on Monday with a performance that was as marvelous as it was stunning.

Ballesteros shot a course record equaling sixty-five, six under par, to win a duel with Nick Price and the 117th Open championship over the churlish links of Royal Lytham and St. Annes.

This was the first time since the Open began back in the days of the Empire—1860, to be specific—that it ever had carried over to a Monday. The reason was a washout Saturday after a rainstorm of epic proportions.

But the delay didn't mean diminishment. Too often in the past, the final round of the Open unravels into disinterest. On the contrary, this one held our attention as Ballesteros and Price held up their end of the bargain.

Seve, now thirty-one, and a winner here nine years ago—and then in 1984 at St. Andrews, his last major—shot an eleven-under-par total of 273, finishing two shots ahead of the star-crossed Price, who three-putted the final hole for a sixty-nine.

Defending champion Nick Faldo of Britain slipped early and finished third at 279, six shots behind, after an ineffective round of even-par seventy-one. And then came the answer to the yearly trivia question: Who was/were the low American(s)?

This year it was Fred Couples and Gary Koch, tying for fourth with three-under 281s. Couples made back-to-back eagles on the short, downwind par-fives, the sixth and seven, and briefly was five-under-par and a shot out of first. But he finished with a five-under-par and a shot out of first. But he finished with a 30-38 for sixty-eight. Koch also shot sixty-eight.

That was the score Ballesteros thought he might need on this glorious afternoon when the sun made its first appearance in days. Seve had started the day tied with Faldo at a seven-under 208, two shots behind Price.

"But the pressure didn't bother Nick," said a gracious Ballesteros. "I was just a little luckier than he was. It is a pity someone had to lose. Someday he will win it."

Who knows? But Price now has finished a close second, once, in 1982, when he blew a three-shot lead the final six holes to Tom Watson, now, in 1988, when Seve blows by him.

And it was not luck that won for Ballesteros. It was that great swing. After Seve and Nick had thrown birdies and eagles at each other like so many pieces of confetti, they were tied at ten-under-par standing on the sixteenth fairway.

Then Ballesteros, standing 135 yards from the pin, pulled a nine-iron from his bag and hit the ball 134 yards nine inches. A tap-in. A birdie. A lead. A victory.

There is great irony here. Tuesday is the 400th anniversary of the clash between the Spanish Armada and the English Navy off the southwest coast of England. Throughout this land, at more than 400 locations, they will light torches as they did four centuries ago to rouse a sleeping nation.

But this time the beacons will signal a Spanish victory, not a defeat. This time the glow will remind us of the battle of Royal Lytham, drivers and putters at close range.

"We were both waiting for the other to make a mistake," sighed Price. "But neither did, except for me missing a short par putt on fourteen. He just played better golf.

"There's nothing better than being able to play the standard of golf we played today in a major championship. It's a shame anyone has to lose. But he won because he played better than I did."

Ballesteros parred the first five holes and then made only one par in the next nine, a stretch that included an eagle, five birdies, and two bogeys.

"We both showed we could handle the pressure," said Seve. "I had lost some confidence since I lost the Masters in 1986. But now I will remember how I played today."

ONE FOR
THE PAST

JUNE 10, 1985

BOSTON—Now the deed is done. The memories are exorcised. Now the Los Angeles Lakers have beaten both cynics and Celtics.

Now it is time to remember. Where are they now, those gallant players of fruitless seasons past? Where are Frank Selvy and Jerry West and Elgin Baylor and Tom Hawkins and Rudy LaRusso? The championship surely belongs as much to them as to Kareem and Magic.

It is one thing to whip an opponent, which the Lakers did so convincingly yesterday, defeating Boston, 111-100, to take the NBA title, four games to two. It is another thing to whip history.

Somewhere in the latticework of rafters at Boston Garden, just beyond the numerous championship banners, perched the ghosts of 1962 and '65 and '69 and '84—and many other seasons in which hope was trampled on the parquet floor.

Sam Snead never won a U.S. Open. Napoleon couldn't beat Wellington. But the Lakers have won the NBA title by beating the Celtics. And grass is still green, and the sun still rises in the east.

The fantasy persisted until the closing minutes. Even with the Celtics trailing, even with the Lakers in control, even with the screaming fans, the sweaty Boston players believed something mystical would happen. Maybe Bill Russell would lope out there in that ill-fitting jersey #6. Maybe Sam Jones would throw in a few bank shots. Maybe Cousy would make the big steal.

Not this time. The fantasy was a fallacy. There was nothing magical about the Celtics. There was only something pathetic. They were weary. They were troubled. They were beaten. Tradition had made them orphans.

The present sneers at the past. Don't remind us, current players admonish. Don't tell us what happened in the 1960s. But for the Lakers there was no escape. Until yesterday.

"All the old Lakers can celebrate with us," said one of the new Lakers, Earvin ("Magic") Johnson. "This championship is for all of them and all the people in Los Angeles. We beat the Celtics, and we did it on their home court. Nothing could be sweeter."

Eight times the Lakers had lost in the championship series to the Celtics, once while the team still was in Minneapolis, the other seven after it moved to Los Angeles.

In 1962, the Lakers' Frank Selvy took a jumper at the buzzer of the seventh game. The ball rimmed and spun out. Boston won in overtime. Elgin Baylor scored sixty-one points in one game of that series. In the Celtics' own building. And Red Auerbach, the Boston coach, said it was a good thing Satch Sanders had defensed Elgin well or he might really have had a big night. But the Celtics won in seven games.

For more than a generation, something always went wrong for the Lakers, invariably went right for the Celtics. And there would be K.C. Jones embracing Russell or Sharman or Heinsohn. And there would be Red Auerbach pretentiously lighting a victory cigar. And there would be the Lakers asking why.

Why couldn't a team of Wilt Chamberlain, Elgin Baylor, and Jerry West beat the Celtics in 1969?

Seven games that series went. The final game was on the Lakers' court, The Forum. Former owner Jack Kent Cooke, certain of victory, ordered balloons hung from the ceiling.

They were never dropped. The only thing that fell was Cooke's face. Final score: Boston 108, Los Angeles 106.

There were no balloons yesterday, there was just relief. And glory. And, for last year and years before that, retribution.

"Oh, boy," chortled Lakers coach Pat Riley to nobody in particular. "I don't believe it."

He can believe it. A year ago in the same cramped locker room, Riley was compelled to explain why the Lakers lost. Now, shirt drenched with Möet champagne, he tried to explain his joy. He couldn't.

"I really just want to savor the moment," said Riley.

Former Lakers everywhere would understand.

TENNIS'S NEXT GREAT CHAMPION

JUNE 27, 1985

WIMBLEDON—They interrupted the rain at Swimbledon again today for tennis. At this rate, the first round should be finished by New Year's Eve.

Hank Pfister already is finished. He had the misfortune to have a match on Centre Court against a young, Teutonic marvel who looks like the guy on the cover of *Mad* comics and hits like a guy on the cover of *Ring* magazine.

Boris Becker sent Pfister out of the men's singles, 4-6, 6-3, 6-2, 6-4, and also sent a message to everybody in the game: Here stands tennis's next great champion.

"Without question he's the best seventeen-year-old player I've ever come up against," insisted Pfister, who played his college tennis a decade past at San Jose State. "Becker's power and poise at his age are incredible.

"I cannot think of anyone worse to play right now besides Becker, McEnroe, and Connors."

Pfister's worries are over. Unfortunately, so are his chances. Becker's chances, however, are superb.

"He could win it," said Ion Tiriac, the former Romanian Davis Cup player who now manages Becker. "He really could."

The last time someone this young made such an impression at Wimbledon, where skepticism ranks only below pretension, was in 1978 when a teenager named John McEnroe played here for the first time. Wonder what's happened to him since then?

Becker is from West Germany, where the exports used to be limited to cars and cameras. Now they've got a golfing champion, Bernhard Langer, who won this year's Masters, and the best tennis prospect on tour. Today sport, tomorrow the world.

Becker and Pfister began the match yesterday at 6:56 P.M. Two hours two minutes later, they departed in darkness and without a decision.

Pfister, trailing two sets to one, then made a major mistake. He came back to the All-England Lawn Tennis Club again this morning. He won't be coming back tomorrow.

"I never played Borg until he was twenty," said Pfister, making comparisons to Becker, "and McEnroe was not that strong physically at seventeen. Boris is on such a confidence high right now, it is almost to a point of arrogance. He takes chances and still wins. You never know what he's going to do."

What he's going to do is give the British a happier memory of a German appearance at Wimbledon than the last one. In 1940, a World War II German air raid resulted in a 500-pound bomb hitting Centre Court and destroying 1,200 seats.

Otherwise, Germans haven't done much around here for a half century, since the late Gottfried von Cramm finished as runner-up in the men's singles finals three consecutive years, 1935 through 1937.

Becker is six-feet-two and has a serve that, contrary to the line about children, is to be heard and not seen. Two weekends past he overpowered Johan Kriek in the finals at the Queens Club. At one stretch during the tournament, he won forty-eight straight service games.

"If Boris plays the way he did today, nobody's going to beat him on grass," Kriek said following the Becker victory. "I didn't have a chance to get near the ball."

With his reddish-blond hair and jug ears, Becker might be a candidate to replace Alfred E. Newman as the man from *Mad*. Instead, with his aggressive style and fluid strokes, he's a candidate to replace McEnroe and Lendl at the top of the computer rankings. Already, five months from his eighteenth birthday, he's #20 on the circuit.

"I made it faster than I expected," said Becker. "There are pressures being #20. I'm expected to play at that level.

"But I'm playing in a lot of tournaments with people like Connors, McEnroe, and Lendl, and there I'm just a nobody. I'm looking forward to not being a nobody."

Becker doesn't always mouth words from Emily Dickinson, but on the grounds of a place where clubby, awkward formality is a way of life, it is wise to start out humble.

Then people admire you when you end up a champion— as Becker surely will.

SLEEPY PLAYS ONE FOR THE SHRINE

MAY 11, 1987

OAKLAND—If this was a last hurrah, it was a loud one. If the Warriors are not to return to their home floor, they depart in glory. If sport is moments to remember, think of Eric "Sleepy" Floyd on a day that will be difficult to forget.

For three games and a greater part of a fourth, Floyd had stood on the periphery of success and of triumph, a pain in his injured left hamstring and an ache in his heart. He hadn't produced. The Warriors hadn't won.

So now it was down to the final quarter, the end of the season, when parting is not so much sweet sorrow as an indication of unfulfilled dreams.

The journey was about to end for Golden State. The celebration had already started for the Los Angeles Lakers.

Basketball may be the ultimate of team games, but teams are composed of individuals. On a memorable Mother's Day 1987, Sleepy Floyd was the individual who made the difference.

He scored fifty-one points, thirty-nine in the second half. And the moribund Warriors arose from what seemed eternal torpor to beat the Los Angeles Lakers, 129-121, before a sellout crowd of 15,025 at Oakland Coliseum Arena that was determined to set an NBA record for noise.

The Warriors remained on a life-support system. They still trail the Lakers, 3-1, in the best-of-seven Western Conference semifinal. And the next game Tuesday is at The Forum, where the Warriors haven't won since last season.

But reality be damned. This was a game for dreamers. For the fans who have been around through the good and lean times and all the in-between times. And for those who only of late have jumped aboard a bandwagon that is constructed well enough to withstand any quick stop.

Whatever happens now, even if the Warriors disintegrate in game five, the memories of the renaissance season will be pleasant ones.

"WIN/LOSE WE LOVE OUR WARRIORS," read a large sign raised high after three periods.

"That sign meant a lot to me," a weary Sleepy Floyd would say. Sleepy meant a lot to those fans.

He was a man possessed, a hero waiting for a role.

"He took it upon himself," said Lakers coach Pat Riley, smiling with chagrin. "There was no stopping him."

And thus there was no stopping the Warriors. From a fourteen-point deficit at the end of the third quarter, from the inevitability of a series sweep, Sleepy shot and they rallied. And the crowd roared. And the season crept forward.

So even if the Lakers march on and win the NBA championship, as they should with that talent and confidence, the Warriors and their followers will be able to cling to this gem of a game like a dowager to her diamonds.

For a brief, shining moment there was Camelot. And there was Floyd riding to save the kingdom.

Eric Floyd, who gained his nickname in an elementary-school baseball game when a grounder slipped past, has large, hooded eyes and a lean and hungry look. Didn't Brutus say such men are dangerous when they get the ball one-on-one?

At Georgetown, under the forceful coaching of John Thompson, Floyd played a disciplined style of basketball, but still set the school scoring record with more than 2,000 points.

In the NBA, he was switched from scoring guard to point guard, although in this league where everybody must dribble, shoot, and rebound, labels are extraneous.

"Going to point guard made me a better player," said Floyd. "And it extended my career. I'm six-three. To play scoring guard in the NBA, you've got to be six-seven, six-eight."

There is more than size to pro basketball. There is skill. There is desire.

"I can't really describe it," said Floyd. "I was not conscious of what was happening, except of the scoreboard and getting back on defense."

The man made thirteen of fourteen from the floor in the last quarter. The man made a difference.

"I wasn't trying to do too much," said Floyd. "It was instinct. I didn't want the season to end."

It didn't. It continues, for a few more hours at least.

"What can I say?" sighed Warriors coach George Karl. "It was guts and heart and Sleepy."

On this day, it was enough.

BOBBY CHACON'S NIGHT TO JAB AND CRY

MARCH 17, 1982

SACRAMENTO—The punches came first, flurries of left-and-rights thrown by a man possessed, and then came the tears. Bobby Chacon asked forgiveness. No one in the room was prepared to deny it.

Chacon had done what he felt obligated to do, fight a boxing match only a day after his wife had committed suicide. How or why was not ours to question.

To some, the results of the bout may be insignificant. To Bobby Chacon, a man of incredible resolve as well as of athletic skill, the results are not. He won. By a knockout, at 1:52 of the third round, over Salvador Ugalde. He won, and then he was heartsick.

All through the day, others had tried to dissuade him from going through with the fight. No man could be expected to perform under such conditions. But Chacon refused. He would mourn the tragedy in days to come. He would cry tomorrow.

But this night the show would go on. He would fulfill an obligation. He would, in his own way, honor the memory of his bride.

Valerie Chacon didn't want her man to fight. Over the years she cajoled Bobby Chacon, once the world's featherweight champ, into retiring. And then when, against her wishes, he returned to the world of knockouts and scar tissue, she would weep and wail.

Monday morning Bobby Chacon was in his motel room in Sacramento when the phone rang. Valerie was calling from the

151

family home, a ranch in Palermo, some ten miles south of Oroville. She begged him not to go through with the bout, to give up boxing for her and the three children. Bobby could only sigh and promise he would be a winner.

In the past, thirty-year-old Valerie Chacon had been treated for emotional distress. When she put down the phone Monday she walked into her room, locked the door, turned up the volume of the television set, and shot herself in the head with a .22-caliber rifle. She died instantly.

The phone rang again in Bobby Chacon's motel room in Sacramento. He was notified of the tragedy. So was Don Fraser, executive officer of the State Athletic Commission and the man who promoted so many of Chacon's fights when Bobby was a champion in the mid-1970s.

"I tried to talk him out of fighting," Fraser said last night inside Memorial Auditorium, a brick neo-Renaissance structure that seemed a bizarre setting for this human drama.

"I recommended Bobby not go through with the fight. I've known him personally for many years. I knew his wife very well. She was a lovely person. Everybody handles things in different ways, strange ways. Chacon had to handle this in his own way."

Normally restrained and patient in the ring, Chacon last night was a wild man, flailing at the bewildered Ugalde and, perhaps, at some imaginary demons. Either the fight would not last or Chacon would not last. The fight did not last.

"I wanted to get it over with," said thirty-year-old Bobby Chacon. "I didn't want to be patient. I couldn't be patient. I told the guys in my corner I wasn't going to get tired. I was just going to keep going. I didn't want to get in trouble. I've had a hell of a lot of trouble.

"I hope my wife was up there watching me. I mean business. That's the only reason I'm in boxing. I had to fight this fight. It was the only way I could keep my mind off of her. My kids wanted me to fight it. My daughter got up on a box yesterday and told me I had to be strong. I was strong.

"I never looked at the guy I was fighting. I didn't want to see him. All I wanted to do was get in there and get it over and see my wife."

He got it over, then a face that had been as emotionless as that of a statue fell against the chest of Alan Ginn, Valerie's brother, one of Chacon's seconds. Bobby wept openly.

"Yes," he would say later, "I cried. If people saw me, I really don't care. I got something to cry about. So if I look dumb or something, forgive me this time. I won't ask again."

The setting for this unnerving evening was one out of a 1940s fight film. In the half-century-old building on a rainy night a crowd of 2,419 was waiting, maybe 500 more than would have been in attendance without the tragic subplot.

In the gallery were a half-dozen journalists from places ranging as far away as Los Angeles and San Francisco, journalists undeniably lured by the circumstances surrounding the match rather than the match itself.

Smoke hung in the air like some translucent white veil. On the front of one balcony of the auditorium someone had draped a sign: BOBBY WE LOVE YOU, THE ENGGASSERS.

Everyone loved Bobby. When he climbed through the ropes, the audience rose and cheered. If they could not quite understand his obsession at least they appreciated it.

Each fighter came in at 133 pounds. That was the last time they were equal. Chacon started from the opening bell, boom, boom, boom. Ugalde went down in the second. Ugalde went down in the third. Ugalde went down again in the third. One ordeal was over for Chacon. Another was just beginning.

"Now I'm going home and look at my wife for the last time. I loved my wife. Boxing is going to be my marriage now, but first I'm going to take some time off. I'm going home to my kids, and we're going to cry. My wife was a beautiful woman."

MUSTER A GEM

NOVEMBER 22, 1987

STANFORD—Do you like Shakespeare? Or music by Scott Joplin? Do you think the world was a better place before punk haircuts and mercenary athletes? Then you'll appreciate Brad Muster.

Muster is the Stanford tailback. Actually, the Stanford offense. Make that past tense. Was. He's finished.

On Saturday, Brad Muster played his final college game. He carried the ball again and again. And then he carried himself into history with dignity.

Brad Muster took a lot of steps forward during a career that ended on a gloriously clear afternoon with Stanford defeating California, 31-7, in the ninetieth annual Big Game.

More important, he was able also to step backward, to make us think of the time when undergraduates belonged in the stories of Horatio Alger and not in the pages of books such as *Less Than Zero*.

Muster didn't tell us how fortunate we were to watch him but how lucky he was to play for us. His values are not defined by dollar signs. He figures there's more to education than reading a playbook.

Brad is from Marin County, across the Golden Gate Bridge, where, according to the clichés, everyone who isn't a materialist is a sybarite. It's a society, we're told, of BMWs, hot tubs, and cool kids.

But Brad never thought himself special, even though he is. He could have been in the pros this year, earning the big money. Instead, he returned to Stanford and earned respect, not to mention accolades.

Muster was literally more than one-third of Stanford's offense. The Cardinal had seventy-three plays from scrimmage. Muster was in on twenty-nine of those, gaining eighty-seven yards in twenty-two rushing attempts and fifty-six yards on seven receptions.

"Overuse Brad?" asked Stanford coach Jack Elway. "Maybe I didn't use him enough."

It was a time to reflect not so much on what had been but what was.

Brad Muster, who stayed in school, tore up an ankle in practice last summer and missed not only several games but a chance at the Heisman Trophy.

Muster never complained. Rather, he competed. He kept trying, kept hustling, even when the ankle wouldn't permit him to exploit his speed and elusiveness. And he went out a winner, with his helmet held high in an upraised hand and traces of tears in his dark eyes.

"I heard about an article written the other day that said I blew it by not turning pro," Muster would comment quietly. "No way."

And then, unintentionally, he offered a pun: "I was interested in the long run."

The long run. Because he was a redshirt freshman in 1983, Muster was eligible for the 1987 NFL draft. But he had promises to keep. And yards to go before he could sleep.

"There's no way I would go back on my decision," insisted Muster. "Money? If I wanted money right away I would have done it. But there's a lot more than money.

"I didn't feel sorry for myself because I got hurt. I felt sorry for a guy like J.J. [Jeff James], who couldn't play in this, his last college game, and had to watch."

Someone wondered, based on Saturday's performance, what Muster might have contributed this season had he not been injured.

"I might have fumbled 800 times," he said, wryly. "That just happens. I did what I could with what I had. I'm proud of this team."

Pro football is next for Muster, and he'd be so perfect for the 49ers, with his size and power and ability to catch as well as run. But Brad wasn't interested in ruminating about the future. He was thinking not about tomorrow but today and all those yesterdays.

"I think Stanford enhanced me," Muster said. "I don't think it changed me too much. There are a lot of class individuals around here and they make you stay on your toes.

"It feels good ending like this because I was able to show

people I still can play at a certain level. I hope I'll be invited to some bowl games and be 100 percent when I get there.

"But I'm sad, too. I'll never play for Stanford again, never play with these guys, before these people. Those fans cheering us on mean a lot more to me than I meant to them."

Not really. The way he plays, the way he acts, Brad Muster means a great deal to everyone. Thanks for the memories.

EDBERG TURNS TIGER

JULY 5, 1988

WIMBLEDON—This was a Wimbledon of irony as much as destiny, a tennis tournament as full of surprises and raindrops as the grass courts were of divots, a time of bedlam and boredom that left spectators with lowered umbrellas and, at last, Stefan Edberg with upraised arms.

It was the Wimbledon in which Steffi Graf wrenched domination of the women's game from Martina Navratilova, the Wimbledon in which the barometer fell like British pride, the Wimbledon one Swede lost a chance at the Grand Slam and another lost a chance at anonymity—which is the price paid for victory.

"How are you going to go out and eat in Kensington now?" a voice asked Edberg early on a Monday evening in which the men's singles final finally had concluded. A day late, but considering the six-figure payoff, something like $183,000, hardly a dollar short.

Edberg shrugged and shook his head of blond hair. Here's the guy who moved from Sweden to London, the chic Kensington district south of Hyde Park, so he could live a normal life, if any tennis player does.

"I like to go about unrecognized," Edberg admitted a few days ago. "I would rather not be known by anybody. It would spoil that if I won Wimbledon."

To the victor, they say, go the spoils, although the definition in this case is a bit unusual.

With his 4-6, 7-6 (7-2 tiebreaker), 6-4, 6-2 triumph over a very bewildered Boris Becker in a men's singles final that stretched nearly twenty-four hours because of rain and gloom and all those other vices unique to an English summer, Edberg was the victor.

Nothing has lasted as long as this Wimbledon since the 1962 World Series between the Yankees and the Giants, which was rained out for weeks. Or was it merely days?

Now I know why England was involved in the Hundred Years' War. They kept stopping to put on galoshes and slickers.

The match between Becker, Wimbledon champ in 1985 and 1986, and Edberg almost turned into a miniseries, sort of a tennis version of "Rich Man, Poor Man." Well, knowing what those guys earn, make it "Rich Man, Richer Man."

First, Becker had to play Friday night and Saturday afternoon to beat Ivan Lendl in the semis. Then Becker-Edberg started at 6:33 P.M. Sunday—and stopped, with Edberg leading, three games to two in the first set, at 6:56 P.M. Sunday.

Overtime. We all came back to the All-England Lawn Tennis and Croquet Club on Monday for the scheduled 11 A.M. continuation. Only at 11 A.M. there was a storm out of the Last Judgment. So resumption was at 1:03 P.M. And fifteen minutes later, with Becker having won a set, the rain fell once more.

If North Dakota could only see us now.

Anyway, the next shot was hit at 2:59 P.M. And, hallelujah, if we didn't finish. And if the twenty-two-year-old Edberg didn't tumble backward in ecstasy. He'd won two Australian Opens, but Wimbledon is Wimbledon.

"It's hard to believe I really won it," Edberg would sigh. "I played well today."

And so the wrong Swede takes another major.

Mats Wilander won the Australian and French Opens, and there was talk of a Grand Slam—which Graf will complete, when she wins the U.S. Open in September.

Wilander tumbled in the quarters. But along comes Stefan. "He seemed to get to every ball," said Becker.

Boris was more tired than disappointed. We had conceded him the crown, figured he and fellow German Graf would combine to prove in tennis, indeed, it was "Deutschland über Alles."

"He started playing well," said the twenty-year-old Becker, "and I was a step slow. I'm still human. I beat the defending champ in the quarters [Pat Cash] and the #1 seed in the semis [Lendl], and when the final dragged on, I started to ask myself, 'What the hell am I doing out here?' "

Some might have asked that of Edberg. Supposedly he had no guts. The French have a term *le grand méchant loup,* which means "big, wicked wolf."

Only for Edberg, the French journalists altered it to *le grand méchant mou*—"big, wicked softy."

He was said to lack conviction. But against Miloslav Mecir, down two sets to love in the semis and against Becker, down a set, Edberg proved he had the heart to go with a marvelous return of serve and some great volleys.

Three weeks ago, in the warm-up to Wimbledon, Queens, Becker beat Edberg in a three-set final, Stefan double-faulting the match away. Hey, baby, said the critics, he choked. But Monday he swallowed hard.

"I played well on the big points today," said Stefan, "and I made him play worse. I believe in myself."

Another knock against Stefan is his personality. Someone suggested he undergo a charisma transplant.

In a sport in which arrogance, obnoxiousness, and a complete vocabulary of four-letter words can be as useful as a two-fisted backhand, Edberg is, to quote his coach, Englishman Tony Pickard, "an exceptionally nice young man."

Too nice, a great many of us said. But we were wrong. How ironic. How delightful.

ONE FOR THE AGES

APRIL 14, 1986

AUGUSTA, Georgia—Jack Nicklaus is walking the eighteenth fairway, out of the past, into history. Great cheers accompany his approach. An April sun glows orange in the late afternoon. The moment is to be treasured.

An athlete for the ages has returned. Time has been reversed. Reality has been suspended. We are younger now. The world is a better place. Jack Nicklaus has won the Masters.

This may have been golf's greatest day. Certainly it is Nicklaus's most memorable. Fantasy dances in the Georgia pines. The improbability of sport will forever tantalize and amaze.

Augusta National Golf Club is a young man's course. It requires strong swings and strong nerves. It is the domain of golfers in their twenties and thirties. No less an expert than Nicklaus himself expresses the opinion.

Jack Nicklaus is no longer young. He is forty-six and seemingly unable to putt. He has been written off frequently.

Yet he comes flying over the back nine, a man possessed, a golfer enlightened, holing putts, eliciting shouts, ennobling the game.

He does what we know he cannot do. He beats the young men. He conquers the course. He wins the Masters for a sixth time.

The emotion is nearly palpable. Tears well in Nicklaus's eyes. He is overwhelmed by the response of the gallery. Competitor and audience share the enjoyment and both are richer for the experience.

On Masters Sunday a potential for frenzy is never far away. Too often it stays hidden, perhaps in the azaleas, maybe in the magnolias. An ending evokes yawns. Golf can be a very dull game.

But yesterday it was a very exciting one. Jack Nicklaus helped make it so. This was the United States–Soviet Union at ice hockey, all over again. Do you believe in miracles? Do you believe in fifteen-foot eagle putts?

Herbert Warren Wind is America's most knowledgeable golf writer, a man who has chronicled the greats from Hogan to Ballesteros. He is conservative by nature, a New Englander given to understatement.

The final round of the 1986 Masters, however, brings an outpouring of hyperbole from Wind.

"There is no question in my mind," insists Wind, "this is the biggest golf happening since the Grand Slam."

That took place fifty-six years ago. Bobby Jones won the U.S. Open and Amateur, the British Open and Amateur. The game jumped from the society pages to the front pages. The country had a hero.

Jones created Augusta National and the Masters. His legacy is the course and the tournament.

In 1965, when twenty-five-year-old Jack Nicklaus set a Masters scoring record of 271, Jones, old and crippled, shook his head and told the winner, "You play a game with which I am not familiar."

Twenty-one years pass. Jack's game is familiar to us all. He has not won in two years. He has not won a major championship in six years.

His sporting obituary appears consistently. He gropes. He frowns. He receives a loving son's compassion and a public's admonition. Please, Jack, we plead, don't get out there and embarrass yourself. Don't dream of what cannot be.

Jack sneers at the cynics. He tells us he can still play. He tells himself he can still play. He is right. We are wrong. Along the fairways, the cheers are deafening.

Xenophobia is evident. American golf is being dominated by foreigners. After fifty-four holes, the Masters leader board displays an Australian, a Zimbabwean, a Spaniard, a German, and only one American. It is not Jack Nicklaus. Jack Nicklaus is four shots behind and has no chance.

The Masters: Dogwood and wisteria blossoms, three-putt greens and one-swing disasters, Jack Nicklaus doing his patriotic best.

His twenty-four-year-old son, Jackie, caddies. Through the day, he whispers advice, speaks encouragement. When the final putt is holed, when Nicklaus has a seven-under-par and a nine-under-par total of 279, they hug on the edge of the eighteenth green.

Hanging back, Barbara Nicklaus, wife and mother, is caught between expectation and relief. The round is over, the tournament may not be. Norman still could birdie, Tom Kite still could birdie. Neither does.

Jack Nicklaus has won seventy-one Tour tournaments, twenty major championships, but only one matters. Barbara Nicklaus smiles.

"It's almost like the first one," she says. "He's been so confident. The things they say about him hurt. Missing the cuts hurts. But this is wonderful."

This is remarkable. Jack Nicklaus has won the Masters. Treasure the moment.

LEGALIZED
MAYHEM

MARCH 11, 1986

LAS VEGAS—It's a tough way to live. Or to die. Boxing is less a sport than a tragedy, a compromise between what the body can endure and what the market will bear.

Learned men have sung its praises. Author and critic A.J. Leibling was moved to call it the "sweet science." But the sweetness sours with the punishment the boxer must take and the money the promoter must make.

Long after the championship card was history last night, after Marvelous Marvin Hagler and Thomas Hearns and Gaby Canizales had sent opponents crashing to the canvas and the crowd fleeing into the dampness, the man who put the show together, the Harvard Law graduate, Bob Arum, felt compelled to talk about himself.

"I hate to gloat," gloated Arum, "but to those who said the closed-circuit telecasts would not attract anyone, well, I will take the credit for this. We had large grosses. We drew big crowds all over the country."

Wonderful. And that a young man had earlier been carried out of the ring on a stretcher, had incurred brain damage, however minor, what about that, Mr. Arum? How much is a person's life worth? How much is boxing worth? When will it ever end?

When will kids from ghettos and barrios stop trying to use their fists to find fame? When will guys with Harvard diplomas or pinkie rings stop trying to use those kids to find the pot at the end of the rainbow?

Boxing escaped last night. More important, so did twenty-five-year-old Richie Sandoval of Pomona. He took one punch too many. And there was panic in the ring as he lay there, motionless, while doctors worked with rapid skill.

Sandoval had been unbeaten. Irony. So had John Mugabi, who was knocked out by Hagler, and James Shuler, who was knocked out by Hearns.

But Richie Sandoval was beaten last night in that outdoor ring out beyond the pretentious glamour of Caesar's Palace casino hotel, beaten into unconsciousness.

This was the second bout of what Arum had listed as "The Fights," three championship bouts of varying weight levels. Sandoval was defending his World Boxing Association bantamweight title against Canizales. But he had no defense.

Whether Sandoval had lost too much weight trying to make the 118-pound limit or whether Canizales was simply too quick and too strong doesn't really matter. The suppositions are academic.

The fact is Sandoval was knocked down in the first round, the fifth round, and three times in the seventh. The last time he was knocked out, painfully, pitifully.

"They should have stopped the fight after the second knockdown in the seventh," sighed Canizales, who took a battering himself. "I knew he was really hurt. I hope to God he's okay."

So do we all. What boxing doesn't need is another walking vegetable. Or another death. But it will have both, of course. In an activity where the prime function is to destroy the other man, to batter him into submission, injuries and fatalities are inevitable.

Even though Canizales knew Sandoval was hurt, he wouldn't let up. He couldn't let up. "His legs were wiggly," said Canizales. "But I still have to go after him. That's why I'm out here. To take every opportunity to win."

Sandoval was taken to the hospital. One doctor said the boxer had stopped breathing for sixty to ninety seconds. Another denied the contention. But there was no denial Sandoval was hurt. Badly.

A CAT scan indicated a slight swelling of the brain. "He's alert and not paralyzed," reassured Dr. Kazen Fathie, a neurosurgeon who was at ringside. "But he didn't know where he was."

That's what we derive from the fight game: Kids who can't tell you where they are. Or older men who can't tell you anything.

Muhammad Ali is the most famous boxer of the era—in his own words, "The Greatest." He could dance. He could jab. But now, after years of blows to the brain, he can hardly talk. And he's not even fifty.

Ali appeared at a testimonial banquet in Las Vegas two nights ago. He stood up in front of a microphone. And he slurred his words. The Greatest is now The Saddest.

Carlos Padilla was the referee for the Sandoval-Canizales fight. He could have stopped the bout. He didn't.

"I asked Sandoval if he was okay," said Padilla. "He said he was. He seemed able to fight."

Sandoval wasn't okay. Boxing isn't okay. It leads young men down a pathway to broken dreams and battered skulls. And yet it goes on and on.

BEWITCHED, BOTHERED, BEATEN

NOVEMBER 21, 1982

BERKELEY—The twilight zone has descended upon Memorial Stadium. Scoreboard lights flicker with the miraculous news. California has beaten Stanford, 25-20, and standards by which games are judged have been blasphemed.

Reality dictates it could not happen. But reality exists no more. Fantasy has strangled truth. The impossible has become ordinary. The descriptions of mortals are rendered useless.

This was a game for the ages, perhaps of all time, a game that ended in a manner so preposterous it had to be the work of witchcraft. This was the only Big Game they'll recall, whether in triumph or, in the case of Stanford, anger and helplessness.

Stanford had this game, or God doesn't make little green apples, and it don't snow in Minneapolis in the wintertime. Stanford had this game on a thirty-five-yard field goal by reliable Mark Harmon with four seconds left.

Stanford had this game, 20-19, and it also had a bid from the Hall of Fame Bowl, whose representatives were expectedly grateful when Harmon's kick flew over the crossbar of the northern goalpost.

And then, unbelievably, Stanford had nothing.

The game was stolen from the Cardinals on the most unusual kickoff return in memory, a play of total implausibility, a play that made the Immaculate Reception seem like a trifle and Bobby Thomson's pennant-winning homer run-of-the-mill.

It was something out of a Disney movie, the sort where the ball carrier leaps tall buildings, soars over tacklers, and finally lands in the middle of the sousaphone section. Okay, the script was changed slightly. When Cal's Kevin Moen finished the play, he was not only in the end zone but in the lap of a trombonist from the Stanford band.

Football evolved from the English game of rugby, a sport where the ball is lateraled from one player to another each time a tackle is made. Yesterday on the final play, football regressed.

What do you do when there's only four seconds left, you're in front and required to kick off? Squib the ball, naturally, kick it on the top half so it bounces crazily, especially on AstroTurf, and becomes impossible to return.

Then you celebrate the victory.

Harmon did kick the bouncer, and when the ball landed in the arms of Moen, a defensive back, it seemed he would be swarmed under.

But as he was about to be tackled, he lateraled to Richard Rodgers. And as Rodgers was about to be hit, he lateraled to Dwight Garner. And now time had ended, but the play was still alive. Or was it?

Garner, stubby (five-foot-nine, 185) and mischievous, was engulfed by numerous white-shirted Stanford players about midfield and started to fall. Impetuously, the Stanford band, an irreverent group if ever there was one, surged into the south end zone, to celebrate the victory.

"We thought the play was dead," a contrite musician would say later. "We would never do anything to hurt our team." The play wasn't dead. If there would be epitaphs written this day, they would be for Stanford, not Cal.

"I swear, my knee never hit the ground," said Garner. "I was just about to fall, and then I saw Rodgers."

And for the second time on this play, Richard Rodgers was off and running. Along with seemingly everyone else in the stadium, band members, fans, and even a couple of Stanford players coming off the bench onto the playing surface. It looked like Times Square on New Year's Eve. But the game hadn't ended.

Rodgers pitched the ball to Mariet Ford who headed for the right, or western, sideline. In front of him was, yes, the Stanford band.

Ford got the ball to the man who started the entire chain reaction, flipping it over his shoulder to Moen about the 25-yard line, or next to the woodwinds. And with musicians fleeing in all directions, Moen scored.

Surely this was a joke. This didn't happen. In the press box, journalists stood with mouths open. On the Stanford sideline, coach Paul Wiggin waited for an official to call back the play. But the only call that was made was for a touchdown. Cal had won. And now the field was choked with humanity.

Fans poured from the seats. Stanford players wandered aimlessly, as if to appeal to some higher authority. Wiggin was aghast, demanding a recount. This was chaos. This was history.

The result would have to stand. No official would have the fortitude to order this one replayed. Hell, they couldn't even clear the field to try the extra point. If you wanted to see it again, you'd have to watch the videotape.

That's exactly what Paul Wiggin did. And then he went after the officials again. But the bitterness would have to be accepted. Stanford would never end up ahead if Wiggin argued until the year 2000.

Dwight Garner may have been stopped, but he never went down. And it was the Stanford band that made the mistake of screening off Stanford defenders. The game was over.

"Whatever happened on the last play," said Cal athletic director Dave Maggard, "we deserved to win this game. We outplayed them. And no matter what anybody says from now on, the score will stand. Cal will always be the winner."

Stanford simply finished second. In this game, the only loser was reality.

THE SECRET OF 49er SUCCESS

DECEMBER 28, 1987

The music pounded into the downpour. "They built this city . . . they built this city . . . they built this city on rock and roll. It was San Francisco's song for San Francisco's team, the 49ers, who were built, on the contrary, on muscle and sweat and brains.

Another division championship, another dominating win, and another appearance, down on the field, by the man at the top, the owner who cares, Eddie DeBartolo, Jr.

Any organization, sports or business, is only as good as its leader. And leadership. You're not permitted room at the top, only direction.

The 49ers have it. And so, with a frighteningly easy victory over the Los Angeles Rams, 48-0, at Candlestick Park Sunday night, they have the best record in the NFL for 1987, 13-2.

Vignettes: The 49ers humbled at Giants Stadium, 49-3, in a play-off game last season. The 49ers searching for answers during training camp. The 49ers beaten in the opening game by Pittsburgh. The 49ers winning on the final play against Cincinnati. The 49ers jogging off the field Sunday evening while Eddie DeBartolo jogged his memory.

It only takes money to own a sports franchise, but it takes so much more to own a successful franchise.

Dollars and cents are no substitute for common sense. Or perception. Or affinity. Or genuine affection. "Nothing's more important to me than my family," said DeBartolo, "and I consider this team a part of my family."

DeBartolo not only understands his role, he relishes it. You acquire the best people available and then step back and allow them to weave their magic. Laissez-faire football. But not lazy-fare football.

In New Orleans, the owner attempts to hog the spotlight, doing his dances in back of the bench. In San Francisco, Eddie D. is content to stand in the end zone with raindrops falling on his head and the glory tumbling on the athletes and coaches.

Sure, the 49ers are "his" team. But only in a paternal definition. So he tries to make his players bonus babies by offering to match their play-off receipts? Just a father helping out his offspring.

Moments before this final regular-season game, two of the 49ers' injured players, Keena Turner and Keith Fahnhorst, exhorted their teammates with brief, emotional speeches. Those who seek simple answers will suggest that's the reason the 49ers breezed to their fifth NFC West championship in seven years. Put it this way: It didn't hurt.

But football, like life, is complex. "Win one for the Gipper" occurs only in movies.

Don't you think Rams coach John Robinson tried to motivate his club? And L.A. incurred its worst regular-season loss in history.

The 49ers triumph because Eddie D. hired Bill Walsh, who hired the assistants. Then the coaches obtained the personnel.

The 49ers triumph because egotism is subordinated to the common good.

You know the similarity between the Rams and the 49ers? Well, both teams started quarterbacks who wore #8. And early in the second quarter both teams had three time-outs remaining.

The Rams have an owner who used to be a chorus girl and now is a miser. Their best player walked out on his teammates. Another refused to report. It's not so much a football team as a study in chaos.

The 49ers work together. They never seem to lose sight of the primary goal, even when they fail to reach it.

"This team was molded," said DeBartolo. "Any team that wants to stay good has to stay in transition. There have to be changes in players. Moves have to be made, even though sometimes you hate to make them."

The 49ers got Steve Young for their backup quarterback—and he started the last two games. The 49ers got rookie linemen in the draft, and they've been starting.

"They know I'm their #1 supporter," said DeBartolo. "I think Bill Walsh knows I'm his #1 fan and critic. We're also very close.

Bill Walsh knows I'm his #1 fan and critic. We're also very close. I don't try to meddle, just lend support."

Walsh lends expertise. Asked a few days ago whether Joe Montana or Jerry Rice was the 49ers' most valuable player, former San Francisco receiver Gene Washington said, "It has to be Jerry Rice . . . but the real MVP of the 49ers is Bill Walsh."

"Our strength," said DeBartolo, "is that everyone in this organization communicates with each other."

Walsh communicated this: "Football is a game in which you don't have the comfort of wishful thinking. You go day to day, piece by piece, and see where that takes you."

Where it's taken the 49ers is to a great regular season. Again. Good people make good organizations. Nothing could be more obvious.

You Can't Choose Them All

HE KNEW AFTER HIS FIRST FIGHT

MARCH 11, 1981

You can dress it up with euphemisms, like "the manly art of self-defense," or "the sweet science." You can say that it develops character, or at the least physical prowess. You can even vindicate it with remarks about the aggressiveness of the human animal.

But no matter what the embellishments or the justifications, no matter what the rewards or the prizes, boxing is and always will be an activity of malevolence, a sport in which the object is to get the other man before he can get you.

Critics call it a blight on society, legalized barbarism. But as long as there are people, there will be people wanting to test themselves and test others, people wanting to fight, people like Larry Virgil.

For a long time Larry Virgil, who is twenty-one and married and presumably should know better, wanted to get into a boxing ring, wanted to hit and, possibly, to be hit, to know the pain and the pleasure that are inextricably interwined.

And last night at the Cow Palace, in the second bout of the *Examiner* Golden Gloves card, before friends and strangers, Larry Virgil received his opportunity. It was anything but successful.

The Golden Gloves competition is held for guys like Larry Virgil, guys with a dream or a reputation, guys with maybe more guts than sense. The Golden Gloves is boxing's version of the U.S. Open golf tournament, of someone boasting he can lick any man in the house. The Golden Gloves is when you stop talking—that mouthpiece makes communication difficult, anyway—and start popping.

Larry Virgil, twenty-one, graduate of Westmoor High in Daly City, a grocery clerk at Bell Market in San Francisco, started popping last night. And then he started getting popped. His

174

opponent in the 156-pound weight class, Pedro Viramontes of Santa Rosa, knocked him down in the first round. And then he knocked him down in the second round.

And Virgil, who wanted to know what it was like to be a boxer, a fighter, knew quite well. Blood covered his nose and mouth and dripped onto his trunks. The referee had no choice. He halted the bout. For Larry Virgil the fight was over. Probably, too, his short, unhappy boxing career.

Down in the audience, where others were shouting, Karen Virgil, Larry's wife, gasped and shook her head—and then smiled. Her husband was standing, bloody, as they say, but unbowed. He had survived, had reached his goal. Under the circumstances, that was about as much as anyone could have hoped.

Larry's father, Joe, who works in the composing room of the *Examiner* and *Chronicle*, fought in the Golden Gloves nearly thirty years ago. Joe didn't want Larry to fight. Joe's wife, Millie, especially didn't want Larry—her son—to fight. But Larry wanted to fight, and that was that.

"So we trained in the garage every evening." said Joe Virgil. "We worked on mats, and with the bags. And he would spar against me or against Dominic Yassolino, who fought before. The trouble was, he didn't have any experience. He really had never been in a ring."

That made Larry Virgil a novice. But you can't compete as a novice if you're older than twenty. So Virgil entered as a junior, and he was matched up against Viramontes, who'd had a previous bout. And it showed.

It showed in the crimson that painted Virgil's face. It showed in the manner Viramontes moved inside to stick and stick—and stick again.

Larry Virgil wore a singlet undershirt and white Nike basketball shoes for his first supervised fight. When he came out of the ring and into the dressing room, the undershirt was spattered with blood.

But he wouldn't change it, wouldn't take it off, wouldn't give up this special garment, just as a few moments earlier he wouldn't give up the fight to Viramontes.

Joe Virgil was proud of his boy, even in defeat. He had reason to be. Larry lost, admittedly, and he bled. But he got up when he was knocked down, and he smiled. He almost seemed to be enjoying the agony.

175

"Really," insisted Larry Virgil, "I feel fine. I wanted the experience of fighting, and now I have it. The worst thing was the waiting, not the fighting. I was here Monday night and they told me I was supposed to fight, but I didn't. Tonight, I finally got my chance."

It's a chance most of us would pass up, a chance to get smacked around. It was also a chance to be cheered by his buddies, by his fellow employees, to earn the respect only a boxer can earn.

"Way to go, Larry," someone yelled as he walked into the stands after the fight. A cheer grew. Karen Virgil ran over and grabbed her husband. They would go home soon. Larry's bruises would heal. Life would go on as it had previously.

For all intents, Larry Virgil was finished with boxing. He had learned that it's a tough, brutal sport, a sport that may teach self-defense and character but extracts a high cost in the process.

Before he left the building, Larry Virgil once more looked up at the boxing ring where maybe a half hour earlier he had learned his lessons. Two other young men were now inside, throwing punches and taking them. His moment had passed. Boxing, however, will always be around—no matter what you say about it.

ONE LAST LOOK BACK

WIMBLEDON—She dipped properly at the service line, the obligatory curtsy to dukes and duchesses on high, then surreptitiously got a look at the arena where on this overcast day she couldn't get a break. Billie Jean King was about to leave Centre Court, perhaps forever.

"The tumult and the shouting dies," wrote Rudyard Kipling, an Englishman, "the captains and the kings depart." The king who was once the queen of tennis is gone, under the most unfortunate of circumstances.

It was not that Billie Jean, five months from her fortieth birthday, lost in a women's singles semifinal today at Wimbledon. It was that she proved entirely ineffective, falling to the exuberance and two-handed rips of Andrea Jaeger, 6-1, 6-1. In less than an hour an opportunity had become a disaster.

"Losing the way I did," sighed Billie Jean, "it was probably my worst Centre Court match ever."

They used to dislike Billie Jean at this fortress of British tradition. She was so intense, so successful, so American.

Triumph is literally foreign to the English, who have watched visitors steal their crowns. The Brits seem to appreciate defeat more than victory, if done properly. That means playing well, but not well enough to win, the philosophy of "good show, old sport."

But Billie Jean offered a flapping jaw instead of a stiff upper lip. Losing was unacceptable, and to hell with decorum. Nothing would stop her, not even booing.

Nobody booed today. The sellout crowd tucked beneath the grandstand roof came to cheer King. It had few chances.

Mostly it offered the sounds of silence, quiet acceptance that what the press had hyped as the dream match, between King and Martina Navratilova in the Saturday finals, would never be realized.

Martina, once more unleashing the blitzkrieg, kept her end of the bargain, battering Yvonne Vermaak, 6-1, 6-1, in only thirty-six minutes. But King was not up to the quickness and excellence of the eighteen-year-old Jaeger.

"I had a bad day at the office," Billie Jean would concede.

As she prepared to leave that office, Centre Court, where six times she had achieved the women's singles title at Wimbledon, Billie Jean did an unusual thing, for her. She glanced back.

"I took a last look all around," explained King. "I never had done it before all the times I played. I usually look to the right and left as I leave but never behind me. I wanted to take another look, because I don't know if it will be the last."

Was she cryptically announcing her retirement, conceding the years and tears were too much of a burden? Not exactly. "I reassess my goals in tennis every six months. I'll have some decisions to make."

Her announced goal the last few days had been to make it to the finals for a ninth time. But her first serves missed and her volleys were soft and her forehands down the line always seemed to be wide.

She wiped her glasses, grimaced, occasionally hollered at the umpire. She even changed rackets in the second set, but it didn't bring a change of luck, or direction.

"I hit shots I thought were great," said King, "but they went out three feet. I said, 'Uh, oh.' They felt great on the face of the racket but they went out. She's not the fastest player I've played, but she anticipates well. She played well. I didn't execute."

Andrea was a year old when King won Wimbledon the first time in 1966. As Andrea went through elementary school, Billie Jean went through one opponent after another. But reputations don't mean much any longer. Only execution matters.

"These kids," said King, half laughing, half sneering, "don't know me at all. They were two years old when I was #1." But isn't there some veneration, some recognition? "I don't think today's kids are in awe of anybody anymore, except maybe rock groups."

And, if you correctly interpret a King remark, Martina Navratilova.

"I don't think Andrea believes she can beat Martina. You have to believe it will happen, or it won't."

Billie Jean believed, until just before 3 o'clock. Then, in a match that had taken only fifty-six minutes, she was beaten and out of the tournament.

All that was left was to take one last look backward and walk away.

HOLLYWOOD ENDING NOT IN THE SCRIPT

NOVEMBER 18, 1979

And now the game was the thing. Sure, the wine had been good and the sun had been warm and the halftime show exciting. But nobody was thinking about pageantry or tradition now, just victory.

Stanford was heading down the field, inexorably, it seemed, for the touchdown that would end this madness. And the crowd was standing and hollering. And in the huddle Turk Schonert was thinking about getting the job done. And thinking about the future, a future where he would never again be in this stadium, in this uniform, in this situation.

And he was dropping back to pass. And then it was fourth down. And then he was dropping back to pass again. The seconds kept clicking off, the minutes kept clicking off. And Turk Schonert, staying calm while 85,577 spectators at Stanford Stadium could not stay calm, kept throwing or running. And Stanford kept getting closer, ever closer.

But this was not to be a Hollywood ending. This was not to be a fairy tale. No carriage drawn by a team of golden horses was to haul Turk Schonert away. This was reality, defeat, disappointment. This was a fourth-down pass from the one-yard line, a pass one yard from success, a pass that went incomplete.

And now the players from the University of California were leaping wildly and hugging. And now, even though thirty-five seconds remained, the eighty-second Big Game was as final as if the gun had sounded hours previously. And now Cal was a 21-14 winner over Stanford.

Turk Schonert's collegiate career was finished. Like that. The possibility he dreaded had become actuality. There was never to be another pass to Ken Margerum, that most agile of receivers. Never to be another handoff to Vincent White. Never to be another victory.

Certainly there was a record, a statistic that would clutter some record book until it was effaced. Certainly Schonert had completed 148 passes in 221 attempts, 67 percent, in this season, his one season, to break a school record set last year by Steve Dils. But at this moment that was not to be mentioned, even considered. The only thing Turk Schonert could talk about was feeling, emotion that practically had leaped from teammate to teammate. Emotion that had now dissipated.

"It kept coming down to fourth down on that final drive," said Schonert. "And we'd look at each other in the huddle, and someone would say, 'This is it,' and we knew it. We knew this could be the very last time the eleven guys in that huddle would be playing together. We kept going out and getting a first down. We kept going out and doing it."

Until the last time. Until it was fourth and goal on the Cal one-yard line. Then Stanford didn't do it. A mistake. A breakdown. A great maneuver by Cal defender Ron Coccimiglio. One of the above? All of the above? It didn't really matter.

It didn't matter either that hours before, Rod Dowhower, the first-year Stanford coach, told his team that if it came down to this, came down to last-minute hysterics, the Cards would go for the two-point conversion, the victory. It would be win or lose. It wouldn't be a tie.

Dowhower had the play selected. A fake pass to the tight end, and then, in a fitting climax for gutty, determined Turk Schonert, a quarterback sweep into the end zone for two points. But there was to be no conversion attempt. There was to be no touchdown. For Schonert and Stanford there was to be only disappointment.

"Everything kept building and building and building," said Schonert. "I had no doubt we were going to get in the end zone. But then when we didn't get it, well, it was like all the air had been let out of the balloon."

So now the game was long over, maybe an hour, maybe more. And inside the stadium the band played on, serenading several hundred members of the student rooting section who refused to leave, refused to let the day end.

The sun had settled beyond the hills to the west and the sky was growing dark. And Turk Schonert, a beer in hand, was backed up against a white Camaro, talking about the agony of defeat — and the thrill of competition. It is a long way from the stadium to the locker rooms, and Schonert hadn't even started on that way. There had been one interview after another. And then an embrace with his parents and friends.

There would be no victory. But there would be the remark from Cal assistant coach Gunther Cunningham that Turk Schonert is the most competitive quarterback he'd ever seen. And there would be a hint from a reporter that had he gone to another school, Schonert would have had headlines and not just years on the bench behind Guy Benjamin and Steve Dils.

But Schonert didn't want to go anyplace else. He enjoyed the campus, the camaraderie, the institution that is Stanford University just as much as he enjoyed putting on the red-and-white uniform and trying to throw and run.

"I didn't come here just for football," said Turk Schonert. "I love Northern California, the atmosphere, the students, and the relationship with my teammates. I'm going to miss it."

And Stanford is going to miss Turk Schonert, the man, the athlete. "It got emotional out there in the huddle," said Ken Margerum, "but Turk stayed cool. I never knew him when he wasn't."

At the beginning of the season some people were pleading for the removal of Turk Schonert. They wanted freshman John Elway at quarterback. But Dowhower went with his conscience. You can't knock him now. You can't knock Turk Schonert.

"I would have been very disappointed if I hadn't gone the distance today," said Schonert. "When a guy's a senior, I think it's only right to let him have that last game."

Turk Schonert had it. And he came one yard short of keeping it forever.

ADMIRATION VERSUS TRUE LOVE

JULY 7, 1985

WIMBLEDON—She stood alone in a crowd, isolated by her reverie in this noisy temple of sport, once more clutching a runner-up medal and the despondency of failure.

Her opponent, the incomparable and nearly unbeatable Martina Navratilova, paraded about the well-worn grass at Centre Court, hoisting the winner's plate, perhaps as much for personal satisfaction as at the requests of photographers.

Chris Evert-Lloyd would say later that her thoughts at this moment were "unprintable." Surely they were understandable. The scene had been repeated too many times, outtakes from a life story that somehow found their way into the final editing.

With the fans, who shouted approval when the announcer finally paid deference, Chris is surely #1. Yet on the well-trod patch of history, she remains #2.

This year as in years past, Navratilova defeated Evert-Lloyd in the women's singles final at Wimbledon.

Martina wins the tournaments, Chris wins the approval. Nothing could be more clear—or more illogical.

For Martina's fifth victory over Lloyd in five Wimbledon championship matches, for her sixth victory overall in six championship matches, the spectators' response was applause that could be preceded by the adjective restrained.

For Lloyd's quest of what each succeeding time seems more and more an impossible scheme, the fans awarded cheers that carried far beyond the green-ivied walls of the All-England Club.

Everybody loves Chris Evert-Lloyd, who comes across as more woman than athlete. Martina, in contrast, seems more athlete than woman. People may admire Navratilova; they don't love her.

183

Martina did not speak of that deficiency after grinding down Lloyd. She tended to dwell on the positive, her elation, her domination. Nevertheless, in private moments this lack of public adoration becomes a special torture.

"I could never understand it," she said once. "If Chris and I do the same thing, I'll be criticized, and she'll come off smelling like a rose."

Women competitors must make peace with the conventions of femininity. "Rightly or wrongly," said Billie Jean King, the matriarch of tennis, "we're still in the business of beauty."

In a man's game, winning may be the only thing. But when the ladies get on the court or the field, the value system changes. They are expected to be beautiful as well as skilled. They are expected to follow what is considered a normal lifestyle.

Martina was not at all pretty when she arrived at Wimbledon as a teen-ager eleven years ago. Frank Keating of *The Guardian*, one of England's more literate journals, depicted her as a "chirpy, chunky, Czech chick . . . a tubby tomboy with a tomahawk of a left-handed service."

The description of her serve remains true. The rest of the phrase basically is inoperative. She still talks considerably, and, showing her intelligence, in English far superior to that of many native-born Americans. She has dieted her way to what might be called unconventional beauty, looking at times like some European movie star. Her problems would seem to arise from her unconventional ways, a fact emphasized anew when her biography was released last month.

Honesty is hardly the best policy when you're in the limelight. Perhaps as much attention was given yesterday to Navratilova's "friend," Judy Nelson, a ravishing blonde from Texas, as was given Martina.

THE BLACK PRINCE

JULY 7, 1986

WIMBLEDON—He played the match so well, so doggedly, that even in defeat one should admire Ivan Lendl. But he plays the game of life so poorly, with so much bitterness and suspicion, the admiration must be withheld.

He is a great tennis player even in defeat—which was, once more, to be his fate at Wimbledon.

Lendl may never win this oldest of tennis championships. His loss to the effervescent Boris Becker, in straight sets yesterday, 6-0, 6-3, 7-5, came at a time when Ivan was the most dominant man in his sport.

Except on grass. Which means except at Wimbledon.

This should be of little consequence. Sam Snead never won a U.S. Open golf championship. Ernie Banks never even got into a World Series. We don't hold it against their reputations.

The public appreciates winners, but it can accept defeat. One finds it difficult, however, to accept Ivan Lendl.

So he lost to Becker, whose serve is as terrifying as Lendl's stare. Ivan didn't quit. He produced numerous spectacular shots. The guy is something special. As an athlete. Not as a person.

We learn more about an individual in defeat than in victory. This is what we learned about twenty-six-year-old Ivan Lendl: That he is unhappy. That he is obsessed. That he makes the worst of everything.

Grace. Ivan Lendl doesn't have it. He has a devastating forehand and superb footwork. But Ivan Lendl is graceless. Not to mention cheerless.

If there is one thing more important at Wimbledon than tennis, it is tradition. The tradition at Wimbledon is that, after each match on Centre Court, winner and loser, sportsmen both, leave together.

Not yesterday. Not after the men's finals. Becker, properly elated following a second-straight men's championship, paraded about the arena and displayed the gold trophy. It was custom.

Lendl glowered at his runner-up award and then, inexplicably, departed, heading for the shadows. Good-bye, black prince.

Later, Ivan the Terrible arrived at the press interview. Question. Answer. Question. Answer. Lendl was doing quite well, thank you, holding his distrust, belying his image. Had defeat made him a better man? Hardly.

A journalist asked Ivan to describe Becker "as a person," a harmless request. Not to Lendl.

"I don't know Boris as a person," said Ivan. Fine. An honest reply.

"I don't know how to describe him because I would probably be very inaccurate. I don't know the man—young man, boy, whatever you want to call him. Call him champion."

Wonderful, Ivan. Poignant. Memorable. Stop there, while you're ahead, while you can walk out with respect.

That's impossible for Ivan Lendl. Why? Is it thoughts of his childhood without a childhood in Czechoslovakia? Is it his fear of failure? Is it his inability to enjoy other victories of a career that has not been unimpressive?

Lendl wouldn't stop. Wouldn't let go.

"It would be very unfair for me to judge him, not knowing him. You journalists are good at it. You don't know him, either. But you do it anyway."

And Ivan was gone. To sulk. To hide behind the walls of his Connecticut mansion with six killer dogs. To prepare for the U.S. Open, where the surface is cement and a big serve is a smaller weapon.

Lendl plays with a haunted look of anxiety. On his sleeve he wears not his heart but a patch advertising Avis, which on this day was appropriate. The company always advertises itself as #2.

Ivan is #1. In the pro-tennis computer rankings. On courts and in stadiums throughout the world. But not in England. Not at Wimbledon. Not at the biggest tournament of them all.

"To be the best player in the world," Ivan Lendl said when someone asked the inevitable question, "you have to play very consistently over twelve months. You have to win on every surface, not just one.

"Boris Becker won today. There is no question about it. For

186

the second time in a row. But I'm still not prepared to give up the title or whatever you want to call it."

Lendl won't give up. Lendl won't give in. But under duress he gives an utterly convincing imitation of a cornered rat.

He is so skilled. So successful. So unloved.

"I'm disappointed and tired at the moment," sighed Ivan Lendl. "Maybe by this time next year I can play better. I don't know."

Maybe next year he'll be a better person. That would be wonderful.

That would be impossible.

THE SAME OLD STORY

OCTOBER 26, 1986

NEW YORK—Fate kicked the Boston Red Sox in the teeth once again. They are a Greek tragedy in double knits, a baseball version of Murphy's Law.

They were one out from winning the 1986 World Series, and then they were in shock.

New England can put away the plans and pick up the sackcloth, because, among other things, Bill Buckner, a sure fielder, couldn't pick up a ground ball.

Red Sox fans are fatalists. Now we know why. Boston isn't a team, it's a malediction.

Somebody in Salem put the Red Sox under a spell years ago, but instead of turning into a frog they turned into a nuisance.

There's no way the Sox could have lost to the New York Mets Saturday night in game six of the World Series. But lose they did.

The night the nation turned back its clocks one hour, we were convinced the Red Sox had turned theirs back sixty-eight years— the last time they won a World Series. Rather they turned back into flawed heroes.

Boston was ahead, 5-3, bottom of the tenth, two Mets out, nobody on. Don't start the celebration without us.

A hit by Gary Carter, a hit by Kevin Mitchell, a hit by Ray Knight, a wild pitch by Bob Stanley, and then, gawd almighty, an error by Buckner on a dribbler down the first-base line that was moving at the speed of the average tortoise.

A hundred times out of a hundred Buckner would have picked up the ball. But this was the 101st.

"Anything can happen," said Buckner. "That's what makes it a great game. I was playing extra deep, and he dribbled it down the line. It was bouncing, and bouncing, then it didn't bounce, it just skipped."

This was the old curse in new form.

This was Johnny Pesky clutching the ball in 1946 as Enos Slaughter scored the winning run. This was Jim Lonborg trying to go on two days' rest in 1967. This was Bill Lee throwing a blooper that Tony Perez hit for a homer in 1975. This was the Boston Red Sox drinking hemlock when they should have been drinking champagne.

This was the Mets winning, 6-5, at 12:29 A.M., after four hours and two minutes of bewildering and tantalizing baseball and sending the Series to a seventh game.

For five previous games the Series of 1986 was as lifeless as week-old beer. The team that got ahead stayed ahead. There were no rallies and very few cheers. Then came game six.

All the drama of an entire World Series was distilled into one marvelous evening of emotion and erratic play.

Boston's best pitcher, Roger Clemens, couldn't hold a lead and eventually Boston's last pitcher, Bob Stanley, couldn't hold the ball, throwing the wild pitch that in the tenth permitted the tying run to score.

Poor Stanley, maligned by the fans for years for his frequent sins on the mound. Poor Red Sox, taunted once more with thoughts of what might have been.

"That was my dream," sighed Stanley, "to be out there when the final out was recorded and we won the World Series. But it didn't work out that way. I just let the ball get away a little inside. It just happened."

It just always happens to Boston. A manager makes the wrong move. A player makes a mistake. It's tradition. It's terrible.

Red Sox manager John McNamara Saturday night pinch-hit Mike Greenwell for Clemens in the eighth with the Red Sox up, 3-2, and Greenwell struck out.

But later in the same inning, with two out and the bases loaded, McNamara permitted the sore-footed Buckner, a lefty, to bat against Jesse Orosco, a lefty, instead of bringing in Don Baylor. Buckner flied out.

Then, in the bottom of the eighth, Clemens's replacement, Calvin Schiraldi, gave up a single, made a bad throw to second on a force, and permitted the Mets to tie the game, 3-3.

Earlier, Dwight Evans, a great fielder, flubbed a bouncing ball in right field. And, finally, Buckner, a great fielder, flubbed a trickling ball to first.

It was Chinese water torture all over again. It was a classic Red Sox collapse.

"What are we going to do, cry out about it?" asked Evans. "Give the Mets credit. They came back. We got a bit of our own medicine. You hear again and again: It's never over."

He was talking about the game. He could have been talking about Red Sox agony. About the World Series Boston has lost since the end of World War II. About that fourteen-game lead Boston squandered the final weeks in 1978.

McNamara, the quiet, proud man who has managed the Red Sox to the jagged edge of success, would not be bothered with the past—whether it was a few hours or many years. "I don't know nothing about history," snapped McNamara, "and I don't want to hear anything about choking or any of that crap."

But he will hear. He will be reminded the jinx is still about, that to be a Red Sox fan is to step once more into the breach.

"This game was as close as we could come to winning," said McNamara. "We needed one out and didn't do it."

In Boston that's a story as old as the one about the midnight ride of Paul Revere.

BIGGER GOALS
FOR GIANTS

OCTOBER 15, 1987

ST. LOUIS—"Oh, somewhere men are laughing, and somewhere children shout . . . . "

Outside, on Walnut Street, the cacophony of automobile horns and human shouts reflected a city's unfettered excitement. The St. Louis Cardinals had won the pennant.

"But there is no joy in Mudville . . . . "

And the San Francisco Giants had lost it.

Died with their boots on. Or, as one imaginative journalist suggested, left their *art* in San Francisco.

The Humm Baby has settled down for a long winter's nap. And we are left with thoughts of what might have been.

But baseball, like love, means never having to say you're sorry. And the Giants, in their reverie, needed make no apologies.

"The long season," they call it, day after day, week after week, month after month. And then it is over, severed by defeat, tinged by disappointment, dashed by unrealized dreams.

But this 1987 Giants season that came to an abrupt end Wednesday evening beneath the rockets' red glare, the booming fireworks of the Cardinals' victory celebration, was one of greatness, not sadness.

Oh, two times zones to the west, by the shores of San Francisco Bay, disbelief must have been the standard response. Expectation had been whirled into dejection. The Giants had gone two entire games without a run. And now they would go into oblivion.

But progress must be measured not only in where you finish, but the distance you've traveled.

When the Cardinals defeated San Francisco, 6-0, Wednesday evening to take the National League Championship Series, four games to three, the tendency was to think only of the moment, of a pennant squandered.

Rather, the emphasis should be on the accomplishment, not the failure.

Two years ago, the Giants may have been the worst team in baseball, a 100-game loser with no future. Now, they are among the four best. And they'll get better.

Give them two years. They'll be in the World Series. The Detroit Tigers, who won more regular-season games than any team in baseball, could only last five with the Twins in the American League play-offs.

But the Giants, young, inexperienced, playing four games in the hatred and hysteria of Busch Stadium, still carried the National League series to the limit. And even led, three games to two.

Naturally the clubhouse scene was depressing, as various players, many still in their road grays, sat silently. After 162 regular-season games and seven play-off games, few could accept the reality that tomorrow wouldn't come.

The Domaine Chandon sparkling wine that had been carried in the cargo hold of their United Airlines charter Sunday evening would not be opened in celebration, but given away.

The Giants drank only some of Augie Busch's brew, not quite drowning their sorrows but quenching a literal thirst while the thirst of victory could not be slaked.

"We hurt," conceded Chili Davis. "But I know all the fans hurt more.

"I'm not known for being too considerate about fans," he said with a sardonic smile, alluding to his criticism of them in 1986, "but I feel sorry for the fans. And Bob Lurie, Al Rosen, and Roger Craig.

"I don't feel angry. I feel like my wife-to-be left me at the altar and ran away with another guy."

And then Chili ruminated the way so many Giants fans will when the days grow short and the memories grow painful: "The door was open. All we had to do was step in."

They couldn't get over the threshold.

The Cardinals, calling down the echoes, used their experience and subtle skills. And some marvelous pitching by first John Tudor and next Danny Cox.

And the Giants had been shut out twice. And the next flight would be not to the Metrodome, for World Series game one against the Twins, but back to San Francisco.

"We've got nothing to be ashamed of," reminded Giants

manager Roger Craig. "Not many people thought we would get this far."

Not at all. Only they didn't quite go far enough, which is the reason St. Louis is that somewhere men are laughing and children shout.

In San Francisco it's time to think of 1988.

INDOOR HORRORS

OCTOBER 18, 1987

MINNEAPOLIS—The St. Louis Cardinals got stuck where the sun doesn't shine. They thought they were going to the World Series. Instead it was a little shop of horrors.

The first Series game in history to be played under a ceiling, the billowy roof of the Hubert H. Humphrey Metrodome, was a great example of why baseball was not meant to be played in the great indoors.

Also why the San Francisco Giants should have been here instead of the Cardinals.

The Minnesota Twins beat the Cardinals, 10-1, Saturday night to take a 1-0 lead in a Series that may set a record for high decibel levels and higher earned-run averages.

The Twins are a bunch of no-names. Actually no-vowels, if you think about people like Gagne and Hrbek. This team is a credit to anonymity. And the miracles of science.

Unlike baseball's other domes, the Astro and the King, the roof of the Metrodome is Teflon-coated fiberglass kept aloft by powerful blowers.

Unlike baseball's other teams, the Twins are kept aloft by fans who can rival a jet engine for noise.

The focus of this eighty-fourth World Series is big, immobile, and white. No, it's not one of Mike Tyson's sparring opponents, but a stadium, where players have a hard time following a fly ball against maybe the worst background in the game.

Twice Saturday night the Cardinal outfield did its impression of old ladies swatting at gnats in a meadow.

Isaac Newton told us what goes up must come down. Vince Coleman showed us what comes down will probably fall for a bloop double.

Over the seasons, with great moments for the Babe, Willie, and DiMaggio, the World Series has been labeled the Fall Classic.

But this year the climax to the baseball season may be a classic fall.

One of the highlights of this opening game was the Cardinals starting a rookie pitcher, Joe Magrane, who used earplugs so he wouldn't be bothered by the din in the dome.

It turns out he should have tried a blindfold.

Magrane was taken out in the bottom of the fourth after giving up four consecutive hits and a walk. In came Bob Forsch. Out went the baseball.

Dan Gladden, the man for whom the Giants couldn't find a spot, trading him to Minnesota during the spring, found a spot about fifteen rows deep in the bleachers.

It was the first World Series grand-slam homer in seventeen years. Move aside, Reggie.

Watching from an area just behind home plate were Giants president Al Rosen, who dealt Gladden for a handful of colored beans and three minor leaguers, and Giants owner Bob Lurie.

Watching from the pitching mound was Forsch, who subsequently gave up another homer, this one to Steve Lombardozzi—whoever he is—and thereby kept intact his postseason earned-run average of twelve.

Someone had the temerity to ask Cardinals manager Whitey Herzog what was wrong with Forsch.

Herzog had the temerity to ask Cardinal manager Whitey Herzog what was wrong with Forsch.

Herzog had the clarity to respond, "I don't know."

That's the response you get from some people when you ask how the Cardinals arrived here—and no, smart alecks, don't answer, "By jet plane."

The Giants, of course, should have beaten the Cardinals in the National League play-offs after leading three games to two.

But San Francisco scored one fewer run in the final two games of that series than St. Louis scored in the first game of this.

So the Cardinals win the National League and get the dubious honor of appearing in a place that from the outside looks like a loaf of freshly baked bread and from the inside sounds like a room full of angry Doberman pinschers.

"I don't want to blame the dome for losing the ball game," contended Herzog, a stand-up guy. "They just beat us. A good old-fashioned ass-kicking. That's all that is. But I'll say this. The place is loud."

And the Twins are hot. They've got the citizens up here almost as excited as at the opening of walleyed-pike season.

The Cardinals, fortunately, only have to play one more game here before heading home. Don't bet they'll be back. As if anyone in his right mind would want to return.

Minnesota: Land of 10,000 lakes and one domed stadium where the Twins and chaos reign.

THE HEARTBREAK KIDS

FEBRUARY 19, 1988

CALGARY—The disasters piled one upon the other Thursday in surrealistic fashion, sad songs of human drama that make victory and defeat only trifles.

In the morning, the best of America's female alpine racers, Pam Fletcher, broke her right leg in the most bizarre of ski accidents, colliding with a course worker nearly two hours before scheduled race time.

Half a day and sixty miles away, the kid whose grief and misfortune touched the world, Dan Jansen, once more crashed to the ice during another speed-skating race, the men's 1,000 meters.

And all you could ask was, "Why?"

Why them? Why these two young athletes who had given their blood and sweat? Why were they rewarded with tears?

Why, when there is so much evil in the world, do two good kids get trashed by fate?

It's a given that life isn't fair. But how unfair does it have to be?

Why should twenty-five-year-old Pam Fletcher end up crying and cursing as they haul her off to a hospital? Why should twenty-two-year-old Dan Jansen end up sprawled on the ice of a skating oval as the race goes on without him?

Fletcher was so confident, so sure. She had won the U.S. National downhill a few days earlier. She was going to upset the field, stun the experts. But she never got the chance.

Jansen was not quite as certain. He's the best sprint skater in America. But his life has been turned upside down. Probably he shouldn't even have been competing. Still he showed an athlete's courage.

These have hardly been momentous Olympic Games for the United States. We're losing in hockey, in speed skating, in skiing, and in practically everything else where you slide on snow or glide on ice. Yet the Fletchers and Jansens refused to concede. They gave their bodies. We should offer them our hearts.

Sunday it was when Jansen learned of the death of his older sister, Jane Beres, from leukemia. He went out in the 500-meter race, winner of the world championship earlier in the month, leaped from the starting line—and splashed to the ice on the first turn.

Panegyrics were numerous. The tale wrenched our souls. We were reminded again of the frailty of life and the insignificance of the games people play.

Still, that doesn't mean you stop playing. And Dan Jansen, in a sport Americans barely understand and rarely appreciate, came back to try once more.

And we were given the most ironic of promises by his coach, Mike Crowe of the U.S. skating team: "Dan won't let it happen again."

Past the halfway point of his race Thursday evening, Crowe seemed vindicated and Jansen seemed triumphant. He was in the fourth twosome of the competition. And his splits at 200, 400, and 600 meters were the fastest of the night. And the crowd was screaming. And Jansen fell. Again.

"Oh, no." A thousand voices cried out in unison. Oh, yes. It couldn't happen again. Mike Crowe said it couldn't. But it did. And you winced and cursed silently. And a teammate walked over and embraced Jansen. And we knew there was no justice.

In the December 1987 issue of the *Olympian,* the glossy magazine published by the U.S. Olympic Committee, are articles on America's top prospects. One after another, back-to-back, there they are: A story on Jansen and teammate Nick Thometz followed by a story on Pam Fletcher. Fate is a lonely hunter.

Jansen showed up for a postrace press conference while the crowd cheered the medal winners, all from Eastern Bloc nations.

First was Nikolai Gouliaev of the Soviet Union, second Jens-Uwe Mey of East Germany, third Igor Gelezovsky of the Soviet Union. While they received cheers, Jansen got questions.

"I'm leaving tonight to spend the weekend with my family," said Jansen. "I'm not sure what I thought at the moment. I can't remember.

"You train so hard and you don't even finish a race. But what happened in the past week has put everything in perspective. I don't feel as bad as I would have.

"I've had so much support all week, from friends and family and people I don't even know. From people throughout the world, and the United States and Canada. It's really helped a lot. They told me how proud they were for me to go out and do my best. It lifted my spirits."

You lifted our spirits, Dan. You and Pam Fletcher and the other kids who gave it their ultimate and got little back.

A TRIUMPH OF SPIRIT, NOT SKILL

FEBRUARY 29, 1988

CALGARY—And so the flame is extinguished, the flag is pulled down, and the captains and the kings and the figure skaters depart. Good-bye to the Land of Oz and the Province of Alberta.

UNTIL WE MEET AGAIN, said the signs in languages from Danish to Spanish. But if and when we do, the circumstances will be different. And the protagonists will have changed.

The Olympic Games now is too commercial, another prime-time miniseries, seemingly designed to sell American cars and the East German political system.

But the Olympics is also wonderful, two weeks of small triumphs and big disappointments that put the rest of life in perspective.

The closing ceremonies Sunday night were the usual blend of joy and sadness, athletes carrying candles and rapt smiles as they marched into McMahon Stadium wearing eclectic apparel ranging from cowboy hats to blankets.

This was their last hurrah. The moments can never be recaptured.

The great shame of any Olympics, winter or summer, is that most of the world experiences it from a nineteen-inch screen.

In Moscow, U.S.S.R., or Moscow, Idaho, the viewer sees what the director would have him see, skiers tumbling on a mountain or skaters stumbling on a turn.

And yet the XV Winter Olympics, which came to the traditional end with memories of yesterday and thoughts of tomorrow, was so much more than a test of athletes or a quest for medals.

It was a brief victory for a troubled world, a window of time in which the door to the Tass office may never have been open, but hearts, even of Soviet journalists, always were.

"You know something about biathlon?" someone wearing a

"You know something about biathlon?" someone wearing a parka with CCCP asked yours truly. "At home I do speed skating."

"No," the Soviet was told, "but I can tell you about baseball . . . . "

This was an occasion when people could gather and appreciate bobsledders from Jamaica and a ski jumper from England, when a skater from China climbed aboard a horse for the first time, when royalty could walk through downtown and demand no special privilege.

Calgary ain't Paris. Under a blanket of snow there may be an imagined charm. But when the warm wind, the chinook, burnished the prairie, we were left with superficial ugliness, barren trees, and brown fields.

Beauty, they say, is in the eye of the beholder, and no one was more beautiful than the good citizens of Calgary, honest, gracious, who gave their best even when the competitors did their worst.

There was no singular hero in these Winter Games, although speed skater Yvonne van Gennip of the Netherlands and ski jumper Matti Nykanen of Finland departed with three golds each. There was no Eric Heiden or Olga Korbut or Carl Lewis.

The Calgary Games, then, belonged to us all. To Eddie Edwards, the British ski jumper who can barely clear his throat, and to the Greek and Cypriot slalom skiers who could never get around the poles.

Canadians get chided by their neighbors to the south. "Adam was a Canadian," goes the line, "because who else would stand in a tropical garden with a naked woman and talk about an apple?"

But, oh, Canada, you did a fine job on this one, extending a welcome that swept away the usual hassles when people from more than fifty countries bring their egos and eccentricities.

One weekend the Canadians were dejected because one of them, Brian Orser, finished second in men's figure skating. The following weekend the Canadians were elated because one of them, Liz Manley, finished second in women's figure skating.

"If it ain't Alberta, it ain't beef" is an advertising slogan on more than a few billboards. Calgary had a steak in our future. How can you dislike a town where the food and the people are both of high quality?

There's pressure in the Olympics. Sadly, Debi Thomas was

crushed beneath it. There's pleasure in the Olympics. Debi goes back to reality with a bronze medal, and how many Americans— or Bulgarians—will have one of those to cherish?

America didn't do as well as the U.S.A. or ABC would have hoped. Not since the 1936 Winter Olympics have we gained as few medals as the six of 1988.

Still, our kids did themselves proud as humans if not as athletes. They may have fallen down on the slopes or the ovals, but they accepted their fate without a whimper.

"I have no excuses," Debi Thomas explained. Neither did the other entrants. They lost, they lost. It was time to start training for 1992.

The scene that will be remembered from these two weeks of midnight dinners and postponed ski jumps was of Bonnie Blair, the little lady from Illinois, gliding around the track to cool down after winning the women's 500-meter speed-skating gold.

Her two rivals, both from East Germany, Karin Enke Kania and Christa Rothenburger, skated along and, one after another, embraced her. They, most of all, knew what she had accomplished.

What the XV Winter Olympics accomplished was to bring East and West together for two weeks of friendship and laughter. Who can find fault with that?

The I's Have It

DOWN, BUT NOT OUT

MAY 18, 1987

The *Examiner* Bay to Breakers has my number. Or maybe Howard Street does. One thing is certain. I don't have it. But I do have two bloody knees and a sore back.

Nobody told me running was a contact sport. Most years when I finish this race I think I should see a psychologist. This time I needed a general practitioner.

I knew it was going to be a bad day when I took the escalator to the second floor of the Hyatt Regency down there at the Embarcadero, went to the men's room, and it was locked. Way to go, Hyatt people. Just don't stop by my home and ask to use the bathroom.

I should have asked to use some shoulder pads and a helmet from the 49ers, several of whom were standing with me in the seeded section a few minutes before the start. There was Ray Wersching, jogging soccer style. And Tom Holmoe, ready to play defense against 100,000 people prepared to run a trap up the middle.

I was right at the front Sunday, maybe two feet behind Rod Dixon. And we were off and, well . . . he was running. For me, *falling* is the appropriate word. I took a couple of strides and the next thing I knew, I was tumbling faster than the Giants. And it's not even June.

Was it Henry Kissinger who warned us about the domino theory? Or was it Henry Rono? Or John Henry, the horse? I should have listened.

Somebody shoved, somebody stumbled, and, splat, I was stretched on the pavement with seemingly everybody else crashing down upon me. Chicken Little was right. The sky was falling. Help!

I lay there for what seemed an eternity while dozens of people used my sacroiliac for a pathway. The Aggie Track Club centipede dropped in, you should pardon the expression. By the time those runners got going again, they had no chance to win.

Neither did I, of course. But I never expected to. Then again, I didn't expect to be involved in an experiment in terror.

By the time I regained my feet and my senses, I had lost maybe a minute and a half, and, more significantly, the number, 212, from the front of my T-shirt. But I wasn't going back to retrieve it. I may be stupid, but I'm not crazy.

Uhm . . . strike that last independent clause. Dripping more blood than Dracula after a midnight feed, I ran the entire seven and a half miles. My time was fifty-seven minutes forty-five seconds, but don't look for it in the results.

An officious sort at the chute on Great Highway wouldn't take my name.

"Hey, I got run over, and my number got torn off," I panted.

"Tough luck, buddy," he sneered. "Rosie Ruiz tried that line in New York a few years ago. I know a phony when I see one."

"But," I protested, "I write a column for one of the San Francisco papers."

"Get out of here," he sneered. "You don't look anything like Herb Caen."

I don't think Herb competed, but I can't be sure. Hobbling up the Hayes Street Hill, I saw someone wearing a sign that read, WILKES SPORTS, WILKES BASHFORD.

Could it have been a worker in the city assessor's office?

Although the Bay to Breakers is an *Examiner* promotion, that doesn't prevent employees of the *Chronicle* from entering.

One of that paper's sportswriters, Ira Miller, was someplace in the rat pack. He complained later it took him almost as long to get to the starting line, twenty-nine minutes, as it did to run the last three and a half miles.

Journalists never have a nice thing to say.

The T-shirts of the runners, as usual, said plenty. REAGAN KNEW was one of the more cryptic messages. Knew what? Not to fall at the start of the Bay to Breakers?

One entrant knew something else. He had hired a limo to wait for him at the corner of Lincoln and Great Highway. Of course, if he were really smart, he would have *taken* the limo to Lincoln and Great Highway.

There seemed to be an abundance of Chicago Cubs

paraphernalia along the route. One woman, in fact, waved a 1984 National League Eastern Division championship pennant. Did she think this was the victory parade?

I didn't. And because I didn't have a number, I couldn't get a victory Bay to Breakers T-shirt with the words, "I Survived."

And I did survive. Anyone have some Band-Aids?

CHASING PAR IN ASIA

MAY 30, 1986

Did the sayings of Chairman Mao allude to double bogeys? Can a country once worried about five-year plans find satisfaction from five-iron shots?

There I was, inside the People's Republic but outside the fairway. The site was Chung Shan Hot Spring Golf Club, where the distances are in meters and the advice from caddies is in English. But who would want to say "fore" in Mandarin?

Opened in 1984, Chung Shan was the first course on the mainland since the Communists took control in 1949.

Five courses then in existence were turned into rice paddies. Now, in an experiment in capitalism, rice paddies are being transformed into golf courses. Three are completed. Three more are under construction.

Nestled against the lower slopes of the Laoshanwei Hills, the Chung Shan is indistinguishable from other courses throughout the world—eighteen holes, water hazards, doglegs. The setting, however, is plenty distinguishable.

Peasant women in conical straw hats tend fairways by hand. Not far away, water buffalo haul wooden plows through flooded rice fields. In the distance a steam engine puffs away at a lumber mill. Could this be the Great Leap Forward?

Hong Kong tycoon Henry Fok financed Chung Shan. Arnold Palmer helped design it. For the nonce, very few play it, with the exception of weekends when several dozen Japanese businessmen make the seventy-mile drive from Canton.

The clubhouse is gray stone with a red tile roof. The ambiance is American. On the walls of the pro shop are photos of Palmer and Nicklaus and advertisements for Titleist and Spalding.

Did Confucius say the longest journey starts with a single step? Ours began with a ride on the Star Ferry from Kowloon, at seven cents U.S. currency for the ten-minute trip to Hong Kong perhaps the best value in the world.

Two sportswriters, Ira Miller and myself, had been invited to make a cultural exchange. Also innumerable bad shots. We had our visas. And our American Express cards, which, yes, are accepted in China.

From Hong Kong, it was a fifty-five-minute hydrofoil ride to Macao, the Portuguese colony that is not more than a pimple on the great dragon of China. After a passport check, we took a Mercedes limo for the five-minute trip to the border.

The customs building was gray, dull, and bleak, with primitive plumbing and uncovered wiring. A glum nurse sat beside a smiling inspector, who kept confusing me with Tom Selleck. I'll just have to shave the mustache.

Once into China, the guy at the wheel of the Mercedes made the best move of the day. Without blinking, he switched the vehicle from the left side of the road, where they drive in Macao and Hong Kong, to the right, where they drive in China.

Not for him that bumper sticker: "If you think I'm a lousy driver you ought to see the way I putt."

China is making progress. Slowly. The forty-minute ride from the border to Chung Shan is also a trip into the past. The road is under construction. Water buffalo are in abundance. So are bikes and pedestrians and tin-walled shacks. Some day there will be modern, high-rise buildings to greet the tourist, but not now.

To greet us in Macao and share the ride was Aylwin Y.C. Tai, a native of Hong Kong and the course general manager. We were not surprised he spoke our language. He was educated in our country at UNLV. Tark the Shark will recruit everywhere.

"To get the job I had to learn to play golf," laughed Tai. "I'm not very good, a fifteen handicap." The two sixteen-handicappers in the car smiled inscrutably.

Caddies were waiting. They were two of the eighteen teenagers selected by Chung Shan pro Peter Tang, also of Hong Kong, to become China's first native golfers in forty-five years.

Eight months ago none had seen a golf ball. Now some are shooting in the seventies. Twenty other young Chinese have been sent to Japan to learn. "The game will grow," said Tai, "when the people here start playing themselves."

Our scores grew immediately. Rented clubs, street shoes, and, alas, a rainstorm. We had excuses. We needed them. Could I take that last tee shot over? A water buffalo snorted in the valley.

For sixteen holes, the day was a disaster. On the seventeenth, a charming par-three alongside a pond full of water lilies, I finally parred Asia.

Was the trip worthwhile? Indeed. My score was terrible, but how many people are privileged to begin a conversation, "The day I played golf in China . . . . "

A SLICE
OF SWISS

So there I stood near the top of the Lauberhorn in Grindelwald, Switzerland, knees as weak as the dollar. Like life after forty, skiing is all downhill. And just as frustrating.

This is the land of the giants. Talk about your peaks and valleys. Nobody around here stays on the level.

Think of Switzerland and you think of cold efficiency and hot fondue. There are glaciers on the ridges and glacial expressions on the faces, men to match those mountains, as it were.

Grindelwald is a town as quaint as it sounds, with a lot of weather-beaten wooden homes and well-organized hotel managers. The place became famous as the starting point for expeditions up the Eiger, which is a block of granite as imposing as the price of a good meal, or in these days of a declining U.S. economy even a bad one.

In March any male citizen of the United States is supposed to be thinking of baseball. And so I was, even across the ocean and above the clouds in the Alps.

"Have the A's signed José Canseco?" I asked Urs Hauser, the multilingual, single-minded director of the Hotel Belvedere. But Urs, whose family has owned the place since the beginning of the century, didn't know the A's from a sitzmark, which is a hole in the snow.

The three massive peaks, the Eiger, Mönch and Jungfrau, each above 13,000 feet, seem to poke holes in the sky. The North Face of the Eiger gave its name to a clothing company and rise to all sorts of terrifying stories.

Numerous men died trying to conquer the sheer rock wall, including, say the natives, a pair of Korean climbers who last fall were some 200 feet from the summit when a storm swept in. The two disappeared and may never be found.

Such sobering items figuratively dim the view even on a sparkling afternoon when from the groomed areas at Kleine Scheidegg, hard below the North Face, you can see practically forever. And ski about the same distance.

From top to bottom, it's more than four miles of winter wonderland. The only things that stop you are aching thigh muscles and the enticement of a beer or a wurst at numerous inns on the way down.

This may not be the best place in the world to ski, but it will do. You take a twenty-five-minute train ride to the skiing summit and then take your time cruising down.

A real snow job, and no experts need apply. The runs are gradual. Only the prices are steep. At the current rate of exchange, it's remarkable Oliver North could afford to open a Swiss bank account for the Contras.

The Swiss, on the other hand, can afford to be magnanimous. When they're not making money, they're making tracks down a mountain. Everybody skis, from babies to old ladies. Doesn't anyone stay at home making cuckoo clocks anymore? Switzerland is the residence of the best skiers on the globe, starting with a man named Pirmin Zurbriggen, who is to the sport what Don Mattingly is to baseball.

"What else is there to do in winter here?" asked a young man in English clearer than anyone in Mississippi has ever spoken. "You either learn to ski or you move to Spain."

From Kleine Scheidegg, the tophill terminus of the railway, you can move on skis either toward Grindelwald or Wengen down the other side of the mountain. That's where Mary's Restaurant is located at the bottom of a run. On a sunny afternoon, skis and skiers invariably are stacked outside Mary's, where a small bottle of beer is $2 and the jokes are free. Paradise? Not quite. Europeans, for all their virtues, unfortunately have never learned the value of queueing up properly. Pushing and shoving are endemic to the Continent, even in lift lines. That plays hell with your skis, not to mention your disposition.

The only solution would be to respond Teddy Roosevelt style: Get out of your skis, then walk softly and carry those big sticks.

FROM THE
HORSE'S EYE

APRIL 15, 1982

I now understand what my sports editor, Charles Cooper, meant when he suggested I would see eye-to-eye with a colt named Cassaleria, who's entered in the California Derby this Saturday at Golden Gate Fields.

I mean, between us, Cass and myself would only need one pair of glasses, that is if horses could wear glasses.

Neither of us moves to the left very well; we don't see to the left at all. We'd spend more time drifting right than Ronald Reagan.

We'd make a great team if someone decided to hold a race at night without lights. Or if I ever learn to ride. I wonder if they've ever auditioned a horse and sportswriter for a Hathaway ad?

Cassaleria and I have more in common than a lack of binocular vision. We both are claustrophobic. I break out into a cold sweat when I walk down a dark hallway or sit in the back seat of a Volkswagen. Cassaleria can't handle a stall without windows.

Everywhere he goes, including Golden Gate Fields where we discussed ophthalmologists yesterday, Cass stays in a special pen, open on all sides.

"He was what we call a stall walker," said trainer Ron McAnally. "It's not a unique problem, but we couldn't stop him from moving around.

"We tried a live sheep to calm him, and that worked for a while, but then he practically stomped the sheep. We put bales of hay in the stall, but he knocked them over. We hung a ball from the beam. That didn't work. Finally, we took him outside."

For me it was easier. I bought a car with a sunroof.

Cassaleria (pronounced Cass-ah-LAIR-ee-ah) has done something with his career. Here he is, only three years old, with a physical handicap of some significance, and Cassaleria has won more that $300,000. In eleven races, he's finished third or better ten times.

The exception occurred a few days ago in the Santa Anita Derby. Cassaleria was practically mugged coming into the home stretch. He backed away from the jostling and came in sixth, which is out of the money even if you have dementia praecox.

Foaled in Kentucky, where the colt may possibly return the beginning of May for a rather large race known as the Derby, Cassaleria scraped the left side of his head against a board when only a few days old and damaged what then was a good eye. The eye had to be removed by a veterinarian.

The name Cassaleria was provided by the sister-in-law of breeder Jim Brady. According to one report the name refers to a flower that, when it blooms, gives the appearance of an eye. The story, even if fictional, makes the colt even more intriguing.

Horseplayers, you see, do have a certain amount of compassion for animals. They may not lavish a great deal of emotion on some plater who runs up the track, but equines such as Silky Sullivan and Seattle Slew had their own fan clubs.

Cassaleria has developed his own particular following, led by McAnally, who also trains the great horse John Henry. McAnally originally felt sorry for Cassaleria. Now he feels only admiration.

"When he first arrived in California," said McAnally, whose training facilities are near Temecula in San Diego County, "I thought, 'You poor devil, you've got to go through all the wars of racing, and you've got this handicap.' And what if something happened to his good eye.

"But now I have a real soft spot for him. I think others do too. Everybody likes an underdog."

Everybody also likes a winner. That's what Cassaleria was in the $136,000 El Camino Real Derby last February at Bay Meadows. Lagging ten lengths off the pace, the horse, ridden by Darrel McHargue, who will be his jockey Saturday in the Cal Derby, made his move. It was as if he had tried to ride through a brick wall.

"It got rough," recalls McHargue. No rougher than The Charge of the Light Brigade. To hear reports, a racing writer couldn't have described the situation as well as Alfred Lord Tennyson. There has been less action in a demolition derby.

A horse named Speed Broker ducked out from the inside,

crashed into Cassaleria and lurched broadside. Cassaleria nearly turned sideways to escape, and another entrant, Domiant Roni, was jolted out of contention.

You figured Cassaleria would be lucky to stay upright, much less finish. But he came on in the final seventy yards to pass two other horses and win by half a length. According to Bob Wuerth, the publicity man at Bay Meadows, there has been more demand for film of that race than almost any movie this side of *Chariots of Fire*.

Said McHargue, in a quote not soon to be forgotten, "He showed a lot of guts for a one-eye horse." It wouldn't have been a bad performance for a horse with two eyes, either.

Journalists without a left eye prefer to keep people to their right. But horses seemingly like it better the other way around.

Going in the counterclockwise direction of U.S. tracks, Cassaleria, of course, has his bad side to the rail, or inside. But he runs best outside.

"It's true he doesn't see horses inside him," said McAnally, "but this way he doesn't get dirt kicked in his good eye either.

Life is not easy for a one-eyed racehorse.

KING OF THE HIGH 'CEES'

MARCH 5, 1981

CASA GRANDE, Arizona—"Cee" basketball is what they called it, a game for squirts, for runts, for guys who stopped growing but didn't stop dreaming.

It was competition and gratification and for most of us a verification that our athletic careers were nearing an end if not already there.

For most of us, but not for Don Buford. For Don Buford, "Little Donnie" Buford as we called him, Cee basketball—which was down at the end of the ladder from varsity and JV and even Bee—was only the beginning. Skill and talent will out.

Now it is 1981, and Don Buford, five-foot-seven Don Buford, a new coach on the San Francisco Giants, is a bit pudgy and graying and forty-four years old. But in the mind's eye, he is sixteen and slender and my teammate on the Cee basketball team at Dorsey High School in Los Angeles.

Twenty-eight years have passed, and here we are once more, brought by who-knows-what-fate along circuitous routes to be reunited at the Giants training camp. As kids we were so outrageous as to imagine ourselves as sports heroes. Fortunately, one of us made it, Don Buford.

He was a talent, you could sense it then no matter the limitation of his height. He was voted the top athlete as a ninth grader at Mount Vernon Junior High.

The rest of us were just pretenders, kids who belonged on the same floor as Buford only because we had the same misfortune to be short.

The delineation came quickly enough. For most of us, the most that could be achieved was a seat on the bench in the next classification, the Bees. For Don Buford came places in the starting lineup on the varsity football and baseball teams and an opportunity to run the low hurdles in varsity track.

215

Our days as jocks were concluding. Buford's were just beginning. From Dorsey he went on to Los Angeles City College. And then to USC. Not only to play baseball, but also football, five-foot-seven Don Buford facing Notre Dame and Monte Stickles. And I, sitting in the press box, was as delighted as I was envious.

From college came the minors, and then the majors, the White Sox and Orioles. And a place in the All-Star Game. And a spot in the World Series. And from locales hither and yon, I would read his name in box scores, see his face on television—and remember.

Dorsey High, southwest Los Angeles, in the mid-1950s often used as an example that people of race, creed, and color truly could get along. We had them all at Dorsey then—whites, blacks, Asians, Hispanics, Jews.

Maybe we were naive. Maybe there was repressed hatred, latent racism, but we were oblivious. We were too busy chasing grades—and talking about the baseball team.

At most high schools, admittedly, the big sport is football. Or maybe basketball. But at Dorsey it was baseball.

George Anderson came from Dorsey. You know him better as Sparky Anderson. Billy Consolo came from Dorsey. So did Marcel Lacheman and Rene Lacheman. So, later, did Derrell Thomas. So did a half-dozen other kids who never made it above the high minors. And so did Don Buford, who, when you study the record, may be the best of the whole lot.

He played ten years in the majors. He played in three World Series. He finished second one season in stolen bases to Campy Campaneris. He was named to the 1971 All-Star team.

Buford says it's all because of a series of accidents. It's also because, unlike the rest of us, he was skillful and gutty.

After Cee basketball in the tenth grade, Don made the varsity team as an eleventh grader. But one day he asked the coach when he could scrimmage. And the coach read him the riot act. So Buford quit and went out for Bee football.

He played varsity baseball, of course, since size was of no consequence, and in 1954, his senior year, Dorsey won the L.A. City championship, beating a Van Nuys team led by Don Drysdale in the semifinals.

After a year at junior college, Buford entered USC to play baseball—without a grant-in-aid. Baseball didn't have scholarships. But football did. So what if he was five-feet-seven? Don made the team, played—in those days of one-platoon—halfback and defensive back, and was a teammate of people like Monte Clark, Ron Mix, and the McKeever twins, Mike and Marlin.

Now, he figured, it was over. Upon graduation in 1959, he would go into teaching or coaching. But the White Sox persuaded him to sign a contract. And four years later he was in the American League. For ten seasons.

Four more years were spent playing ball in Japan. Then, finally, Don Buford retired and began to work full time at a position that he previously had held part-time, personnel manager at a Sears store. Sports? He coached his sons' Little League teams.

But new Giants manager Frank Robinson, a teammate of Buford's on the Orioles a decade past, called him up and asked Don to coach. And though he had a good job, Don consented. Why? Because a new opportunity had been presented and if there is something Don Buford likes it's a new opportunity.

Well, he has it. And I have the chance to reminisce, to remember the Dorsey High Cees. It may not mean much to Don Buford, who eventually was to become a major leaguer, but for at least one dreamer from that team it means some great memories.

Piques and Valleys

THE QUESTION MAN

JULY 27, 1980

Whatever happened to satisfaction? To understanding and laughter and social graces? Whatever happened to athletes who are happy? And fans who are friendly? Whatever happened to sport? Whatever happened to society?

Where are the ballplayers who said they loved their job so much they'd perform without a salary? Where are the fans who loved the games so much they'd cheer the opponent? Where are the sporting journalists who didn't have to belittle everything they report?

Why does every game have to end up as a war? Whatever happened to sportsmanship? Why does there have to be a controversy after every play or every pitch or every forehand? Why does there have to be a holdout by every first-round draft choice of every twenty-game pitcher?

Whatever became of the good guys? Why do so many of our heroes seem to be big mouths with big salaries and big egos? Why do we glorify athletes who flip the bird or throw a tantrum? Has arrogance become a substitute for appreciation?

Why does Dave Parker want to leave Pittsburgh? Why did the Reds allow Pete Rose to leave Cincinnati? Why did Ken Stabler have to leave the Raiders? Why do the Raiders want to leave Oakland? What's wrong with stability and loyalty? Why are we so self-serving, so greedy? Why can't we compromise even just now and then?

Why does every baseball game have to have a beanball, every hockey game have a brawl, every tennis match have an argument? Why have we made heroes out of Jimmy Connors and Muhammad Ali? Why can't we have heroes like Jackie Robinson and Stan Musial?

Why is everyone so worried about everyone else? Why can't we be concerned with ourselves? If Dave Winfield's making a big salary, why should he care if Reggie Jackson's making a bigger salary? Why should writers and fans care what either Winfield or Jackson is earning?

Why is there so much jealousy and distrust? Why do we claim every horse race is fixed, every football game is shady, every athlete is on the take? Why are we so opposed to legalized sports gambling, and then make millions of dollars of illegal bets? Why do we bet if we think everybody is dishonest?

Whatever became of the work ethic? Why do athletes who have problems give up so easily? Whatever happened to trying to improve, instead of just trying to find an excuse? Why can't people ever give credit, or give thanks? Why are we so critical, so vitriolic, so suspicious?

Why does Dave Kingman get publicity for being antisocial? Why do the enforcers in the National Hockey League get publicity for being vicious? Why are all the new sports books only exposés about violence or sex or drugs? Whatever happened to Frank Merriwell or The Kid from Tompkinsville?

Where have you gone, Joe DiMaggio? And Ernie Banks? And Rafer Johnson? And Joe Louis? Why don't we have any more Brockton Blockbusters? Any more Pride of the Yankees? Any more Four Horsemen?

Must we have a fight every time a pitcher even throws near a batter? Must we have a fight every time two fans disagree? Does a trip to a stadium have to become an exercise in terror? Why do so many people on the field have to get so belligerent? Why do so many people in the grandstand have to get so drunk? Or stoned?

Why is someone always tossing a punch? Or a bottle? Or obscenities? Whatever happened to good-natured chiding? To athletes who willingly gave autographs? To kids who said, "Thank you" after receiving autographs?

Why can't we overlook the little things? Why do we take everything so personally? Why is everybody so intolerant? Why does an athlete who's been benched or been replaced act like his manhood has been questioned? Why do fans boo a guy who's trying to do his best? Why do fans seem to boo everybody?

Why can't we accept individuals for what they are? Why do we always have to compare? Does it matter if Babe Ruth was better than Hank Aaron? Or that Kareem Abdul-Jabbar can't pass like Bill Walton? Or if Tom Seaver wasn't as fast as Walter Johnson? I mean, does it really matter, like it matters if we end world hunger or if we run out of fossil fuel?

Why can't we accept compliments without becoming overbearing? Why can't we accept criticism without becoming irate? Why can't we grin about our mistakes, smile about our achievements? Why does an outfielder who's batting .325—or even .225—care what a sportswriter says? Why does a sportswriter who has a steady job care what an athlete doesn't say?

Why can't we allow our kids to enjoy sport the way we enjoyed it when we were kids? Why can't we take them to a game and give them some insight into the skill and dedication involved? Why can't we let them play a game with some insight into the fun of being involved? Yes, whatever happened to satisfaction and understanding, to athletes who appreciated their good fortune, and to fans and writers who appreciated the athletes? Whatever happened to sport?

Whatever happened, I don't like it.

WHY SPORT?

AUGUST 19, 1984

There may be times, said Sigmund Freud, when a cigar is only a cigar. There may be times, then, when sport is only sport. The Olympics of 1984 was one of those times.

Was there chauvinism at the Olympics? Was there patriotic fervor? Yes on both counts. But there was also splendid athletic competition. Is it possible much of the excitement was generated by an appreciation of the competition with no regard to politics or nationalism? Again, the answer is yes.

The information is hereby presented to a Betty Cuniberti, now of the *Los Angeles Times'* Washington bureau but in the past a co-sportswriter on a morning San Francisco daily.

While marvelously talented, Betty suffers from an ailment common in the industry: guilt. She calls the American Olympians false patriots and decries our value system. We should not be honoring athletes, argues Betty, we should be praising doctors and teachers and social workers.

"You want great Americans?" Cuniberti asked. "You can find them, but they won't be in red-and-blue jogging suits, pouting if they fail to break a record in the backstroke.

"Pediatric oncologists—the human saints who treat child cancer victims—are great Americans. They have far more defeats (measured not in hundredths of seconds but in numbers of dead children) than poor Rick Carey, who won the gold in the 200-meter backstroke but hung his head during the national anthem because he was 1.37 seconds off his own world record."

What do running and jumping and swimming have to do with saving the life of a child? Can't we accept sporting excellence for what it is, only sporting excellence? If we can admire Michael Jackson or Placido Domingo, why can't we admire Mary Lou Retton or Edwin Moses? Do we need a sociological interpretation every time someone crosses home plate or the finish line?

Do painters and violinists make a greater contribution to society than pole-vaulters or boxers? No one worries about idolizing a Paul Klee or an Isaac Stern. So Rick Carey is a prima donna. The definition is directly from music. Some sopranos have egos that make Rick Carey seem humble by comparison.

Betty Cuniberti left sportswriting because she felt confined. She was hauled back during the Olympics.

At the risk of engendering a sexist dispute, I contend too many women sportswriters fail to understand what they are covering. They didn't grow up spitting into gloves or worrying they'd never be able to dunk a basketball. To them, sport is a business. To men, sport is a passion.

It is this simple: Sport enables men to remain boys.

A few years ago, Mike D'Innocenzo, then an associate professor of history at Hofstra University, offered a special course, Sport and the American Character. One of his contentions: "The young men in my class haven't completely freed themselves of seeing athletes as great heroes. The women probably are more insightful—because they didn't grow up hoping to be Joe DiMaggio."

The boys who wanted to be DiMaggio or Mays or Jesse Owens or Johnny Lujack grew up to become oncologists or accountants or politicians or metalworkers. They work hard. For relaxation, for escape, they regress. They turn to sport.

Doctors who perform triple-bypass operations get more excited about saving strokes on a par five than saving a patient's life. Is it wrong for those doctors to idolize Watson or Nicklaus?

In 1819, the English essayist William Hazlitt produced this eulogy upon the death of the famous handball player John Cavanagh: "It may be said there are things more important than striking a ball against a wall—there are things indeed that make more noise and do as little good, such as making war and peace, making speeches and answering them, making verses and blotting them, making money and throwing it away."

In the memory of both Hazlitt and Cavanagh, have a cigar.

A SUCKER BORN EVERY MINUTE

NOVEMBER 26, 1980

NEW ORLEANS—P.T. Barnum hit it right on the nose, which is more than you can say for either Sugar Ray Leonard or Roberto Duran. Indeed, there is a sucker born every minute.

We'll fall for anything, we will. If someone told us we could fly, we'd not only agree with him, we'd buy the television rights for a couple million—and then ask Harrah's to give us odds. We're so gullible it's terrifying.

The next thing we'll believe is that Panama is going to give back the canal.

All you need to succeed these days is some high-powered advertising and a good explanation, or, considering what happened last night in the Louisiana Superdome, even a poor explanation.

It may not be entirely fair to call the welterweight championship fight between Leonard and Duran a travesty, but it's quite tempting. Or maybe *farce* is more accurate? Try that script on Broadway, and you'd be laughed back to Peoria.

I mean, you're not going to believe what happened. Duran, the champion, maybe the guttiest boxer in memory, quit. Yes, just like that. He gave up, he conceded. He said his arms hurt from cramps. Or did he say he could fly?

After all the hype, all the buildup, all the insults that led up to this bout, Roberto Duran just quit near the end of the eighth round. He will walk off with his $8 million purse, pending a WBC investigation, leaving Leonard once more holding the title and the spectators holding the bag.

Manos de Piedras, they had nicknamed Duran—Hands of Stone. And arms of what, balsa wood? If he had been knocked down, if he were bleeding, why then no one would have been the least bit surprised. After all, it's better to stop a fight than allow the possibility of a serious injury.

But there was no hint of injury, serious or otherwise. Leonard seemed to be slightly ahead—which was later verified by the judges' cards—and Roberto seemed determined to battle back. And then he shook his head. And then he waved his arms. And then the fight was over.

And then, a half-hour later, Duran, the late, great champion from Panama, was sitting in front of a microphone and saying through a translator that he was retiring from boxing. Fine. But in the middle of a round?

If it weren't so absurd, it would be contemptible. A marvelous career of fourteen years was decimated in one round.

No longer will they talk about the way he knocked out Esteban De Jesus or defeated Carlos Palomino or beat Sugar Ray Leonard to win the welterweight title in June in Montreal. From this moment on, Duran will be known as the guy who gave up.

Unless some justifiable explanation is provided, this bout will go down in boxing's tainted history.

They still wonder if Jack Dempsey had plaster of Paris in his gloves when he beat Jess Willard. And did Muhammad Ali really throw an unseen mystery punch to kayo Sonny Liston in the first round in 1965? No one will ever know.

The only thing definite is that the ending that enabled Leonard to regain the World Boxing Association title was the most bizarre since Liston, then champ, would not or could not come out for the eighth round in his first bout against Ali in 1964. Oh, yes, in boxing, it's always something—and usually something questionable.

Maybe the biggest question is why anyone would pay up to $1,000 to see Duran meet Leonard in a battle the publicists had labeled, "Showdown at the Superdome." And a bigger question is whether anyone would do it again.

Yes, Duran said he was quitting. But Muhammad Ali said he was quitting so many times they could have chiseled it into concrete, and still he came back. There are among us some cynics who might, in fact, contend that what Duran did was set everything in motion for a third bout between the two men. And yet that isn't as logical as it might appear on the surface.

Last night's bout was promoted by Don King, he of the electric hair, big cigar, and pinkie ring. King is affiliated with Duran, or vice versa. But Leonard refuses to deal with King. Thus, the loss by Duran works to the disadvantage of King and Duran. So much for the conspiracy theory.

Leonard, of course, was properly irritated by all the innuendo. Admittedly, he was in front after seven rounds, although not by much, and, unlike the previous fight in Montreal, seemed to be in some semblance of control. That Duran would take the easy way out was not his fault.

"This doesn't take anything away from my victory," said Leonard. "I'm the champion. I beat him fair and square." Well, we shouldn't go that far, but you get the idea.

Leonard's remarks, naturally, were cheered by the entourage that is as obligatory to every boxer as roadwork. It's amazing how many people want to share the glory—and maybe the earnings—of a winner. If questionable endings are a very big part of the sport, so are sycophants.

If someone dared ask Leonard whether he believed Duran was hurt or had a reason to retire, Sugar Ray would growl a quick denial—and his traveling show would cheer wildly.

What some individuals might cheer is a simple explanation as to why the people in boxing keep getting away with, well, not murder, just our trust and our money.

Six weeks ago, millions of dollars were spent to watch Muhammad Ali do nothing. Last night, additional millions were spent to watch a walkout.

We are an amazing species. As P.T. Barnum knew so well. Cramps? Sure, sure.

NO FUN?
WELL, TOUGH

APRIL 10, 1988

AUGUSTA, Georgia—A man named David Forgan said this about golf: "It is a test of temper, a trial of honor, a revealer of character."

It is a game where a player is alone, with no substitutes and no teammates, where every swing is counted, every imperfection recorded. It is often discouraging and only infrequently rewarding. It is, like life itself, inscrutably unfair.

A bad bunker shot may hit a flagstick and drop into the cup while a well-played shot catches a spike mark and spins off the green.

"If you watch a game," Bob Hope once said, "it's fun. If you play at it, it's recreation. If you work at it, it's golf."

The players in this fifty-second Masters have been working, working at trying to keep from losing their cool and losing shots, working at trying to win this first major championship of the year. And isn't that the way it's supposed to be?

Fuzzy Zoeller isn't sure. The 1979 Masters champion, he is displeased with the tournament, more specifically with the men who run it. He says they've tricked up the course, made the greens like cement so balls infuriatingly bounce away from the target. He says he's *piqued,* only he didn't use the word piqued. He says golf at the Masters isn't fun.

And Zoeller is one of the leaders after three rounds, tied for fourth place, four shots behind the leader, Sandy Lyle.

Fuzzy is one of golf's good people. One of sport's good people. He can raise a glass with his friends or, as we've seen, a ruckus in the press room. He's won a Masters and a U.S. Open and an army of friends. But this time Zoeller is wrong.

The rules of golf are ancient—dating from the 1700s—and voluminous. They say what to do when your ball flies into a hazard or when a bird flies off with your ball. But nowhere do they say you're supposed to have fun.

You want to have fun, go to the beach. Or to a ball game. Not a Braves game or Padres game, of course. Those aren't fun. And neither is golf fun. For the players in a major tournament.

You think basketball is fun for the Celtics in the NBA finals? Or baseball was fun for the Cardinals and Twins in the World Series? Sports are fun for the pros after the game is over, after they have had time to reflect.

Each of the first three rounds of this year's Masters—Thursday, Friday, and Saturday—somebody has broken seventy. If the course were tricked up, that would have been impossible.

Augusta National Golf Club has been prepared to separate the great golfers from the good ones and poorer ones. Sandy Lyle is six under par for fifty-four holes. Ben Crenshaw and Mark Calcavecchia are four under. They've played great golf.

In football, baseball, and basketball, the more important the game, usually the tougher the opponent. That's why winning the World Series or the Super Bowl means so much.

In golf, your opponent is the course. There are dozens of tournaments each year. There are four majors—the Masters, the U.S. Open, the British Open, the PGA championship. The courses for the majors are supposed to be demanding. Anybody can beat the Phoenix Country Club, but can you beat Augusta National?

Masters greens always have been evil. This year they're loathsome. Someone said they've been mowed with a razor. Greens by Gillette. Three-putts by the dozen.

Tom Watson, an idealist, disputed Zoeller's claim. The course, said Watson, is not impossible. Saturday, Watson, two under par, four-putted the sixteenth green from ten feet for a quadruple-bogey six.

"I hope he enjoyed every stroke," said a sarcastic Zoeller.

Was the sixteenth green that difficult? Seve Ballesteros and Mark O'Meara each four-putted sixteen earlier in the weekend. But Saturday Fred Couples and Ray Floyd one-putted for birdies.

"They're going to have to redo all the greens," said Zoeller.

No, they're not. Fuzzy is going to have to redo his outlook.

It's not supposed to be easy. This is a tournament for Masters, not moaners.

THE
49ers'
LOSS

NOVEMBER 5, 1986

Do not feel sorry for Wendell Tyler. He has survived before, and with his sense of perspective and his religious beliefs, he'll survive once more. Feel sorry for the 49ers.

They'll miss Wendell more than he'll miss them.

They'll miss his laughter. They'll miss his camaraderie. And, yes, they'll miss his running with the football—even, and here we allude to the fumbles, his running without the football.

Wendell Tyler was with the 49ers three complete seasons. In each they reached the play-offs. That was more than coincidental. Wendell gained yards. Wendell gained respect.

Not from Bill Walsh, apparently, who first tried to persuade Wendell to retire. And then when Wendell refused, Walsh on Tuesday waived Tyler.

Bill offered us eyewash. "We had the most difficult task in my eight-year tenure as head coach of the 49ers," Walsh told us.

"Our reasons are related to the other men playing his position. We have Joe Cribbs, who has shown solid progress each week. Derrick Harmon has returned to full strength."

So? Joe Cribbs will have to progress from here to 2001 to be the running back Wendell Tyler was. And is. And Derrick Harmon at full strength isn't as good as Wendell Tyler at half strength.

Wendell gave the 49ers everything he had. The 49ers gave him the back of their hand. Adios, Wendell, and clean out your locker.

Wendell played with a torn-up knee. Wendell played with a broken hand. He was a profile in courage. He was waived.

Bill Walsh is an excellent football coach, but he has his weaknesses. Primary among them is impatience. Bill is intolerant of anything less than perfection. On occasion, he criticizes his players, by position if not by name.

When Walsh made the trade for Tyler with the Los Angeles Rams before the 1983 season, the 49ers obtained a great running back with a particular flaw: Tyler fumbles.

Bill could never accept the thorns with the rose.

Eric Dickerson fumbles, Tony Dorsett fumbles. Yet Bill Walsh was outraged when Wendell Tyler fumbled.

Three years ago, Wendell fumbled on the one-yard line against the Bears in the first half of a game at Chicago the 49ers were eventually to lose, 13-3. Walsh benched him for the rest of the game.

Tyler made a critical fumble this past Sunday against New Orleans, the 49ers losing the ball on the Saints' twenty-one-yard line—similar to the incident in Chicago—late in the first half. Walsh said the fumble was not a factor in his decision to release Tyler. Hmmm?

Flashback: The end of the 1983 season, Tyler's first with the 49ers after several seasons with the Rams. Wendell ran for 856 yards that year, an average of 4.9 yards per carry, and Bill Walsh said, "That's remarkable on a pass-oriented team. The runners who get big stats usually play for teams that don't throw the ball very well."

Tyler had to do his running behind an offensive line that was created for pass blocking. Once in a while he complained. Most of the time he simply performed.

"He's a tremendously gifted man," Walsh conceded before the 1984 season. "And he's a cheerful man, a good player to have on the team."

Which, of course, is why the 49ers no longer have him on the team.

The best thing about Wendell Tyler is not his skill or determination. It is his exhilaration, his joie de vivre. Nothing appears to bother the man, whether press criticism or a fumbled handoff. He has supreme confidence. He has great equanimity.

In 1983, a fan sent him a football with a handle on it. Someone else suggested that when showering Wendell uses soap-on-a-rope. Athletes normally bristle at sarcasm. Tyler laughed with us.

"I gave the football with the handle to my son," Tyler explained.

"I thought it was a great joke. I once refused to talk to the press, but that wasn't right. I made the mistakes, not the press. I can deal with anything in life."

Until Tyler arrived, the 49er rushing game consisted of eleven men jogging to the bench after an incomplete pass.

Even last weekend, when the 49ers were following the instructions of that old record by the Ventures, "Walk Don't Run," Tyler managed to be the leading ball carrier.

Fumbles? Tyler's original season with the 49ers, a chart was printed. Wendell was only third on the all-time list, with a fumble every 26.3 carries. Number two? Joe Cribbs.

Let us choose to remember Wendell entertaining the kids at the Shriners Hospital for Crippled Children. Or slashing through a seam in the defense for fifteen yards.

Wendell Tyler ennobled the 49ers by his presence.

We will miss him.

Worse, the 49ers will miss him.

A TOAST TO NUMBER TWO

DECEMBER 28, 1986

Our problem is not that we make too much out of winning, but that we make too much out of failing to win.

This is a tribute, then, to the year that wasn't. We reach a time for reflection but not dejection, a contemplation of what might have been.

Here's to the, well, not losers. The word has such a negative connotation. A man who finishes second of 156 entrants in the U.S. Open golf tournament is hardly a loser. A team that finishes second in the World Series is hardly a loser.

Winning is wonderful. But winning isn't everything or the only thing—the slogan presented not by Vince Lombardi in the 1960s but by Red Sanders, the UCLA football coach when I was at the school in the 1950s.

Television, in an endless quest to create an audience for commercials, would have us believe the essence of sport is to be king of the mountain. There is fear we won't watch. So it shills and sells. "The battle for #1." But what is important? The battle? Or the result?

Would a game between Penn State and Miami be as enjoyable if there were no rankings? Does the final score mean as much as the quality and pace of play?

Think back. Yes, for Jack Nicklaus and Willie Shoemaker and the Boston Celtics it was a very good year. At one time or another they were champions.

The year was no less significant for John McNamara and Gene Mauch. Or for the Houston Rockets. Or Ivan Lendl at Wimbledon. They fought the good fight. They nearly made it to the top.

The difference between victory and defeat often is minuscule. A volley that nicks the net, a putt that rims the cup, a line drive that kicks up chalk down the foul line, a pass caught with only one foot in bounds.

And yet we glamorize the winners and second-guess those who do not win. We seek explanations when there are none. We do psychological profiles on athletes because of a bad bounce that decided the outcome.

So the Red Sox didn't win the World Series? They made it one step farther down the road than the Angels, who in turn made it farther than every other team in the American League. Is John McNamara, the Red Sox manager, a bum because Boston couldn't retain a three-run lead in the tenth inning of game six? No more than he would have been a genius if the Red Sox had held the lead.

During the baseball meetings in Florida, McNamara was a readily available foil. He was asked again about the fateful tenth against the Mets. Once more unto the breach.

What is it about society? Are we incapable of understanding? Could it be the Mets won the World Series rather than the Red Sox lost the World Series? Is it possible to congratulate the Red Sox for the excitement they provided?

Sport is supposed to be a diversion. It has grown into an obsession.

How many people ever say, "That was a great game," or a "great race," or a "great fight"? What they invariably say is, "We won." Or "We lost." Or "What a choke."

I say, "What a joke." I laugh *with* McNamara and Lendl and the New England Patriots, runners-up all, and not *at* them. I thank them for the skill and effort. For the precious moments of pleasure they brought to a hectic world.

I commiserate with Columbia University's football team, which has now gone so long without a victory that the media and skeptics can dwell on nothing else about the school.

I sympathize with the seniors on the USC football team who, walking over for the traditional farewell from the student body, were instead booed after the loss to Notre Dame.

The realm of sport is not entirely peopled by Larry Birds and Martina Navratilovas. Most of those in the arena are struggling to make it, and many of them fail in that struggle. They still must be admired.

First place is where we'd all like to be. Second is where most of us end up. You don't have to be a champion to be considered a winner.

GREED TAINTS IMAGE OF SPORTS HEROES

OCTOBER 26, 1982

So the Warriors traded Bernard King, who wouldn't sign a contract, for Micheal Ray Richardson, who wants a new contract. And the NFL strike may go on forever. And the Giants have raised ticket prices for next season.

That's the wonderful world of sport, circa 1982, a world of mercenaries and greed and attitudes so selfish you wonder if team play is even possible. For damned sure modesty isn't.

Yes, it's a world of supply and demand. And if you can run from end zone to end zone in ten seconds or dribble a basketball through your legs you're more valuable to society than some guy who discovers a cure for cancer.

And everybody else has his, which means you want yours.

But that doesn't make it right. In fact, it makes it wrong. It takes the enjoyment out of the game. It poisons the air, destroys a trust. They say there is honor among thieves. But there certainly isn't honor in professional sport.

Standing outside the visiting locker room at Cal's Memorial Stadium, you could hear the UCLA football team singing a school fight song. It was a moment out of Grantland Rice or John Tunis, young men savoring a victory. College kids still play the game for fun. The pros do not.

Pro sports now is symbolized by the word *more*. The logotype ought to be an open palm. It's an activity of dissatisfaction, inflated egos, bloated salaries, and athletes who think they have been granted divine privilege.

Whatever happened to players like Lou Gehrig, who stood there dying and in appreciation of the fans' affection called himself the luckiest man on the face of the earth?

Whatever happened to people like Jackie Robinson, who accepted insults and hardship to advance a cause and a marvelous talent?

Whatever happened to humility, sportsmanship, good manners, and the idea an athlete should be a role model for kids, not somebody prancing up and down the sidelines waving at the TV cameras?

If an athlete can earn a billion dollars, more power to him. But why can't he earn it with dignity, with understanding that he is fortunate to be in the right place at the right time? Why shouldn't he honor a contract? Management is expected to do so. Why do negotiations always have to drag the parties through the gutter?

It isn't the amount of money that turns people against the pros, it's the amount of gall. They walk out on $500,000 contracts because a teammate is earning $600,000. They're too envious of the other guy to find happiness.

Calvin Murphy, the little big man of the Houston Rockets, expressed a common theme of athletes when asked about salaries.

"I get upset when people say we are being overpaid," Murphy explained some time ago. "People don't know the frustrations and the fatigue in the game. People don't know the preparation a ballplayer goes through. They only see the finished product—a two-hour basketball game.

"People really feel that we're stealing something, that ballplayers are being paid outrageously. But somebody must think that these guys are worth it, if they pay them. And everyone wants to get paid what he thinks he's worth."

There's the key phrase: "What he thinks he's worth." Too frequently these guys perceive themselves as a gift to mankind. That we should fall to our knees when they walk by, praise them for deigning to put on their Nikes or Pumas.

I don't think athletes are stealing. I do think some are remarkably self-centered.

Preparation? Does Murphy think a physician gets his license by sitting around? Hard work? Spend a day on the assembly line at General Motors, or, as is now the case, the unemployment line.

We wouldn't care what an athlete made if only he comprehended his good fortune, was grateful instead of grating, stopped whining about every minor difficulty.

Sport is supposed to be a microcosm of life, only a symptom of our problems rather than a cause. But if some secretary decides to sulk at home because she's unhappy with her pay scale, she'll be looking for another job. And I'd like to see an attorney renegotiate his salary with the Department of Justice.

At first, Maurice Cheeks of the Philadelphia 76ers refused to report to camp because the team gave Moses Malone everything except the Liberty Bell. And Warriors rookie Lester Conner hasn't even put on a uniform because he doesn't like what he's been offered.

Fine. Conner can sit this one out. Nothing personally against Lester, a decent sort, but let him go out in this world of double-digit unemployment and find a job that pays anywhere near what he could earn with the Warriors.

In his book *Farewell to Sport,* the late Paul Gallico, rhapsodizing about the Golden Age, the 1920s and 1930s, wrote, "What a world! What heroes and heroines!" Today it could be changed to "What heroes? What heroines?"

Bernard King is a great basketball player. But if the Warriors hadn't given him a chance when he was in trouble, no one might ever have known how great he could be.

We found out. We also found out his primary interest was a bigger contract. Good-bye, Bernard. Good-bye, logic. Good-bye, loyalty. Good-bye, pro football season. Good-bye, money. The whole business stinks.

DOUBLE STANDARD

APRIL 17, 1987

The talk always is of sending a message. And so we have sent one. We have told the people who can throw baseballs or catch footballs they live outside the society for which they perform.

"The rich are different from us," said F. Scott Fitzgerald. So are athletes. They are not restricted by the rules of law or the boundaries of good judgment.

They are governed only by one mandate, the one so succinctly expressed by Al Davis of the Los Angeles Raiders: "Just win, baby."

Just win, and we'll take care of those cocaine charges or that rape accusation. Just win and we'll give you a standing ovation although you're more deserving of a jail sentence.

Four football players at the University of California last fall were accused of rape. If they were ordinary students, they'd probably be in San Quentin. But they're jocks, so the chances are good they'll be at Memorial Stadium.

Dwight Gooden confessed he uses drugs. Tsk, tsk. Don't worry, Dwight. We'll send you to a rehabilitation center and pay you a million dollars so when you emerge you'll have more money to spend on—drugs? Why would anyone think that way?

"We love you, Dwight," is what the Mets, individually and as a group, told Gooden before he was hustled away to learn what he already was supposed to know, the difference between right and wrong.

"We love you . . . and come back soon and help us win a pennant."

My friend Leonard Koppett, once of *The New York Times,* argues that this is absolutely the worst thing we could tell Gooden and those like him. We've advised Dwight it's okay to use drugs, to break the law, if you can strike out 200 people a season and help the Mets get to the World Series.

I think it's admirable Gooden recognized his need for assistance, as did so many others. I hope he stays clean. I hope he wins twenty games.

But what about the millions of addicts without Gooden's fame or resources? What about the kids who stood outside the New York hospital to wave farewell to Gooden?

The message we're sending them is that we have a double standard.

Win the Cy Young Award, and we'll hire the best attorneys, seek out the best doctors. But if you're poor, if you're anonymous, well then, tough luck, baby. Go straight to jail, and never mind the $200.

The charade begins at an early age, when athletic skill beomes recognizable.

Grades are doctored. Speeding violations are dropped. Teenage pranks—sexual assault and theft are pranks, aren't they?—receive a pardon, not a reprimand.

The message? Stay eligible and help beat Tech, and please, easy on the beer.

Did you notice that quote from the Cal freshman who was allegedly raped by the four football players?

The players were to have received sexual counseling and to have performed community service as ordered in a settlement with the woman. Apparently they have not fulfilled the obligation.

"I felt naive," the woman said. "Like they were going to learn something from all this. Now I don't really think so."

She is naive. She believed athletes were treated like ordinary students. She probably believes in Santa Claus, too.

Chris Washburn of the Warriors got into North Carolina State with a score of 470 on the Scholastic Aptitude Test. The test is supposed to be culturally biased, and maybe it is. But you get 400 points just for signing your name.

If Chris Washburn didn't play basketball do you think he would have been accepted at North Carolina State?

Send a message. Tell the world that if you're clever enough to be born with great hand-eye coordination, able to leap tall buildings in a single bound, can run from here to there in a blink, you've got it made.

As long as you can score touchdowns or sink baskets, somebody will take care of you.

Vince Lombardi, we now know, was absolutely correct: Winning is the only thing.

That's what we tell our youth.

They've heard it. They've followed it.

And we suffer for it.

Someday, maybe, we'll understand the message is absolutely wrong.

DISTORTION OF SPORTS

JANUARY 20, 1988

It was Eric Sevareid who said television transformed American journalists from critics on the aisle to actors in the play.

Is there a better, or more unfortunate, example than Jimmy "The Greek" Snyder?

Television is not content to report the event, it must create the event. So instead of commentators we have stars, many of whom shouldn't even be permitted cameo appearances.

Let us give Mr. Snyder the benefit of the doubt and accept his argument he is not a racist. He then is merely insensitive and stupid. If Snyder had simply remained an oddsmaker in Las Vegas, his numbers might be important but his thoughts would not. So who cares about some bookie's viewpoint on physiology?

But TV seeks out people like Jimmy the Greek, people who can be exploited for a price, people without qualifications, people who are *personalities*—whatever that word means.

The public equates recognition with responsibility. Hey, there's that guy we saw on TV. He must know something.

Right. What he knows is how to make $500,000 a year without talent.

Jimmy the Greek is seen so often he becomes bigger than the events. And the next thing, he's being questioned about politics and finance and, heaven help him, black athletes. And, instead of conceding his ignorance, he takes himself seriously. And then, of course, millions of Americans do, too.

Television executives have no qualms about what is on the set, only that the set may not be on. To keep us watching the commercials they'll show us almost anything in between.

For the average American male, *anything* means football, baseball, basketball, logrolling, Australian rules football, golf tournaments, karate, boxing. I mean anything.

And then TV tries to give us self-esteem with close-up shots of the crowd. If those people, we're told subconsciously, are getting hysterical about some prepubescent teenager performing a double axel, then we too should care. And we do.

Television has distorted sports in America. It has persuaded a generation that games are a method of self-gratification instead of an opportunity for teamwork. It has given us high fives ad infinitum, double-pump jump shots, and—oh, gracious—wimpy dances in the end zone.

Humility has gone the way of the nickel Hershey bar. The cameramen encourage the guy on the bench to mug for the audience. Is there anything more disgraceful than for a player of a team down 27-7 to go into a pantomime routine on the sideline?

Once upon a time a man who scored a touchdown was content to drop the ball and return to his teammates. A man who scored a basket was content to run upcourt and play defense. No longer.

Now it's show biz. Now it's double-pump dunk shots and "Cabbage Patch" dances in the end zone. Now it's pom-pom girls who only jump and scream when the Minicam is aimed in their direction. Now it's only a paper moon hanging over a cardboard sea.

Every play in football, every score in basketball inevitably is followed by a view of the crowd. See Dick and Jane. See Spot. See the director pander to the lowest common denominator.

The other evening on ESPN, Ohio State was upsetting Michigan in basketball, only the man in charge seemed obsessed with the undergrads in the stands. Announcer Dick Patrick felt obligated to remark, "If we can get back to action on the floor, you'll notice . . . . "

Television is a lot of people saying, "Look at me." And when we look we see oversized egos, in the action and in the announcing booth.

CBS is the network that gave us people carrying refrigerators and called it competition. CBS is the network that gave us Phyllis George and called her justified. CBS is the network that gave us Jimmy the Greek and called him competent.

Jimmy the Greek fell victim as much to the system as to his own unawareness. TV showed him up as a false prophet and a real fool.

Levity, the Role of Wit

CAUGHT IN BASEBALL'S DMZ

OCTOBER 22, 1980

PHILADELPHIA—It doesn't matter if you win or lose anymore, just if you escape. If you think it's terrifying taking a ride on a New York subway at midnight, you ought to take a seat in the grandstand at a major sporting event.

I don't know what Alexander Cartwright thought about the final game of the World Series last night, but Leonid Brezhnev would have loved it. By the time Tug McGraw struck out Willie Wilson for about the zillionth time, Veterans Stadium had more people in uniform than Red Square on May Day.

It was baseball's version of a demilitarized zone, Selma, Alabama, of the early 1960s. There were riot police, attack dogs, horses, and enough arms to overthrow Castro. The only thing missing was a shortwave broadcast from Radio Free Philadelphia.

And do you know why they were there, the officers in their helmets and face guards? No, not because of a Russian invasion. Or an escape from the city jail. No, the police and the weapons were ordered because authorities were worried about the Phillies winning the World Series. That's right, winning. Not losing.

If you can figure that one out, you might be able to end the war in the Mideast. Or stop inflation. I can't figure it out. But then I don't live on the East Coast. And after seeing the way they prepare for a victory celebration, all I can say is thank heaven.

Officials were worried that what should have been the greatest moment in the city's history might turn into its worst. For the first baseball championship in the ninety-eight years in Philadelphia, there had been predictions of rioting and looting and vandalism. In other words, the people were going to celebrate.

According to mental-health experts quoted in a Philadelphia paper yesterday, the Phillies might be the best thing for the city since electroshock therapy. Or at least a couple of smacks over the head with a billy club.

"We have very little control of our own lives," said Stephen P. Weinstein, an assistant professor of psychiatry at Jefferson Medical College in Philadelphia. "But people in Philadelphia feel good because they've identified with the team, which is assuming control of something very real, the game."

Shortly after the Phils assumed control of the game, taking a 4-0 lead that eventually became a 4-1 win over the Kansas City Royals, the police assumed control of the stadium. No one ever minds a little precaution, especially since the tumultuous climax to the 1977 World Series at Yankee Stadium, where patrons ripped up seats and grass. But this wasn't precaution, this was a show of force.

The open areas along the left- and right-field lines toward the foul poles were packed with policemen. Before the bottom of the seventh, a mounted posse big enough to capture the James gang galloped blatantly from the right-field corner along the outfield fence to the left-field corner.

Then, just before the hysterical climax, when Tug McGraw would send up pulse rates before setting down the star-crossed Wilson with his record twelfth strikeout of the Series, another group of police leading German shepherds swept onto the AstroTurf field. Someone was trying to make a point. I'm not quite sure what it was.

"Even I lost my concentration a little bit when those horses came onto the field," said Larry Bowa, the Phillies' feisty shortstop. "I was worried they might trample me. Or I might get bitten by a dog. These are tough fans, but . . . . "

But. But this is supposed to be baseball, America's Pastime, the Fall Classic—not an exercise in terror. What have we come to in America of the 1980s?

True, the Phillies are a team of abrasion, of guys who seem to dislike each other or their manager, Dallas Green, more than they dislike the opposition. And true, the sporting public in Philadelphia is known to be a trifle intolerant. Once, during a Christmas celebration at an Eagles football game, they even booed Santa Claus. But . . . .

This is the land of the free and the home of the brave. This is a place where supposedly you're innocent until proven guilty. This is a country where in theory the people control the police and not the other way around.

Someone justified the zealous display of power by pointing out that when the Phillies played their final game at Shibe Park, in September 1970, before shifting to Veterans Stadium the following spring, the fans literally tore the place apart, dismantling seats and railings even before the final out. This, said a resident, was not going to happen in 1980.

It didn't happen. Veterans Stadium still stands unsullied, save for a few uncollected hot-dog wrappers. Of course, a couple of kids were roughed up by the city's finest, some of whom seemed intent on doing more celebrating than the other spectators.

In the Phillies locker room a policeman, a regular at the park, had shed his coat and was guzzling from one of the champagne bottles being passed around by the ecstatic Phillies. And if the reporters didn't like it, he'd take care of them.

Some of his colleagues already had taken care of a young man who must have done something terrible. The guy's arms were handcuffed behind his back and he was being held by two policemen. But that didn't prevent the young man from softly chanting, "Go, Phillies . . . Go Phillies."

You wanted to tell the kid to be quiet. Otherwise they might bring in the cavalry.

TURNBERRY SETTING RECORD— FOR FUTILITY

JULY 17, 1986

TURNBERRY, Scotland—A sportswriter asked the late Tony Lema how he found the golf course. "Easy," Lema cracked, "I walked out the clubhouse door and there it was." Ho, ho. Not at Turnberry, he wouldn't have.

They sent 153 guys out of the clubhouse today in the first round of the British Open. Most of them are still looking for the course. And their pride. Also for a few dozen balls.

On a place that served as a Spitfire air base during World War II, we had a new version of the Battle of Britain. Where is Winston Churchill when we need him? Where is Bobby Jones?

There's no question where Jack Nicklaus is. At seventy-eight, or eight over par. And he finished eagle-birdie.

"I'm lucky I finished," said Jack. "This is not what I traveled several thousand miles from the United States to shoot, seventy-eight."

Ray Floyd also is at seventy-eight. And Roger Maltbie is at seventy-eight. And at wit's end. Alluding to the setup of the course, Maltbie sighed, "Either I have a real misconception of what the game is all about or they do."

"They" means the Royal and Ancient Golf Club, which runs the tournament. The Open was held at Turnberry in 1977 and Nicklaus and Tom Watson broke the tournament record. This year, the R & A was determined to break a few hearts. The fairways were narrowed and the rough was lengthened. "Hardest

247

course I ever played," said former U.S. Open champion Larry Nelson. And that was on a calm day. Today was anything but calm.

A chilling west wind, crashing in from Ireland and picking up speed as it crossed the Firth of Clyde, sent golf balls flying, temperatures dropping, and scores rising.

If this had been a boxing match, someone would have ruled the course a winner by a TKO. The weather bureau said there were gusts up to thirty-five miles an hour. The golfers said there were shots that couldn't be made. There definitely were scores that shouldn't be reported in a family paper.

Ian Baker-Finch, who led the Open two years ago, almost trailed it this year. He shot an eighty-six. And he was in front of Tony Johnstone and George Richie, who had eighty-seven.

Somebody named Andrew Broadway could have shot a lot higher than that. Broadway went out in forty-nine. But he never came in. For a while it was rumored he blew out to sea. But in truth, Andrew withdrew. No "Lullaby of Broadway" this week.

Plenty of dirges, however. And people stomping around in grass up to their knees. Ray Floyd lost a ball on the fourteenth. Maltbie lost a ball on the tenth. And they were the lucky ones.

Broadway found his in the hay off the seventh fairway. The only problem was he tried to use a sand wedge when he needed a scythe. In four swings he never moved the ball.

"I found my ball in the rough on fourteen," chuckled Craig Stadler. "I wish I hadn't. Took a swing at it with a wedge, the ball never moved, and I nearly broke my wrist. Had to play the rest of the way one-handed. I don't know why I finished." Persistence, you guess. Craig shot eighty-two.

Vaughan Somers, a Brit, had a seventy-three. Not without considerable embarrassment. "I had a one-and-a-half-footer on the eighth green," said Somers. "The wind blew my rain pants, my putter caught in them, and I missed."

He wore rain pants even though it wasn't raining. Thank heavens. Anyone who tried to open an umbrella would have been blown halfway to Kilmarnock. Mary Poppins must have practiced flying around here.

Greg Norman only practiced his humility. He had two double bogeys and a seventy-four. That was one in front of Deane Beman, who finished birdie-birdie-birdie for seventy-five. Beman is supposed to administrate golf. He's the PGA Tour commissioner.

Today, he played it three shots better than the men who this year won the Masters and the U.S. Open.

"What happened out here is amazing," said Norman. "We're talking about some of the best players in the game being humiliated.

"I said to Ray Floyd on seventeen, 'Have you ever played golf anywhere in the world under these conditions, when you've been so humiliated you feel like a nonentity like this? Hacking it around in the rough. Hacking it on the green. Two-putting.'

"He said, 'Never,' and Ray's been around a long while."

The game of golf's been around longer than Floyd, 500 years or so. It started in Scotland, on the other coast, and has been played in the gales and the gusts ever since.

"In a way," laughed Roger Maltbie, "it's so ridiculous it's kind of fun."

How did you find the course, Roger?

DEAR BILL: TRY A PUNT, A PASS, AND A PRAYER

NOVEMBER 29, 1983

Take a memo, Ms. Jones. Send it to Bill Walsh, coach, San Francisco Fumble-Niners. The address? Number 2 Western Division is good enough.

Dear Bill:

Have you thought about retirement? No, I didn't mean it. Just a joke. The 49ers need you.

Before you arrived, they used to lose to teams like Detroit and St. Louis.

But you changed all that. Now they lose to Philadelphia and Chicago.

Not that it's your fault. The athletic director who arranged this year's schedule is completely to blame. He signed the Jets and the Dolphins. You need a home-and-home arrangement with the Oilers. Or Stanford.

You also need a running attack, but that's stating the obvious. This kid Tyler you got from the Rams has a lot of class and some great moves. The problem is they're with the football, not his feet.

Of course, it's easy to criticize. Wendell doesn't give it up all the time. He didn't fumble once in the fourth quarter Sunday against Chicago.

Maybe you should try Wendell at offensive tackle. This way you know at least one person would never be guilty of holding.

One word of advice. If somebody on the Rams tries to sell you a gold watch, don't buy it. Don't let Wendell buy it, either. He'd probably drop it.

Perhaps you could get Jim Brown. Or Bronko Nagurski. I mean, when nobody on your club has more than twenty-one yards rushing, anybody with a pulse rate should be a candidate.

Some of the press is knocking you now, Bill. They say you can't coach, which is stupid. How could a man who can't coach win the Super Bowl? You devised the offense of the eighties, and I don't mean the 1880s. They don't call you "Genius" for nothing.

Just because some Bear defensive assistant takes a few cheap shots doesn't mean you should change your strategy.

Buddy Ryan's the guy's name and, after the game Sunday, he said the Chicago defense knew exactly what the 49ers were going to do. Baloney! He never knew you would bench Wendell the last period.

"The 49ers are heavily typed," is what Ryan said, "and nobody knows it." If the guy's so smart, why couldn't he figure out a way to stop Eric Dickerson? Or the rain at Soldier Field?

You do have to admit, however, that when you play Mike Wilson in the backfield you're going to pass. Even a couple of dumb journalists know that. It's just that they're too shy to tell you. No writer would ever second-guess a football coach.

The great thing about you, Bill, is your splendid sense of humor. That stunt when you dressed up like a bellhop in Detroit was a real thigh-slapper.

Still, borrowing the game plan for the Bears from Mel Brooks may have been going a bit too far. Then again, you were the only team in the NFL this weekend with more laughs than points.

Mike Ditka, the Bears coach, has a reason. "They wanted parity in the NFL," Ditka said, "they got parity." What that means is eleven of the twenty-eight teams have records of 7-6 or 6-7. Bill, is that parity or mediocrity? At least you don't have to feel alone.

I hate to bring this up, Bill, but that's the way Russ Francis feels. He never caught a pass Sunday, which some people think is surprising since Russ is a tight end.

But it was understandable. You need Russ as a blocker, to establish the running game and to protect the quarterback. The plan worked swimmingly. Joe Montana only got sacked five times and called for intentional grounding one time.

The rule of thumb in sport is to keep the opponent off balance. Cleverly, you've done the same thing to the fans and the writers.

When people belittled the 49ers after they lost the first game of the season to the Eagles, you showed us. Won six of the next seven, and everybody said you had one of the best teams in football. Then, you old card, you lost four of the next five, which was really confusing.

Are the 49ers great or a gang of stiffs? Trying to figure it out is worse than Chinese water torture. Do we take the points or give them? Is Joe Montana going to get any protection? Is Dwight Clark ever going to get open? Is anybody going to get a touchdown?

But hey there! You do look great in those Volvo commercials. And we know what's important, don't we? Maybe you could import a running back from Sweden.

Or a bottle of glue. Or an offensive scheme that keeps fewer than three guys from getting to the quarterback.

You play the Tampa Bay Bucs Sunday. They're terrible. Which is the reason you should worry.

Three yards and a cloud of dust . . .

—Amos Alonzo Spander

STAMPEDING MEDIA

JANUARY 16, 1985

Early morning comin' down. "You can't roller-skate in a buffalo herd," Roger Miller advised us once in a song. You can, however, sprint across Candlestick Park in a journalistic herd. Dear Boss: Are you sure this is the way Ernest Hemingway got his start?

The sun was peeking above the rim of the Oakland Coliseum. Don Shula was peeking from under the brim of a baseball cap. "Awesome," said Don. Lafayette, we are here. Take the right flank and watch the Minicams.

A new twist to an old tale. Give me your wretched masses yearning to meet deadlines. Hundreds of guys looking for angles and finding clichés. Did Dan Marino really say, "I think I have to improve every part of my game"?

It happens every January. Hundreds of reporters clamber aboard buses and hustle off to the camps of the Super Bowl teams. This year, with the 49ers on one side of the Bay, the Dolphins on the other, we get—you should pardon the expression—the abridged version, transpontine madness.

The Coliseum at dawn. Jeff Greenfield, the author and TV critic, is there wearing a trench coat and enough credentials to get through the Pearly Gates. St. Peter, don't you call me 'cause I can't go, I still have to interview Tony Nathan.

"You can't get a story out there," Dave Kindred, the columnist of the *Atlanta Constitution*, complains later. "There's too many people, too many interruptions."

But like gamblers standing next to the crap table at Harrah's, we keep trying. Seven come eleven. As the guy who cleans up after the elephants was supposed to have said, "Quit now and get out of show business?"

Those who don't learn from history, warned George Santayana, are doomed to repeat it. Wasn't Santayana the defensive coordinator under Halas? We're never going to learn. Over the loudspeaker a disembodied voice advises, "Buses leave in fifteen minutes." Onward through the tule fog.

At Candlestick, the troops bivouac in a tent, waiting to enter through a portal over which is a sign, ENTERTAINMENT GATE. Grumbling, shivering writers, announcers, photographers, and advisers—that's entertainment? As Don Rickles jokes, we could have been on the Ed Sullivan Show but our bear died.

Our pioneer spirit lives on. Where's the beef? Where's the story?

Joe Montana wanders out of the locker-room door and is surrounded. He begins to run toward the opposite end of the stadium, the left-field bleachers, picking up followers faster than Gandhi. Montana the quarterback has more people, cracks one observer, than Montana the state.

Joe climbs into the $1.50 seats and, like some monarch on his throne, tosses bons mots to the media the way he tosses passes to Dwight Clark. Step right up and hear about life, love, and interceptions.

No face in the crowd: Alan Kennedy, the offensive lineman, stands apart, a lonely sentinel. He has not been asked even one dumb question. Tell us once more how football is a team game.

Guy McIntyre, the guard-turned-fullback, is telling half a dozen people how they hauled him out of a three-point stance into a dream. "When it was all explained to me," concedes McIntyre, "I didn't think they were serious."

They were. The 49ers had the best three-guard offense since the 1982 Lakers. Could McIntyre now clear interference to the locker room?

"Freddie," a man with a microphone inquired of a bemused Freddie Solomon, "does this media crush bother you?" The 49er receiver carefully considers the question, then responds, "No."

The man is a diplomat, as well as a football player. Of course it bothers him. It bothers everyone, including the media.

I would go into greater depth, but I don't have the time. I have to chase Joe Montana back across the field at Candlestick.

WHAT HAPPENED TO HUMOR?

FEBRUARY 21, 1982

Asked once how he would like to be remembered, Jimmy Cannon, the late, great sporting columnist, never hesitated: "I'd like people to say I gave them a few laughs." It is fortunate then, for Jimmy Cannon, that he's no longer around.

Sports has ceased to be a world of fun and games, the place to create a few laughs or to have them. Sports is now serious business, with the emphasis on business. Sports simply is money or image—or both.

Laughing, a comedy writer insisted some time ago, is the only form of revolt we have in this country. Well, haul out the white flag. The revolution is over. We've lost. That's because we've lost our sense of humor.

You don't expect people to guffaw about the economy or the Middle East or their PG&E bills. Some things cannot be approached lightly. But supposedly that's why we have sports, to give us a break from the real world. The problem now is that sports is considered the real world.

The legends deal with the oddballs, the flakes, the incidents. Casey Stengel once tipped his hat to the crowd and a bird flew out. Billy Loes claimed he lost a ground ball in the sun. A golfer in the Masters took off his shoe and rolled up his pants leg to play a ball out of Raes Creek—and then stepped into the water with the other foot.

Sports used to be Abbott and Costello reciting "Who's on First?" Or Dizzy Dean standing up in the announcing booth and shouting at Tony Cuccinello. Or nicknames like Puddinghead or Schnozz or even Dr. Strangeglove.

Sports used to be people playing for the love of the game, not deferred interest payments.

Now sports is agents who think they are negotiating the peace settlement between Israel and Egypt, not simply a contract for a twenty-one-year-old left-hander. Now sports is a group of individuals who get pushed out of shape every occasion a journalist doesn't treat them like royalty.

Mention that they grow corn in Iowa or that soccer isn't about to replace football and invariably the remark will be taken as a personal insult. You expect to receive a set of dueling pistols, C.O.D.

Because I suggested that, tongue-in-cheek, the North American Soccer League next year wouldn't go indoors it would go underground, one reader canceled a subscription. Because I chided the University of Iowa for laying an egg in the Rose Bowl, a woman insisted I apologize to the whole state, including the hogs and cornstalks.

An old rule of thumb is that you're supposed to take what you do seriously but never yourself. But that idea went out with Fred Allen and Jack Benny. Now, if you so much as smile when a center fielder drops a fly ball, you're reprimanded.

It's our basic application of the theory about whose ox is being gored. Knocking somebody is acceptable, but don't knock me, you jerk. We're about to fight World War III.

Why is everybody perpetually on a soapbox? Why can't we accept losing, accept laughing? If Washington beats Iowa in the Rose Bowl, or Al Davis wants to move his football team to El Centro, why shouldn't we become satirical?

It's all song-and-dance these days, people shilling and selling. Advertising means more than laughing. You have to think positively. You have to appeal to the consumer.

There are billboards around the Bay Area advertising Golden Gate Fields racetrack on which is painted a young couple smiling and the words, WE WON. That, of course, is the power of positive thinking, but it is not exactly accurate.

The billboard should read, WE LOST, since most of us do lose when we spend a day with the ponies. But that would present a negative image, and management would be livid. That the rest of us might think someone at Golden Gate still had a sense of humor is totally insignificant.

Bethel Shine of Concord felt obligated to write after a certain columnist attempted to have some fun with what basically was a mismatch in the Rose Bowl game—or should I say that since she emigrated from Iowa, she felt outraged.

"I need your help in explaining to my eighty-four-year-old father, an Iowa farmer, the motive behind your article following the Rose Bowl game . . . . I believe your assignment was to write a column about the game. I fail to understand why you developed a column deriding farmers and the clothes they wear and their economic judgment. Please explain how this relates to your coverage of the game."

It doesn't, Bethel. No more than talking about San Francisco's unusual lifestyles relates to the 49ers' winning the Super Bowl. Tell your eighty-four-year-old father that my motive was to offer a few smiles, and maybe increase membership in local 4-H clubs. Tell your eighty-four-year-old father he's fortunate he doesn't have to live in California.

But also tell him that what was said about the state of Iowa or the football team won't matter a bit in the great scheme of things, that the snow still will fly in winter and the flowers bloom in spring.

Tell him not to take anything personally, although that would make him unique, since everyone takes everything personally, especially in sports.

We're not allowed to laugh, or even smile. We've got to get out there and try to become #1—and earn a million dollars. It's fortunate Jimmy Cannon is no longer around.

THE APRIL ASCENT

APRIL 27, 1986

Hello, Bureau of Missing Teams? Officer, I'm trying to find the San Francisco Giants. Right, the club that gave Rennie Stennett $3 million and gave Willie Mays the gate.

No, I don't have an address. They moved. Not to Denver. Out of last place. Yes, it's important. They're ruining their reputation. Also San Francisco's.

This is supposed to be the worst baseball town in the country. The fans normally lose interest after opening day. The team simply loses.

A year ago, upon hearing that manager Jim Davenport was leading the Giants, the normal response was, "Yeah, and so is everyone else in the division." They were almost mathematically eliminated by Mother's Day.

Now they're threatening to stay around until the Fourth of July. Maybe even the first of October.

I know it's not even May, but this is serious. By now, the Giants are usually a half-dozen games under .500. People are thinking about the NFL draft. Or about next year.

But the fans are thinking about—please don't say this too loudly—a pennant.

Sorry. I know I can get locked up for using that word in public. But people keep asking, "Are the Giants for real?" And they're coming out to Candlestick Park. For baseball, not football.

No, officer, I haven't been drinking. There were 40,000 people for a game against the Padres. And 27,000 on a Wednesday afternoon against the Dodgers. Last year, there were times when the Giants didn't draw 40,000 in a week, much less one day.

No, Candlestick wasn't moved to Puerto Vallarta. It's still sitting there near a dock of the Bay with Otis Redding. The weather? Terrible. Foggy, cold, damp. The team? Amazing.

That's the trouble. It's written in the Book of Genesis that unless you're wearing shoulder pads and helmets and playing the Rams, you can't draw at Candlestick. Bad egress. Lousy sight lines. For years we've been telling everyone that not even winning would help.

The public is even worried about the "June Swoon." That was a tradition in the late '60s and early '70s. Giants teams would play well until the end of May and then exit like a guy doing a half-gainer off the three-meter board.

But the "June Swoon" became the "April Sag." By the time school was out of session, the Giants were out of contention. We didn't have any Boys of Summer. They couldn't survive spring.

No, officer, Bob Lurie hasn't sold the team. We thought he was trying to sell us a bill of goods. He hired a general manager named Al Rosen who kept telling us the Giants were going to be improved, which is sort of like telling Reagan that Khadafy is going to be a barrel of laughs.

Rosen got rid of Manny Trillo and Matt Nokes and brought in Will Clark and Robby Thompson. He also brought in Roger Craig as manager. Baseball litany proclaims one manager is pretty much like another. Don't believe it.

Actually, Roger's not a manager, he's a magician.

Craig's virtue is supposed to be in teaching pitchers the split-fingered fastball. In truth he's taught the Giants how to win. What's he trying to do, get a job with the Yankees?

The Giants didn't win their tenth game in 1985 until May 7. This year they won it April 22. This year the Giants were the first team in the majors to win ten games. We're not prepared for results.

This is out of character for the Giants. What's happened to Spec Richardson and Tom Haller? What's happened to Joe Strain and Allen Ripley?

When I think of the Giants, I think of trading Fred Breining for Al Oliver in February and then Al Oliver for two minor leaguers in August. I think of giving up Jack Clark for David Green and an Alcoholics Anonymous membership.

I think of an article in *Sports Illustrated* nearly thirty years ago, 1958, the Giants' first season in San Francisco.

"Overlooking San Francisco Bay and Hunter's Point Naval Shipyard on Candlestick Point," the author, Robert Shaplen, erroneously suggested, "the new park will be located in one of the relatively warm and unfoggy pockets of the city—a better spot than the site of Seals Stadium."

Ho, ho. The laugh was on us. Promises, promises. Mistakes. Bumbling, fumbling, and Frank Duffy.

But now the Giants are winning and the fans are fascinated. More than 22,000 spectators on a miserable Monday night. Remarkable.

Anybody seen the real Giants? Forget it. This group will just have to do for now. Or forever.

IS BING GETTING EVEN?

FEBRUARY 2, 1986

PEBBLE BEACH—Don't you enjoy this, Bing? All these guys tromping around in galoshes and hangdog expressions at your golf tournament and trying to make us believe it's something called the AT&T? Ho, ho.

We know what it is, the Bing Crosby National Pro-Am, alias the "Chattering Teeth Open." Forget the putters. Haul out the unbrellas. Here's mud in your eye. And your socks.

Great joke, Bing, tossing that rain at us, postponing the second round. What's the next stunt? Someone trying to duplicate Porky Oliver's sixteen strokes on the sixteenth at Cypress? Jimmy Demaret tossing down a drink and tossing out a riposte?

Remember when it snowed in 1962 and Demaret looked out the window of The Lodge and cracked, "I know I got loaded last night, but how did I wind up at Squaw Valley?"

The three of you must be cackling up there at what's happened this weekend. "Laughing your butt off" is the way Jack Lemmon phrased it.

People can change the name, but they can't alter the tune. "When the blue of the night meets the storm of the day . . . . "

Any tournament can have sunshine. Yours had character. And characters. Where else did they need a rule for imbedded shoes? Or give away cough drops as tee prizes?

A Crosby wasn't a Crosby without weather that would make the witches in *Macbeth* flee for cover. Same goes for the AT&T. Or the Ma Bell Invitational. Or the MCI Shootout. Or whatever they've labeled it.

I mean, if they get any more rain at Pebble Beach, they may rename the tournament the Titanic Sinkout. Or the Totes Cover-

261

up. And someone will resurrect that line by Tennessee Ernie Ford from a wet afternoon a few years ago: "I worked all my life to keep from walking in the mud," said Ford, "but every year I pay $400 to come here and spend a week in it."

Only amateur entrants now have to pay $1,500 to enter. But their feet still get wet. And their minds still get mangled. And their scores still get ruined.

Very clever, Bing, the way you psyched everyone out, wind and sunshine on Thursday, a downpour Friday morning. What did you think of the double and triple bogeys on the sixteenth and seventeenth at Cypress? And the soggy greens at Pebble? Is that your tournament or isn't it?

You should have heard Dwight Clark of the 49ers when play was called off Friday morning. "What do I do now?" Clark wondered. "Ten o'clock is awfully early to start drinking."

The line goes into the history books, along with the one by Phil Harris about Johnny Miller's deft sand play: "As smooth as a man lifting a breast out of an evening gown."

And the remark by Dean Martin: "I didn't get a par until the fifth hole. Then I brought out the vodka and played great the rest of the way. Those Russians have all the answers."

Some of the younger entrants thought the weather was bad the first two rounds this year. They should have been around in 1952, right?

"We didn't have any casual water on the fairways," said Cary Middlecoff. "That's because it was all frozen. Slabs of ice were blowing around. One pro slipped and broke his arm."

Wasn't it four years later you hired somebody named C.K. Leong to set up Chinese anti-rain rockets and launch them? Didn't Leong promise it wouldn't rain a drop? He was right. It rained buckets.

C.K. never stayed around to watch Middlecoff slog in for the win. He had to return home because he was susceptible to colds. Pass the Comtrex. And the con job.

Bing, wasn't 1960 the best year for the worst weather? Ken Venturi shot a five-over-par seventy-seven the final day. And won easily. Somebody said that tournament was the Dunkirk of golf: Get off the beach with what you can save.

Personally, I liked 1974, when it hailed, and 1969, when some kids floated a life raft on the eighteenth hole at Pebble. But the golfers didn't have smooth sailing.

Do you recall when everyone complained about the drought

in 1976 and 1977? The courses were as dry as a well-made martini. Now they could be confused with the Everglades.

"And we shouldn't play winter rules," chuckled Craig Stadler, "because we got in one round without being allowed to move the ball."

They did use winter rules. Too bad, huh, Bing? Golf is playing it as it lays. And in your tournament, now as then, it's usually laying in a puddle or the ice plant.

Phoenix and Palm Springs may have blue skies. The Crosby has distinction. Even when it's called the AT&T.

GEORGE
PLAYS
THE HEAVY

JULY 9, 1987

OAKLAND—George Foreman is the Prince of Paunch, an eighth of a ton of, well, to his opponents, he's hardly fun.

Foreman used to be the heavyweight champion of the world. Now he's simply a heavyweight, with the emphasis on *heavy.*

If Sugar Ray Robinson was the greatest fighter in the world pound for pound, then Foreman is the heaviest fighter in the world punch for punch.

Call him the boxer from Weight Watchers, or since he's an evangelist, perhaps God's Fighter. You can also call him unbeaten. He hasn't lost a fight in ten years. Of course, he's only had two.

The first was in March at Sacramento when George, at 267 pounds, doing his impersonation of the battleship *Missouri,* knocked out someone called Steve Souski in the fifth round.

The second was Thursday night at Oakland Coliseum Arena when Foreman, at a mere 247 pounds, knocked out someone called Charlie Hostetter in the third round.

Hostetter is your average sacrificial lamb, who, forty-five pounds lighter than Foreman, spent more time running backward than an NFL cornerback. Unfortunately, there was no place to hide. Next week, Charlie's going to apply for work as a punching bag.

To Hostetter, Foreman probably looked like the right side of the 49er offensive line. Or a steamroller.

"He's determined," mumbled Hostetter after Foreman turned Charlie's solar plexus into a conga drum.

"If he dropped fifteen or twenty pounds," sighed Hostetter, "Foreman might be able to challenge Mike Tyson."

Why not? And I'm going to take on Jack Nicklaus without any strokes, and you can grab a bat and face Bret Saberhagen.

Foreman is nearing forty. He's either thirty-eight, if you believe him, or thirty-nine, if you believe *Ring Record Book.* Whatever, he's a generation removed from Mike Tyson. Some people, in fact, might call George an old man.

One of those people is not Archie Moore, who was winning titles when many simply were trying to spell the word *geriatrics.* Archie, the Old Mongoose, held the light-heavyweight championship at age forty-eight. A year later, Archie fought Muhammad Ali, who was still called Cassius Clay.

Archie is seventy-three now, and the way things are going in boxing you expected him to announce he was coming out of retirement. Sorry. He's just coming out in support of thirty-eight- or thirty-nine-year-old George Foreman.

"It isn't how old you are," said Moore, "it's how you treat your body."

Archie sat elfin-like next to Foreman's incredible bulk in a postfight press conference that offered the usual inanities.

"This man here, he's very religious," said Moore, after Foreman left to clean up, reportedly at a car wash since he'd never fit under a shower.

"Those religious laws and doctrines preclude gallivanting around. You don't mess your body up. He's been away from boxing for a while, so there's been no one to destroy his body.

"And George has learned. He's had time to think. He knows what he's doing."

But do we? Charlie Hostetter isn't going to make anyone forget Gerry Cooney, much less Mike Tyson. George Foreman literally spent more time posing for postfight photographs than he did boxing Hostetter.

"The sky's the limit now," Foreman advised. "If I was offered a fight tomorrow for the championship, I would take it."

Don't hold your breath. Foreman is going to continue his comeback against the Souskis and Hostetters, guys who are adept at counting to ten.

"Hostetter is a smart fighter," said Foreman. "He wanted me to throw a lot of punches and tire myself out. Then he was going to sneak in with a right hand."

Brilliant strategy, Charlie, taking all those jabs and uppercuts to the chin and stomach. I'll bet George really got tired hitting you. If you guys meet again, just send your head.

Foreman insists he's made his comeback to help boxing, which has been in trouble since the departure of Muhammad Ali.

At the start of the third round, the fans, few that there were, started chanting, "Ali, Ali, Ali." Or was it "Ollie, Ollie, Ollie"?

Sure. I can see it now. Oliver North versus George Foreman. Winner takes Hall.

Index